Introduction

When reading the usual histories of colonisation, it's the successful ones that dominate. We read how the Pilgrim Fathers survived against the odds, of the ordeals of the convicts and their overseers in Sydney Cove. Yet the successes of colonisation are outweighed by the failures. Scattered throughout the world are the stories of settlements that were founded but never made it: ghost colonies.

Few books have looked at failed colonies from as broad a perspective as this. In these pages are twenty-five varied tales of colonies that were lost, destroyed, overtaken or abandoned. Some of them, such as the Cossack colony of New Moscow on the Red Sea coast of Africa, or Sullivan Bay in Port Phillip Bay, Australia, lasted only a matter of weeks. Others such as the Norse Viking settlements in Greenland survived for centuries before the interaction of entrenched cultural practices, environmental change and the arrival of the Inuit wiped them out.

The reasons for the failure of these colonies often came down to nature. Europeans seldom prospered in the tropics, where mosquitoes and fevers gained a small revenge on behalf of the locals for the smallpox and other viruses European civilisation exported. Dysentery, infections and scurvy also turned many colonists to ghosts. Starvation was frequently a factor: with supplies from the mother country often erratic and the new colonists lacking the knowledge of what to grow where. Their crops were often defeated by the elements or, in the case of Dutch Mauritius, for instance, eaten by rats.

Most of these colonies, however, came to grief due to human nature. Some of them foundered because the prior inhabitants didn't always take kindly to intruders, especially when their visits began to look permanent. In the great carve-up of the world by the European powers which began with the Spanish and Portuguese at the end of the fifteenth century, a colony's demise often came about because its existence conflicted with the strategic interests of another power. Sometimes the destruction of a colony came down to complex patterns of alliance and antipathy between rival colonial and local politics.

Unsurprisingly, many of the problems were internal. These colonies were sometimes like a perverse anticipation of reality TV shows such as *Survivor*—except that the consequences of the petty rivalries that developed between small groups of people clustered together out of range of everything familiar to them could be deadly.

In some cases, such as the Darién venture, the leadership group was cowardly and inept. Other leaders went mad, perhaps most notably in the bizarre suicides at Jonestown, Guyana in 1979. At other times democracy proved counter-productive to survival and colonies were undone by bickering and indecision. Other colonies, such as those of Providence Island and Port Essington, arguably were destroyed by the slow reaction times caused by the insistence on remote rule from England.

Yet these failures in history teach as much about ourselves as the successful ones do. And when the absurdity of human behaviour under the microscope becomes all too apparent, it's worth trying to imagine how we would have acted if put in these unfortunate shoes ourselves.

The construction of Fort Caroline on an island in the St John's River in 1564

CHAPTER 1

Erik the Red and the Viking settlements of Greenland (985–c. 1500)

The Vikings were the first recorded explorers to set off into the unknown with colonial ambitions. Sailing from Scandinavia, they island-hopped across the Atlantic, first settling in Iceland. From there they travelled westward to Greenland, where two colonies were established on the southwestern coast. The settlements lasted over 400 years, but they eventually lost contact with Europe. When the Danish resettled Greenland in the eighteenth century, they half-expected the Norse colonies to still exist. Instead they found the ruins of abandoned farms and churches. Archaeological evidence subsequently showed that the settlements died out at some point in the fifteenth century. The question was, after four centuries of settlement, why did Greenland become a ghost colony?

According to the Viking 'Sagas', on which much of our knowledge of the Norse colonies of Iceland and Greenland is based, it was in 982 that Erik the Red, a violent man, was banished from Iceland for unlawful killing. Having already been banished from the Norse mother country of Norway for the same offence, there were few options remaining to him. In most of the other extant Viking colonies, the distribution of land and the social hierarchy were already established, and an interloper like Erik, with a bad temper and a desire to climb the social ladder by any means available, was hardly likely to be welcomed with open arms.

Perhaps Erik realised this himself, since instead of heading for some place already populated by Vikings, he set out in his longship to explore a land spotted by his compatriot Gunnbjörn Ulfsson, when he was blown off course several decades before. It was a risky venture. As recently as 978, Snaebjörn Galti, another Viking banished from Iceland for murder, had tried to settle Greenland; his party survived the winter, but in the spring all but two of them were massacred by *skraelings*—most probably the indigenous 'Dorset' people who inhabited the area prior to the Inuit.

Erik spent the three years of his banishment exploring the land Ulfsson had named Gunnbjarnarsker, meaning 'Gunnbjörn's skerries'. Unlike Galti, he returned. During the course of his explorations, Erik discovered a number of things that made a more permanent settlement seem tenable, at least on the far

side of Greenland's vast landmass. While the eastern coast was significantly closer to Iceland, just 287 kilometres (178 miles) away at its closest point, the climate there was harsh. But Erik found arable land on the southwest coast—although, despite being considerably to the south of Iceland, it was not blessed with the tempering weather effects caused by the warm currents of the North Atlantic Drift. And thanks to his longship's slim design and small displacement, he discovered that the best farming land lay inland, in the narrow river valleys protected for the most part from the cold winds and salt spray along the fjords.

In all truth, the prospects for settling Gunnbjarnarsker were marginal at best, the vast majority of this land being composed of inhospitable tundra. Nevertheless, when he returned to Iceland in 985, Erik had already determined to succeed where Galti had failed. The problem was getting people to come with him. There was no point in being the chief of a Viking colony if there was no one to show off to, after all. Working to his advantage was the same population explosion that had led to the Norse territorial expansion out to new lands such as Iceland—the need being not just to ensure an adequate sufficiency for their people, but also because status in Viking society, as in most feudal societies, was highly contingent on the ownership of land. While the Vikings would be remembered for their rape and pillaging, to them their farms were more important. Erik the Red also had a touch of the property developer about him: although only a minuscule proportion of the land was arable, he decided to call the place Greenland in order to attract his fellow Vikings to the proposed new colony.

Erik left Iceland for good in either 985 or 986. He arrived in Greenland with fourteen ships full of settlers, livestock and the equipment needed to begin a colony. The initial complement was twenty-four longships, but the journey, although relatively short, was perilous and a number sank, while others were blown off course and turned back for home. The first settlement he founded was at Julianehab, which he called the Eastern Settlement, despite its being on the southwestern coast. This area had the most arable land and it was here that Erik set up his own farm, Brattahlid (meaning 'steep slope'), on meadow land around a fjord he named Eriksfjord. A further, smaller settlement known as the Western Settlement was established at Gothab Fjord, although it was actually around 640 kilometres (400 miles) to the north of the first site. This second settlement never prospered to the same extent, mainly because the colder climate made for a shorter growing season for the grasses on which the Viking livestock depended.

How green was my fjord

The early stages of the colony appear to have been successful. Greenland was enjoying the benefits of what is often referred to as the Medieval Warm Period, which succeeded the colder period marked by the Dark Ages.

Lasting roughly between 800 and 1300 AD, its beginning coincided with the emergence of the Vikings as a colonising force. During this period, relatively warm winters, longer summers and a lack of pack ice in the northern oceans helped Greenland remain viable for a Norse lifestyle.

Of course, some adaptations had to be made, compared with how they'd gone about things in Iceland. To begin with, it was virtually impossible to plant crops. Livestock, the dairy products derived from them, and the hunting of seal and caribou, became the prime sources of nutrition. In his fascinating account of the decline of the Norse in Greenland (*Collapse: How Societies Choose to Fail or Survive*), Jared Diamond has argued that the move to Greenland entailed a change in livestock patterns. Domesticated birds, for instance, were never a feature of Greenland's food culture as they were in other Scandinavian cultures. Of all the meats, the Vikings usually had a preference for pork. However, pigs, while fairly omnivorous, were ill-suited to the colder climate of Greenland; they couldn't be milked, and their skin was not so useful for making warm clothes. Of the remaining livestock, the Vikings valued cows above sheep and goats, yet the latter two were better suited to the Greenland climate, with their thick woollen coats. Nonetheless, as Diamond argues, cows conferred status among the Viking farmers, and while they were an inefficient use of resources, most farmers tried to maintain at least a small herd.

Eric the Red exploring the fjords of Greenland

Life in Greenland followed a strict seasonal pattern. Before the snow melted in spring, the Vikings went seal hunting, since seal meat, although a low-status food, formed a staple part of their diet. In the short summer, the livestock were let out of their stables, while the farmers spent their time cutting grass and turning it into hay (to feed their animals over the following winter) and turning the milk from their cows, sheep and goats into cheese and other products that could be stored during the colder months.

In September and October, the men headed off to hunt caribou. When they returned, the farmers culled their own herds by estimating how many animals the hay they had harvested could support over the winter. They tended their animals inside during the long winter, repaired their turf houses and processed the walrus and narwhal tusks that were their main items of trade with the Norwegian ships that came on average twice or three times a year.

For the first few centuries, it was a system that seemed to work. The population of the Eastern Settlement grew to around 4000 people, who collectively inhabited about 400 farms, while the Western Settlement peaked at roughly one-quarter of that size. Reports talk of green fields and prosperous farms—the claims of Erik the Red appeared to have been vindicated. However, this prosperity was a mixed blessing. It lasted long enough for the patterns of culture and economic production to become sufficiently entrenched that when conditions changed, the Norse Greenlanders, habituated to the viability of their way of life, failed to change with them.

Norse trading

One of the eventual problems for the Norse settlements in Greenland was their spiritual and material dependence on contact with Norway. When ships from Iceland or Norway arrived, the Greenlanders traded their walrus and narwhal tusks, which were in demand as ivory because Muslim control of the Mediterranean prevented Christian Europe from being able to access ivory from Africa and Asia. Other produce they sometimes exported included animal skins and the odd live polar bear. In return, the ships brought the Greenlanders much-needed supplies of iron and timber.

While the Inuit, Greenland's eventual permanent settlers, and their ilk used seal blubber for fuel, the Vikings continued to use timber, despite the fact that it was in short supply. With most of the limited forests cleared for pasture, aside from trading they had come to depend on serendipity in the form of driftwood being deposited on their shores from Siberia, as well as making probable trips to Markland, in eastern Canada. Not only did they use timber for fuel, but in order to get sufficient heat to forge their bog iron (which could contain as little as 1 per cent iron ore), they had first to make charcoal from wood. The making of iron was severely limited in Greenland, and perhaps the settlers' most vital imports were iron implements and weapons.

When they lost contact with Norway and the rest of Europe, they also started to lose their military superiority over the Eskimos.

Another import that ultimately had more disastrous consequences for the Vikings than the lack of timber and iron was the importation of Christianity. Greenland was founded on the cusp of Norway's switch from the pagan religion of Odin and Thor, the God of Thunder, to Christianity. While Erik the Red remained a pagan until his death circa 1001–03, his son Leif converted to Christianity. According to the Sagas, so did Erik's wife:

Eric was loath to leave the old religion, but Thjodhild, his wife, was converted at once and had a church built at a distance from the farmstead. It was called Thjodhild's church, and it was there that she and other converts would pray. Thjodhild refused to live with her husband after her conversion, and this greatly displeased him.

By 1126, a diocese had been established at Gardar, close to Erik's old farm at Brattahlid, and by the end of the twelfth century there was also a monastery and a convent of Benedictine nuns. At the peak of Norse colonisation, in the thirteenth century, there was a total of twelve parish churches in the Eastern Settlement and four parish churches in the Western Settlement, as well as an impressive cathedral at Gardar. In 1261, when Greenland was incorporated into the Kingdom of Norway, one of the inducements

offered by King Haakon IV (who was over the moon, apparently, with the Greenlanders' gift of a live polar bear) was a bishop to reside at Gardar.

The Viking chiefs who owned the large farms and were effectively feudal lords found Christianity useful since, as a monotheistic religion, it tended to support social unity and, despite its creed, the maintenance of the economic status quo. The problem with Christianity for Greenland, though, was that it sucked up a considerable portion of the colony's wealth. Although their export resources were limited, the Greenland farms were forced to pay tithes to the Church. Records show that these were paid in walrus and narwhal tusks, and polar bear skins, which were exchanged for silver once they reached Bergen in Norway. The Greenlanders also had to contribute to a levy raised by the Church to fund the Crusades—the prosecution of which, paradoxically, caused a decline in the value of their chief export because it led to renewed Christian access to African and Asian markets and their superior elephant ivory.

Keeping the Church going in Greenland was also expensive. The cathedral at Gardar, for instance, was as big as cathedrals in towns with many times the population. It seems as if the Greenlanders, insecure at being located on the fringes of the known world, went to greater efforts in order to reassure themselves that they were Christian Europeans. Similarly, valuable resources were used up on expensive items such as bells, in order to maintain a

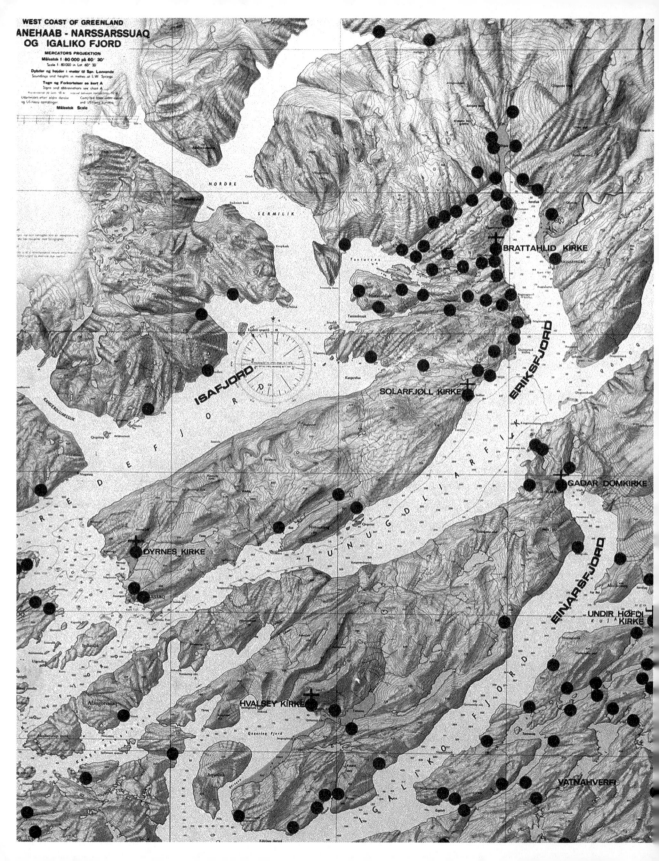

WEST COAST OF GREENLAND
ANEHAAB - NARSSARSSUAQ
OG IGALIKO FJORD

MERCATORS PROJEKTION

BRATTAHLID KIRKE

SOLARFJØLL KIRKE

ISAFJORD

ERIKSFJORD

GADAR DOMKIRKE

DYRNES KIRKE

EINARSFJORD

UNDIR HØFDI
KIRKE

HVALSEY KIRKE

VATNAHVERFI

sense of the favour bestowed by God. Instead of these outgoings, the Greenlanders could have enhanced their survival chances by importing more metal weapons and tools. Finally, the support of Christianity meant that much of the colony's best land was given over to the Church (Gardar being a prime example), a problem that increased later when many of the more marginal farms began to fail.

Flaws in the grass

To some extent, Erik the Red and his descendants had been lucky in the timing of early settlement. But, just as the first decades of the Medieval Warm Period coincided with the start of the Viking age, so the ensuing Little Ice Age signalled another change in Norse fortunes. While the Greenlanders enjoyed several centuries of prosperity, it was a situation that wasn't to last. Archaeologists who have studied the two settlements have found the remains of small birds and rodents, and from this have concluded that the last of the Norse Greenlanders starved to death while shivering inside their huts.

The reasons for the colony's sad demise are multiple, but the two primary ones appear to be soil degradation and climate change. Although there are many descriptions of the verdancy of Greenland's pastures, it's highly likely, given the dependence on grazing

LEFT: Map of the west coast of Greenland with dots marking the Viking settlements

animals to feed and clothe the Vikings, that the land was over-grazed. As in Iceland, the soil in Greenland that supported the farmlands was fertile, yet shallow and fragile. This situation was exacerbated in the beginning by the clearing of trees for fuel and for pasture. Because of this, the soil became more prone to erosion at the hands of the fiercely cold winter winds that blew through the valleys from the fjords. On those farms close to the coast, the wind also tended to dump salt spray, which likewise affected the productivity of the soil. And when the snow melted in the spring, topsoil was washed away, while the presence of masses of hoofed animals in an ecosystem unused to them also worked to prevent the topsoil from holding together.

In addition, the health of the soil was not helped by the fact that the houses and stables had to be re-turfed every ten years or so, at a cost of around 4 hectares (10 acres) of turf per farmstead. Given there were up to 400 farms in the Eastern Settlement and 100 in the Western, this would have amounted to approximately 200 hectares (500 acres) worth of turf per year. As timber became less and less available, turf was also needed to fuel fires for heating and cooking, accelerating the process of erosion even more.

The erosion of the land was undoubtedly a gradual thing. By the time the Vikings noticed anything was wrong with their green land, other destructive factors caused by the onset of the Little Ice Age had probably come into play as well. In order to survive, the

Norse colonists needed to abandon their way of life, but this they were unable to do. By the time they became extinct, sometime during the fifteenth century, many of their former meadows had most likely turned into sand.

Colony on the rocks

The Little Ice Age, which began around the end of the thirteenth century, caused the Greenland Vikings problems in a variety of other ways. Most obviously, the growing season was shortened and the winter lengthened, meaning there was less food to keep livestock inside for a longer time.

If the Greenlanders hoped that help might come from Europe they were mistaken. The incorporation of Greenland into the Kingdom of Norway had come with the promise of annual trade ships, but it also imposed a monopoly on the trade between Europe and Greenland. Although ships were prone to 'accidentally' arrive at Greenland with a full cargo, designated trade routes between Greenland and other ports in Europe weren't developed. And so, as the Arctic pack ice moved south, the usual route between Norway and Greenland became more precarious and eventually had to be abandoned. Unfortunately for the Greenlanders, this also coincided with a diminution of Norway as a sea power, as trade in the northern oceans increasingly came under the control of the ports collectively known as the Hanseatic League, from the turn of the fourteenth century onwards. This meant that the ships

trading between Greenland and the rest of Europe became more and more erratic.

The consequences for the colonists were a chronic lack of iron with which to make tools and weapons, precious little timber to make ships and houses, and a stagnation of their culture.

When the Vikings had settled Greenland, only the northwestern fringes of the island were inhabited by the Dorset people, a Paleo-Eskimo culture who preceded the Inuit in the western Arctic. The Dorset people lacked both the weaponry and the will to attack the Norse. But as the Little Ice Age took hold, the Dorset were replaced by the more warlike Thule Inuit, who had the advantage of weapons such as the bow and arrow, as well as harpoons for hunting whales.

Having reached Greenland from the American Arctic, the Thule moved down the west coast and by end of the fourteenth century, contact and competition for resources between the Norse and the Inuit increased. The Vikings, deprived of adequate weapons and nutrition, were no match for the Thule in these conditions. The Thule's superior mobility in the water from the use of kayaks, their ability to hunt ring seal (who breathed through holes in the pack ice during the winter), their use of harpoons for whaling, and their burning of seal fat for heat and cooking, meant they were far better adapted to the changing conditions than the Vikings.

As with most Christian Europeans when dealing with pagans, the Greenland Vikings were contemptuous of the Dorset and the

Thule, both of whom they collectively lumped under the term skraelings, meaning 'wearers of animal skins' or, more disparagingly, 'weaklings' or 'wretches'. As contact developed between the two peoples, there was no intermarriage between them. Furthermore the Vikings failed to adopt any of the technologies that the skraelings used. As the climate cooled, their pastures eroded and their gene pool narrowed, the Vikings persisted in the lifestyle that had served them for centuries until it was all too late. The northernmost Western Settlement was the first to go, overrun by the Thule and abandoned at some stage during the middle of the fourteenth century. The larger, more temperately situated Eastern Settlement survived considerably longer. Yet by the last decades of the fourteenth century, it too was indubitably on the skids. In 1377, Alf, the Bishop of Greenland, died and wasn't replaced, depriving the Greenlanders of the ability to appoint priests who could preside over the Christian rites for births, deaths and marriages. Two years later, an Icelandic annual records an attack by the Thule in which eighteen Norse were killed and two Norse boys enslaved.

A Viking fighting with a 'pygmy' or Greenland Inuit, from a fifteenth century Scandinavian manuscript

The last ship intentionally to visit the colony arrived in 1385 and left after staying for two years. It would be another twenty years or more before some Icelanders were blown to Greenland by mistake. By this time, timber shortages meant that the Greenlanders were probably without ocean-going ships of their own—so it's easy to imagine the excitement this visitation must have caused. And, given that the Icelanders stayed for four years, one can imagine how difficult the Greenlanders might have made it for them to leave. Was it possible that their departure was only permitted once they had made sufficient promises to return?

These Icelandic traders were the last Europeans known to have visited the Greenland Vikings. When Norwegian Lutheran missionary Hans Egede went looking for the Greenlanders in 1721, in the hope of bringing them the Reformation, he found only the ruins of a colony. The only living people on Greenland were the Inuit.

Even today, with the advantages of modern technology, there are only two small towns on the entire 2700 kilometre (1600 mile) coastline, where the dominant industry is hunting seals. Qaqortog, with a population of around 3000, is south Greenland's most populous town—1000 fewer inhabitants than the Eastern settlement at its height.

✳ THE LAST VISITORS

'The diocese of Gardar lies at the bounds of the earth in the land called Greenland. The people there have no bread, wine, or oil; they sustain themselves on dried fish and milk. Very few sailings to Greenland have been possible because of the ice in the seas and these only in the month of August, when the ice has melted. It is reckoned that no ship has sailed there for eighty years and that no bishop or priest has resided there during this period. As a result, many inhabitants have abandoned the faith of their Christian baptism; once a year they exhibit a sacred linen used by the last priest to say Mass there about a hundred years ago.'

Pope Alexander VI describing Greenland in 1492, by which time it is quite likely that the Norse settlement no longer existed

Vinland, and the Viking missions to North America (1000–13)

It's often assumed that Columbus was the first European to discover the Americas, but what about the Icelanders who founded two Scandinavian colonies in Greenland? According to the Viking Sagas, three separate territories were discovered when sailing west from Greenland: Helluland, Markland and Vinland. The last of these was where Leif Erikssen decided to erect a settlement and sit out the winter; and over the next ten years or more, Greenlanders came and stayed at Vinland on a number of occasions. A permanent settlement failed to eventuate, however, and with the possible exception of lumber missions, the Viking connection with North America duly ceased. Vinland was considered a myth until midway through the twentieth century, which was when archaeologists unearthed the remains of a Norse settlement at L'Anse aux Meadows, in northern Newfoundland—proving once and for all that the Vikings were indeed the first Europeans to found a colony in America.

It was in the period of Viking supremacy on the seas that Iceland and then Greenland were colonised. The Norse settlement of Iceland began with Ingólfur Arnarson, who started a farm in Reykjavík in 874. The subsequent colony was populated by a combination of Norsemen and their Irish and Scottish slaves but, just as in the home country of Norway, before long there were too many young men there and not enough land to go around. By the time that the future founder of the Greenland colony, Erik the Red, arrived in Iceland from Norway, the best land had already been divided up—a fact that no doubt contributed to the violence among Viking men eager to make their mark.

Another of the Greenland colonists was Herjulf, the father of Bjarni Herjolffson. When Herjulf migrated with Erik the Red in 985, Bjarni was in Norway. Hearing of his father's whereabouts upon his return to Iceland, Bjarni decided to follow. Strong winds blew his ship off course and when he eventually made landfall, it was somewhere to the west that, in the words of the Viking Sagas, was 'not mountainous and covered by forest and low hills'. He set sail again to the north, and landed at a place of high mountains and glaciers, before finally finding his way to his father's farm at Herjolfnes, on the western coast of Greenland.

Bjarni subsequently visited Erik at the latter's farm in Brattahlid, where talk of these new western lands eventually inspired Erik and his sons to mount an expedition. In 1000, Erik's eldest son, Leif, set off on a voyage of discovery. Erik had wanted to go too, but he was not well at the time, and stayed behind.

Leif first found the land with the glaciers that Bjarni had seen back in 986. He described it as having great glacier plateaus that plunged over sheer cliffs straight down to the sea. For this reason he named it Helluland, meaning 'flat stone land'. It's usually considered that Helluland is Baffin Island, where recent archaeological finds near the community of Kimmirut, on the shores of Hudson Strait, suggest the possibility of a Viking presence.

From Helluland, Leif sailed south. On his starboard side, he found a second land, flat and covered with forest, that sloped gradually via sandy beaches into the sea. This he called Markland, meaning 'woodland'. It was a more promising proposition than Helluland, especially since Greenland had a serious wood shortage, and the Vikings there had to rely mainly on driftwood and imports to provide the timber necessary for housing, blacksmithing, shipbuilding and keeping themselves warm.

Leif and his men explored Markland before returning to their ships. They sailed south for a further two days until they came to a grassy offshore island shrouded in mist, then a north-pointing cape belonging to a larger body of land. They sailed westwards between the island and the cape until they entered a sound. Their ship ran aground, but they managed to free it and then sailed into a river that took them to a lake. In the words of the Sagas, 'There was no lack of salmon in either the river or the lake, salmon larger than they had ever seen. The land was so rich that they thought none of the cattle would require fodder for the winter.' Unsurprisingly, the Vikings decided to set up camp. Houses were erected from timber and turf sods, stables built, and while some of Leif's men continued to explore, others settled in the village, given the name Leifsbudir.

The territory itself they called Vinland. The etymology of the name, and indeed the location of Vinland, remain the object of historical controversy. While the two Viking Sagas are based on oral history, the Saga of Erik the Red is not always consistent with the Greenlanders Saga. The word 'Vinland' has traditionally been associated with the discovery of wild grapes, which places the Viking settlement further south than it probably was. Some historians have claimed that Vinland was as far south as New England, although the most likely location, given the archaeological finds at L'Anse aux Meadows, is that it was in Newfoundland. In this case, the 'Vin' referred to in the Sagas may have been a generic reference to berries that could be used to make wine. Yet another explanation is that Vinland is derived from the old Norse word *vin*, meaning 'pasture'. The Sagas themselves were not written until 250 years after the events they describe, so there is a good chance that the story has been altered by Chinese whispers across the generations.

In the spring, Leif and his men decamped back to Greenland, bringing with them a cargo of timber and some of the grapes or berries they had found. Leif returned home

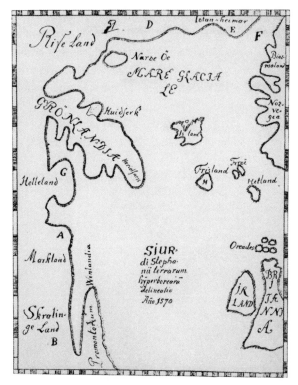

Map of North America based on records of Viking journeys west from Greenland

to discover that his father had died while he was away. He never visited Vinland again. Instead, the next to make the journey from Greenland to America would be his younger brother Thorvald.

A family affair

Thorvald Erikssen argued with Leif that he had failed to reconnoitre the land sufficiently. In the power vacuum created by the death of Erik the Red, there seems to have been some rivalry between the brothers, which in a Viking context could easily prove deadly. Given the family's poor record in conflict resolution, it's possible there wasn't room for the two brothers to co-exist on the limited resources of Brattahlid.

Leif responded to Thorvald's charge by challenging him to do better. Thorvald set out for Vinland in Leif's ship with thirty men and reached Leifsbudir, where they wintered, subsisting mainly on fish. When spring arrived, they explored the territory to the west, discovering more forests and long strips of beach. A wooden grain-holder, however, was the only sign of human presence they found and, with the colder weather

Settlers unloading Viking longships in Vinland

approaching, they returned to Leifsbudir and wintered there in the houses built by Leif.

The following spring, Thorvald and his men travelled north. At one point, their ship ran aground during a storm and the keel was damaged. They landed on a cape and rebuilt the keel, then sailed eastwards until coming across a fjord, which they navigated down before mooring their ship in the shelter of a headland that was again covered in forest. Their excitement at the sight of these forests underlines how sparsely vegetated Greenland actually was, and suggests therefore that the territory they were discovering was full of lucrative goods. Here, they also found the first active signs of human habitation: three boats made from animal skins, each with three men in them.

In typical Viking fashion, they killed eight of the *skraelings*—the derogatory term the Norsemen used for members of the Inuit and the like—and commandeered two of the boats. The surviving Inuit escaped in the remaining boat to alert his fellow tribesmen. Not long afterwards, a whole fleet of boats containing hundreds of *skraelings* descended on Thorvald's party and attacked. Although vastly outnumbered, the Vikings managed to repel the attack. The only casualty was their leader, mortally wounded by an arrow that snuck between the longship's gunwale and his shield.

Knowing he was going to die, Thorvald ordered that the ship return to Leifsbudir. Like his mother and elder brother, Thorvald had converted from the religion of Thor and

Odin to Christianity, and so told his crew to bury him there on the land he had intended to settle. Then he died.

When the ship returned to Greenland, Thorstein, the youngest of Erik's sons, decided to mount an expedition to retrieve his brother's body. He re-provisioned Leif's ship and sailed for Vinland with his wife, Gudrid, and another adventurous crew of men. However, the winds and currents were against them and they were forced back onto the Greenland coast at Lysufjord, where illness spread through the party. Soon Thorstein too was dead, leaving Gudrid to sail her husband's body home.

Further Vinland adventures

The Vikings' attempts to colonise Vinland didn't end with the deaths of Thorvald and Thorstein Erikssen. According to the Greenlanders Saga, Gudrid remarried, to a Norwegian, Thorfinn Karlsefni, who came and stayed with Leif at Brattahlid. The following year, perhaps in 1010, and with Leif's encouragement, the couple embarked on a permanent honeymoon, together with sixty men, five women and a lot of livestock. They travelled to the camp at Leifsbudir and settled in. A temporary food shortage was solved by feasting on the flesh of a beached whale. With timber abundant and plenty of fish and livestock, the first winter passed without remark.

In the spring, the Inuit came to trade the furs of sable and other animals with

SEEING RED—THE VIKING AGE

The story of Erik the Red is a classic tale of Viking fractiousness. If he lived today he might even have been described as a serial killer. Every Viking male was allowed to carry his own weapons and, given their propensity for binge drinking, when arguments inevitably arose they were often deadly. The violence that shaped the life of Erik the Red began in Norway, from which he and his father were exiled due to some undisclosed slaughters. They subsequently settled on the west coast of Iceland. According to the Saga of Erik the Red, when his neighbour Thorgest borrowed a shovel and didn't return it, Erik went in search of an explanation for this breach of etiquette. Thorgest still refused to return the tool, so Erik stole it back. Thorgest then chased after him and in the ensuing struggle Erik slew him. As a result, Erik was exiled to another part of Iceland, where he again ran into trouble with the neighbours. The problems began when one of Erik's slaves accidentally set off a landslide on a neighbouring farm, belonging to a man called Valthjof. Angered by the damage to his property, Valthjof slaughtered the slave. Erik was suitably incensed—most likely, it must be said, not from human empathy for the fate of his slave, but because of the loss of a valuable asset. He slaughtered Valthjof in retribution. For this, the Icelanders banished him from the island for three years. In return, Erik provided the Norse people with the foundation of a new colony in Greenland, one that would remain prosperous for a few centuries to come.

As remarkable as Erik the Red's story is, he was no more bloodthirsty than the society that spawned him. The Vikings were an aggressive bunch. Their summers were spent fighting, trading and pillaging, and during the long northern winters they tended to get on each others' nerves. When they weren't making their own conquests, or fighting among themselves, they were the mercenaries of choice for many medieval potentates. The pinnacle of their power was between the eighth and eleventh centuries. But this prowess came not just from their ruthless combative nature. Viking longships, with their sails complemented by rows of oarsmen to enable them to navigate against the wind, were the finest marine technology of the time.

The Eastern Vikings were mainly from Sweden, and it was this branch that expanded into Russia. Their shipping lanes extended down the Volga River as far as the Black and Caspian seas and into the Mediterranean. Eastern Viking traders reached all the way to the capital of the Abbasid Empire, Baghdad, with its massive population of almost a million people. The Varangians, a troop of Swedish Vikings, were the elite guard of the Byzantine emperors, much in the same way as the Swiss Guard still protects the Pope today.

Then there were the Western Vikings. Mainly composed of Norwegians and Danes, they used their longships to mount raids throughout the Baltic and the North Sea. During the Viking era, their kings ruled Normandy and England. And under their most powerful king, Canute the Great (son of Sweyn Forkbeard), whose reign ended in 1035, the Western Vikings had dominion over Norway, Denmark, England, Iceland, Greenland and some of Sweden. The Normans, who would rout the English in 1066, were also of Viking descent. The Western Viking sphere of influence, in fact, expanded as far south as Sicily and Naples in the Mediterranean.

Eric the Red battling Valthjof, prior to his banishment from Iceland

the newcomers, hoping to exchange them for some of the Vikings' weaponry, as the *skraelings* were yet to develop iron technology. Thorfinn, mindful that his armed superiority co-existed with a vastly numerical inferiority, refused to trade any weapons and the Inuit had to make do with milk. Perceiving that they resented this, he built a stockade around the settlement, just in case.

The Vikings spent a second winter there without major incident, after which the Inuit appeared with more furs to trade. This time, again frustrated by their failure to obtain any weapons, one of the Inuit apparently tried to steal some. He was caught and killed by the Vikings. This slaying provoked the Inuit to attack en masse, but the Vikings defeated them in hand-to-hand combat in the forest. Thorfinn and his company spent another winter in Vinland before abandoning the colony the following spring, returning with 'many valuable goods including vines, grapes and furs', as the Saga records. Perhaps they were tired of fighting the Inuit, or perhaps they were simply homesick.

The story of this mission in the Saga of Erik the Red is rather different. In that version, two ships containing 160 men and women left Brattahlid to establish a colony in Vinland. And rather than camping at Leifsbudir, they stayed at a place called Straumsfjord, where they had found pasture with naturally growing wheat. In this account, the winter was a harsh one, on account of insufficient food, while the whale they found had actually washed up dead, its meat

making even the Vikings sick when they ate it. (No mean feat, given that their Icelandic descendants consider rotten shark meat a delicacy.) Once the winter was over, the party prospered, catching fish and stealing the eggs of birds.

In this version of the colonisation attempt, the would-be settlers split up in the summer to explore. A party of ten men, led by Thorhall Gumlasson, headed north in one of the longships, but they were blown so far off course that they ended up in Ireland, where they were captured and enslaved. The others, under Thorfinn Karlsefni, went south and found an estuary that led to a lake; on the hills surrounding it were vines, while on the flood plains they discovered wild wheat. They decided to call the place Hop, built houses near the lake and settled in for the winter. Thorfinn and his companions were impressed by the fact that no snow fell during the entire winter, allowing their cattle to graze outdoors all year round.

In the spring, *skraelings* came to trade furs, again hoping for arms, but receiving only cloth in exchange for their goods. The natives decided to attack and forced them into a defensive position behind some rocks. But, led by Gudrid, the Vikings fought back and the *skraelings* retreated. The victory was pyrrhic, however, since Thorfinn concluded that, despite the excellent conditions for settlement, the constant threat of attack from the vastly more numerous Inuit would make establishing a permanent base too difficult. The Vikings retreated to Straumsfjord, only to begin fighting among themselves over the winter. Part of the problem seems to have been marital since, according to the Saga, when they left America via Markland the following year, Gudrid returned to Greenland, while Thorfinn went to Iceland.

Fractious Freydis

The Old Icelandic Sagas record one further attempt to colonise America by the Greenland Vikings. This one features Erik's daughter, Freydis, suggesting that there was considerable family pressure to make a go of colonising America. It's tempting to think that the version of America that survived to become part of the Sagas was a gilded one, designed by the Erikssen family to attract possible settlers, in the same way that Erik's naming of Greenland made the place seem more attractive to settlement than it actually was.

On this final trip, Freydis and her husband, Porvardr, were accompanied by two Norwegian brothers, named Helgi and Finnbolgi. However, bad blood soon infected relations between the two groups of settlers. The brothers arrived at Leifsbudir first and put their belongings in the houses built by Leif a decade or more before. When Freydis arrived, however, she laid claim to the whole of Leifsbudir as her personal fiefdom, and kicked them and their entourage out. Helgi and Finnbolgi built their own facilities further away from the sea, towards the lake. Although the two parties were the only Vikings on the fringes of a vast unknown land and remained within sight of each other, they'd stopped talking to each other.

Having asserted her claim to her brother's huts, Freydis began to covet the Norwegians' longship. The Sagas describe her as being both haughty and greedy; and, unlike Gudrid, who had proved herself as brave as any man on the battlefield, Freydis was sneaky. One morning, she put on her husband's cloak and, despite a heavy dew, walked barefoot to Finnbolgi's house, where she asked him outside to talk. Announcing that she wanted to return to Greenland, she wondered if they might exchange ships. Finnbolgi, no doubt happy to see the back of this troublesome and dishonest woman, agreed to the deal, and then went back to sleep.

Freydis returned home to Porvardr, who asked her why she was so cold and wet, as she climbed back into their bed. She claimed that she had offered to buy Finnbolgi's ship, but the Norwegian had become mad with anger and beaten her up. Freydis then berated her husband, saying, 'But you, you weakling would never avenge either my humiliation or your own. I realise now how far away I am from Greenland. And unless you avenge this, I am going to divorce you.'

Unable to bear her taunting, Porvardr decided to seek redress in the only way Vikings seemed to know how. He gathered his men together and went to the camp where the two brothers and the rest of their party were still sleeping. They surprised the Norwegians, tied them up, dragged them

The settlement at L'Anse aux Meadows

outside and, with Freydis no doubt egging them on, slaughtered them. Five women remained, whom none of the male Vikings would kill. Undeterred, Freydis demanded an axe and murdered them all herself.

Having made a good profit through the acquisition of her victims' assets, Freydis Eriksdottir abandoned Vinland and headed for Greenland, where she established herself at Gardar (eventually the seat of the Bishop of Greenland). She tried to cover up the incident by swearing her crew to secrecy, but the details of her perfidy emerged. Given that her brother was effectively ruler of Greenland, it's perhaps unsurprising that she escaped legal action.

Digging for ghosts

The colonisation of Vinland by the Greenland Vikings lasted little more than a decade after Leif Erikssen passed that first winter of

1000–01 there. Perhaps the major problem was that there were never enough Vikings to build a colony big enough to comfortably deal with the Inuit tribesmen. The largest contingent to leave for Vinland was about eighty people—or perhaps 160 if the version of events in the Saga of Erik the Red is to be believed—while at the time the Viking population of Greenland was probably only 500. Add to this the Vikings' predilection for murderous disputes among themselves, as well as the tyranny of distance, and it's easy to see why these colonies failed.

There's evidence that Viking ships continued to visit America for centuries after 1013, probably to acquire valuable cargoes of timber and furs, but no further mentions appear of attempts by the Norse to settle there. In fact, for centuries it was assumed that the Old Icelandic Sagas were simply telling tall tales when they spoke of the settlement of Vinland. All that changed, however, when a new generation of Norwegians, the husband-and-wife archaeological team of Helge Ingstad and Anne Stine, arrived in the far north of Newfoundland in the the early 1960s. Their discovery of an abandoned Norse settlement at L'Anse aux Meadows, the location of which corresponds quite closely to where the Sagas position Leifsbudir, proved conclusively that the Vikings were the first Europeans to leave their mark on American soil.

CHAPTER 3

The Spanish colony of San Miguel de Guadalupe, the Carolinas (1526)

After the Native American Francisco Chicorana was captured on America's Carolina coast by Spanish slave hunters and brought to Santo Domingo, on the Caribbean island of Hispaniola, he used his wiles to create the catalyst for his journey home. Appointed as a manservant to Lucas Vázquez de Ayllón, he filled the conquistador's head with such exotic images of his homeland that Ayllón sought assent from the King of Spain to settle the Carolinas. In 1526 Ayllón set sail with a force larger than that used by Cortés in the conquest of Mexico. The result couldn't have been more different, however. After less than three months, the disease-ridden colony was abandoned, with just a quarter of the 600 arrivals able to set off on the desperate return journey to Hispaniola. The slave Francisco was free, but one of Spain's great conquistadors was dead.

While the explorer Juan Ponce de León's claim to Florida was delayed by his subjugation of the fearsome Caribs from 1515 onwards (see page 36), there were several other attempts to explore the landmass that lay to the north of Hispaniola, and by extension to discover the imagined passage through the Americas and out to Cathay (China). As with all the land the Spanish discovered in America, rumours abounded of unimaginable riches. In 1521 Lucas Vázquez de Ayllón, a gentleman and judge on Hispaniola, was sufficiently intrigued by these reports to hire the navigator Francisco Gordillo to further explore the region.

In the Bahamas, Gordillo met a slave hunter called Pedro de Quexos. Thinking the tasks of slave raiding and exploration could easily be combined for profit, the two men joined forces, despite Ayllón's specific orders not to take slaves, and headed north. In June 1521, they landed at the mouth of a large river, which they named in honour of St John the Baptist. They then sailed north to Cape Fear in North Carolina, and possibly as far north as Chesapeake Bay, before returning with 150 Native American slaves from the Chicora region, near Cape Fear. To their dismay, when they returned to Santo Domingo to sell their cargo, Governor Diego Columbus ordered them to repatriate the Native Americans at their own cost.

Only one of the slaves was detained. He was baptised Francisco Chicorana, his surname derived from the region of his birth. Utterly isolated from his people and eager to return to them, he adopted the brilliant strategy of regaling his master with tales of the riches of Chicora. In 1523, Ayllón brought Chicorana to Spain, where he embellished his stories even further in conversation with the Spanish writers Peter Martyr and Gonzalo Fernandez de Oviedo y Valdez. There were pearls and precious stones, and domesticated deer lived indoors and were valued for their cheese and milk. The stories became more and more improbable. Their chief was named Datha, and he was an enormous man— apparently because his bones had been softened and stretched as a child—while there was also a race of men with immoveable tails, who needed to dig holes in the ground in order to comfortably sit down.

In an era when people were prone to believing in monsters and interpreting storm clouds as the armies of God, these stories were not entirely incredible. In fact, they were enough for Ayllón to petition the King for a grant to explore and settle the region. In return for funding the mission himself, Ayllón was to receive around 4000 square kilometres (1 million acres) of land of his choosing in the new domain. King Charles V also stumped up the funding to ensure that several Dominican priests joined the expedition. Of the importance of their role, and the priorities of colonisation of the Americas in general, the Spanish monarch left Ayllón in no doubt:

Our principal intent in the discovery of new lands is that the inhabitants and natives thereof, who are without light or knowledge of the faith, may be brought to understand the truths of our Holy Catholic Faith, that they may come to a knowledge thereof and become Christians and be saved, and this is the chief motive that you are to bear and hold in this affair ...

The policy on slave taking, however, was ambiguous. Although native tribespeople were to be well treated and paid for their work, a loophole existed in that those people already enslaved by the Native Americans were fair game and could be traded and taken to Hispaniola for sale.

In 1525, Ayllón sent the slave trader Quexos on a reconnaissance mission with two ships and sixty men. In May that year Quexos landed at the Savannah River, then sailed north to Winyah Bay, and then north again in the direction of Cape Fear. Instead of raiding for slaves, he was there to butter up the natives in anticipation of the arrival of the Spanish colony: he handed out gifts, including clothing, and seeds of Spanish plants, with instructions on how to grow them. From Cape Fear, Quexos and his party sailed south, scouring the coast for the inlet best suited to settlement. Having reached the northern limit of Ponce de León's explorations, they sailed back north. In June they entered Chesapeake Bay before returning to Hispaniola via the Bahamas.

Ayllón's folly

In mid July the following year, Ayllón sailed from Puerto Plata, on the northern coast of Hispaniola, with six ships containing 600 people, 150 of whom were sailors. The colonists included women and children, African slaves, doctors, Dominican priests and Francisco Chicorana, whom Ayllón hoped would be their intermediary with the native people. Their supplies included bread made from manioc flour, corn, olive oil, cattle, pigs and goats, as well as 100 horses.

The place they initially chose for their landing (probably near the mouth of the Pee Dee River in South Carolina) proved something of a disaster. The flagship ran aground and all its supplies were ruined. To compensate for this, an open boat with a single mast was built. Designed for both rowing and sailing, it was arguably the first boat built by Europeans in what is now the United States.

Worse perhaps than the loss of the flagship was the loss of Francisco, who, having tempted Ayllón to sail to Chicora, took the wisest course of action and disappeared soon after their arrival. This left the Spaniards unable to communicate with the Native Americans—a big problem, given that trade would be their best chance of survival. The place they had landed at was relatively devoid of native villages anyway. It's unknown exactly why, but possibilities include that the tribespeople were away hunting, they were hiding from the Spanish (perhaps on the advice of Francisco), or they'd been decimated by previous contact with European microbes.

With much of their provisions sunk, the land tending to swamp with fever-carrying mosquitoes, and the season too late for planting, Ayllón sent some of his ships to scout for locations more congenial for wintering. Although they sailed some way both north and south, Ayllón determined to move the colony south to somewhere in the vicinity of what is now Sapelo Sound, in

Spanish colonists disembarking in the New World

present-day Georgia. He sent the men and horses overland, while the women, children, the ill and livestock followed in the ships.

By late September 1526, the sea and land parties had met at their designated destination. A church and houses were rapidly constructed and the village named San Miguel de Guadalupe. However, if the Spaniards had hoped for an improvement in their conditions they were sorely mistaken. The autumn was uncommonly cold. Their provisions gave out and there were no supplies of grain that could be commandeered from the locals. Ayllón was essentially a bureaucrat, excellent at the theory of society, but ineffectual when it came to the task of governing a nascent colony in deep

A Native American village enclosed with palisades

34

trouble. As with many ghost colonies, as much energy was spent on political dissension as on solving a series of problems that threatened the settlers' survival.

Many of the colonists had been weakened by disease, and as the weather cooled and the rations shortened, they began to die in droves. On 18 October, Ayllón himself died and the struggle for power broke out into the open. The lieutenant who was his anointed successor was imprisoned by an ambitious junior officer. The African slaves, perceiving that they would be ill-used by the usurper, burnt his house to the ground while he was in residence, then escaped to live with one of the native tribes—having first set fire to some of the settlement's other buildings by way of celebration.

A number of the Spanish settlers weren't so fortunate. Having sought refuge and, no doubt, food in a neighbouring Native American village, they became too much of a burden on their hosts' resources as winter approached and were killed. The success of the Dominicans in converting the locals to Catholicism, given the benefits on show, was understandably dismal.

A desperate end

Once the Native Americans saw the extent of the shambles to which the Spanish had been reduced, they decided to attack, and were helped by the former African slaves. Persistent raids ate further into the capacity of the colonists to endure. Abandoned by their slaves, fighting among themselves and at constant risk of dying from disease, duel or attack, even before the onset of winter, the decision was made to abandon San Miguel de Guadalupe and return to Hispaniola.

In November, the 150 colonists who had not abandoned the settlement to try their chances with the better-provisioned native tribespeople gathered themselves, boarded their ships and headed south into the fierce winter waters of the Atlantic in search of the sun, society and salvation. Behind them, in the open boat they had built in more optimistic times, they towed the body of their leader. It was an odyssey as harrowing as the colony itself. The ships were lashed by the storms at the tail end of the annual Atlantic hurricane season. Sailing into the wind, in boats that weren't particularly good at it and crewed by weakened men, they made small headway and were flung about on the sea. The funereal barge bearing Ayllón was eventually torn from the other ships and vanished behind the giant swell, never to be seen again. According to the Spanish historian Gonzalo Fernàndez de Oviedo, seven men froze to death on the deck of one ship as it lurched with tattered sails towards the safety of Hispaniola. Corpses were assigned to Davy Jones' locker regularly.

The trip home took almost as long as the colony had lasted. It had taken only three quick months of unmitigated disaster for the first permanent European settlement of North America in half a millennia to come to an ignominious end.

FAILED IN FLORIDA

JUAN PONCE DE LEÓN was the first Spanish conquistador to fail in Florida. In 1514, he secured a patent to colonise Florida and Bimini (in the west of the Bahamas), both of which he had explored the previous year. The establishment of the colony was delayed, however, while he prosecuted a successful war against the Caribs. In 1521, he led 200 men as well as cattle, sheep and horses to the west coast of Florida and tried to found a settlement there. But almost as soon as they landed, the Spanish were attacked by Native American warriors, and driven back to Cuba, where Ponce died from wounds inflicted by an arrow.

PÁNFILO DE NARVÁEZ was described by a fellow explorer as 'cocksure, a braggart and unsure of the line between dream and reality'; and it's fair to say that if it weren't for his colossal ambition, he might have been a relatively harmless, Don Quixote-style buffoon. In 1526, Narváez secured a patent to the lands of Ponce de León and Francisco de Garay, two years after which he landed near today's Tampa Bay with 600 colonists who had signed on with him in Spain. The local Native Americans told him of a treasure-laden province called Apalachen, in the vicinity of contemporary Tallahassee. Far from another El Dorado, it proved to be a village of forty huts. Disillusioned, Narváez found the coast near St Marks Bay and built a fleet of horse-hide boats, having omitted to include a carpenter in his party. He then set out to meet his ships at Pánuco in Mexico and got lost. Many men died of thirst, and others drowned when the fleet was wrecked by a storm on the coast of Texas. Disease, starvation and hostile locals accounted for all but four of the rest, who, after nearly six years of enslavement, escaped across Texas and into Mexico.

HERNANDO DE SOTO, who had been involved in the conquests of Central America and Peru in the 1530s, was the next conquistador to be granted a patent by the Spanish monarch and thus be appointed Governor of Florida. In 1539, he landed at Tampa Bay with a colony of over 600 people. Soto's force set out for a rich province called Cale and kept going for almost four years on the rumours of gold and treasure. He travelled to Apalachen, then the Savannah River, northwest to North Carolina and Piedmont, and south towards Mobile Bay, before heading northwest again to the Mississippi, near

Memphis. He reached as far west as Oklahoma before travelling down the Arkansas River to its confluence with the Mississippi, which is where he died of fever in 1541. Some of the survivors of his fruitless expedition, now led by Luis de Moscoso, set out for Pánuco and eventually arrived there two years later via the circuitous route of Arkansas, eastern Texas, the Mississippi again, and along the coast of Texas.

TRISTÁN DE LUNA Y ARELLANO was sent by Luis de Velasco, the Viceroy of New Spain, to settle Santa Elena (Tybee Island, Georgia) in 1559, along with a fleet of thirteen ships containing 1500 soldiers and colonists. Half of his captains were veterans of Hernando de Soto's mission, although this didn't help. The main body of the expedition landed at Pensacola Bay, where a fort was built. One thousand colonists were then moved up the Alabama River to Nanipacna, from where an expedition was launched to ascertain the fabled riches of Coca. It was a failure: there was local antipathy and disputes among the colonists were rife. In 1560, the colony returned to Pensacola and De Luna was replaced by Ángel de Villafañe, who had arrived from Vera Cruz, Mexico, with supplies. He too failed to make a success of settling Santa Elena and returned, and not long afterwards the garrison at Pensacola was withdrawn. After decades of Spanish failure in the region, King Phillip II ordered the cessation of all attempts to colonise Florida. It was only the presence of the French at Fort Caroline in 1564 that would force him to change his mind (see page 60).

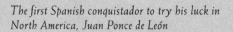
The first Spanish conquistador to try his luck in North America, Juan Ponce de León

Jacques Cartier and the French colony of Charlesbourg-Royal, New France (1541–43)

Being a great explorer is one thing, but founding a successful colony is another entirely, as French navigator Jacques Cartier discovered to his chagrin. The first European to explore the Gulf of St Lawrence, and discovering the territory known as Quebec, Cartier then attempted to found France's first permanent settlement in North America, in 1541. He and his colonists—a mixed bag of criminals and money-strapped noblemen—endured a bitter first winter at Charlesbourg-Royal before concluding that the effort wasn't worth it. On the way home he encountered his superior officer, Jean-François de la Rocque de Roberval, who ordered them all to return to the colony. Instead, Cartier had his ships sneak away at night and continued for France. Roberval went to Charlesbourg-Royal and renamed it to expunge the taint of Cartier. But after another harsh winter, he too abandoned his plans to colonise and returned home, with no trace of the riches or the prestige he'd imagined the venture would bring him.

Jacques Cartier wasn't the first European to discover the Atlantic coast of North America. That honour belongs to the Vikings, who briefly settled Newfoundland in the eleventh century. And when the Breton set out on his first voyage to North America, in 1534, the coast was already known to European fishermen, who had been drawn there by the rich stocks of whale and cod. But no one before him had entered the Gulf of St Lawrence, the large body of water beyond Newfoundland and Nova Scotia.

On that first voyage, like Columbus before him, Cartier was sure he had landed in Asia. He explored Newfoundland and the Atlantic coast of Canada and then entered the Gulf, where he encountered a tribe of St Lawrence Iroquois. The locals were friendly initially but became concerned when Cartier planted a massive cross on their land, effectively claiming it for France. He also kidnapped Chief Donnacona's two sons and took them back to France, on the understanding that he would return with European goods the following year.

In May 1535, as good as his word, Cartier set off for Canada with the chief's sons, along with three ships and 110 men. This time he sailed up the St Lawrence River, as far as Donnacona's village at Stadacona (the site of present-day Quebec City).

Aside from the goal of reaching Asia, one of Cartier's primary motivations was a desire to discover the fabled kingdom of Saguenay, a land said to hold great reserves of silver and gold. He had heard much about

Saguenay from Donnacona, who, like many Native Americans, was fond of telling wild tales studded with jewels and precious metals to European interlopers. The Iroquois chief's skills as a storyteller would ultimately prove his undoing, however.

By the spring of 1536, Cartier was so entranced by the prospect of Saguenay that he brought Donnacona and nine of his subjects back to France with him, no doubt so that he could impress the King sufficiently to fund a third mission. But there was a darker motive behind the explorer's actions. Donnacona and his sons had impeded his mission upriver from Stadacona, probably in order to maintain their trade monopoly with the Europeans and thus gain an advantage over another Iroquois chief, Agona, with whom he was tussling for power. While Donnacona had asked Cartier to help him overcome his rival, the Frenchman showed Macchiavellian traits in deciding that, since Donnacona had been interfering in his explorations, it would be better to support the other side. Part of the reason, therefore, for the chief's imposed sojourn in Europe was to create a power vacuum for Agona to fill.

Donnacona lived well in France for four years, during which time he augmented his description of Saguenay to please his royal host, King Francis I. Not only was it a repository of gold, silver, rubies and copper through which France might achieve economic parity with Spain, but the kingdom's riches came to include spices such as nutmeg, cloves and pepper, as well as oranges and pomegranates. Not content to rest on tall tales of material riches, Donnacona also told the King of marvels such as men without anuses and others with wings on their arms who flew from the trees to the ground, like bats.

Cartier's next mission soon became less about the discovery of a passage to China and more about finding the mythical Saguenay. However, the expedition was delayed, first by a fresh war between Spain and France that lasted until 1538, then by the diplomatic complexities of the peace. By the time Cartier left in mid 1541, Donnacona had succumbed to disease, his two sons had died after getting involved with Parisian criminals, and with the exception of one small girl (whose fate is unrecorded), all the Iroquoian visitors were dead.

Cartier's colony

Although he enjoyed the King's favour, on his third expedition Cartier was outranked by one Jean-François de la Rocque de Roberval, whose pedigree was old French aristocracy and who, despite being a Protestant in an era when they were being severely persecuted in France, remained a royal favourite. Roberval was thus the one granted the commission of Lieutenant General of New France, with Cartier relegated to the role of mere pilot and navigator. It was perhaps a sign of how seriously King Francis had taken Donnacona's stories of Saguenay. Yet it was a move Cartier didn't enjoy.

The explorer's fellow Bretons from the two previous expeditions were less enthused about the prospect of joining a permanent settlement in a place whose fierce winters they were already well acquainted with. Thus, many of the new colonists were 'recruited' from gaol. While those who were guilty of treason, had counterfeited the King's coin or had been detained at his majesty's pleasure were excluded from going, the eventual complement comprised two murderers, others imprisoned on charges of violence, and a variety of thieves and fraudsters. Juxtaposed against the criminals were 150 'gentlemen'. As did Spain, France had a large number of impoverished aristocratic families, the younger sons of which understandably looked to the New World as a way to escape the financial predicaments imposed by virtue of belonging to a social class whose manners prevented many forms of economic activity. In all, a Spanish spy estimated at the time that there were 1500 people on Cartier's five ships. However, this is likely to be an exaggeration designed for diplomatic leverage, as the Spanish still believed that the entirety of the New World belonged to them and the Portuguese.

Roberval had another five ships, but he also had financial problems. Unable to buy provisions and sufficient artillery for his vessels, he sent Cartier on ahead. It would be another year before Roberval could clear his debts and sail, during which time he sold one of his estates and turned to piracy in the English Channel to raise funds.

Jacques Cartier exploring the St Lawrence River

Cartier sailed on 23 May 1541 and reached Stadacona three months later after a rough crossing of the Atlantic. While Chief Agona wasn't upset to hear that his rival Donnacona had died, there was probably some scepticism on his part concerning Cartier's assertion that the other nine Iroquois were living in luxury in France and had therefore decided not to return. The tension between the French and the Iroquois was certainly sufficient for Cartier to change his mind about establishing a colony in the vicinity of Stadacona. After a reconnaissance upstream, he decided on Cap-Rouge (now a suburb of Quebec City), some 14 kilometres (9 miles) further up the St Lawrence River. Cartier provided the following description of the site: 'On both sides of the said River there are very good and fair grounds, full of as fair and mighty trees as any be in the world, and diverse sorts, which are above ten fathoms higher than the rest.'

Having found a suitable location, the Frenchman then brought up the five ships, unloaded the settlers and began to build the colony. The cattle were turned loose to graze on the 'fair grounds', while vegetable gardens were planted. Cartier built palisades around the new village and a fort high on the bluffs above the floodplain. He named the settlement Charlesbourg-Royal, in honour of Charles, the King's son and Duke of Orléans. Soon the optimism of the colony was greatly buoyed by the discovery of what were believed to be diamonds and gold. Two of the ships were sent back to France

that September, taking with them samples of these precious finds. Just like English explorer Martin Frobisher's later discoveries in Meta Incognito in the Canadian Arctic, the minerals from Charlesbourg-Royal would turn out to be no more than iron pyrites (fool's gold) and quartz crystal.

On 7 September, Cartier left his brother-in-law in charge and took off upriver with a couple of longboats in search of Saguenay. They reached the Iroquois village of Hochelaga (meaning 'at the place of the beaver dam'), near present-day Montreal. Hochelaga was a powerful palisaded settlement, comprised of around fifty typical Iroquoian lodges, each lodge 50 or more paces in length and 12 or 15 in breadth, built of wood and covered with bark. Its population is estimated to have been in the vicinity of 3000 people. Cartier had visited there in 1535 and been given more information about the supposed whereabouts of Saguenay.

Frustratingly for the Frenchman, he would get no closer to his Canadian El Dorado on this visit. Their passage was ultimately blocked by the La Chine rapids and, according to local intelligence, the even larger Long Sault rapids, which extended beyond them. The truth was, having told the Europeans such fantastical tales, the Iroquois were often reluctant to let them find out the truth for themselves. The inhabitants of Hochelaga failed to direct Cartier and his men towards the Ottawa River, the waterway that would have taken them further inland without the same degree of obstacles. Their hopes of finding Saguenay disappointed, the party had no choice but to return to Charlesbourg-Royal.

Bailing out

Back at the settlement, Cartier's mood was not improved by the build-up in tension between his colonists and the Stadacona Iroquois. While the native people were happy to trade with the French, they were understandably less happy at the idea of a European colony on their turf. As winter approached and it became clearer to the Iroquois that this was what they were dealing with, they stopped visiting Charlesbourg-Royal to trade furs, fish and game, and instead began to prowl around the fort in a threatening manner.

The record of what exactly happened during the colony's first winter is fairly sketchy. It seems that on one occasion the Iroquois attacked and thirty-five of the colonists were killed. As was often the case, scurvy took hold of many of the survivors, although it's believed that the casualties were limited. Cartier had wintered on the St Lawrence back in 1535–56 and had learned that scurvy could be cured by eating the bark of the white cedar tree. Still, the Canadian winters were far fiercer than anything the colonists had experienced in France, and given the fact that a high proportion of them were violent criminals, it's unlikely that Charlesbourg-Royal was a pleasant place to be at this point.

What is known for sure is that having failed to find Saguenay, yet having loaded his remaining ships with a full cargo of illusory mineral wealth, Cartier and his fellow settlers abandoned the colony in June 1542. They sailed to the fishing port of St John's, Newfoundland, where they were surprised to find three more French ships—commanded by none other than Jean-François de la Rocque de Roberval.

Unaware of the governor's extremely delayed departure from France, Cartier had assumed that Roberval had been lost at sea. He soon wished he had been. The explorer's efforts to persuade Roberval that the colony was a lost cause fell on deaf ears. For Roberval, it was not merely a matter of pride and loyalty to his king to keep going; he had borrowed heavily to fund the expedition and had a responsibility to his backers. Like many who came after him, Roberval had staked his already precarious financial future on an adventure in the Americas, and in consequence ordered Cartier to return with him to the site of Charlesbourg-Royal.

Given what his men had experienced over the course of the winter, Cartier was deeply reluctant to obey his superior. The chances were that if he ordered a return, there would be a full-scale mutiny. Unlike Roberval, Jacques Cartier was a man of some means, and the prospect of spending another

FOLLOWING PAGES: Illustrated map of New France showing Jacques Cartier and his settlers disembarking in New France

43

winter starving and freezing in a wooden hut, surrounded by hostile tribespeople, was no competition for returning to his home in St Malo and enjoying the conviviality of a familiar life. As well as that, Cartier probably believed he had already collected enough wealth to last him several lifetimes. So what was the point in enduring such misery, of risking his health and possibly even his life, simply to rescue the fortunes of an officer who had arrived an entire year late and whose superiority he begrudged?

Under the cover of darkness, Cartier and his ships slipped out of St John's and headed back to France. It was a level of insubordination that could have cost him his head. Perhaps Cartier thought his imagined riches would insulate him from the wrath of the King, but in fact he never was punished for his actions.

Roberval's France-Roy

The desertion of his second-in-command was insufficient to deter Roberval from the mission. After first marooning his relative Marguerite de la Rocque and her nursemaid on an island as punishment for an amorous indiscretion, Roberval and his ships navigated their way through the Gulf of St Lawrence using Cartier's charts. From the mouth of the St Lawrence River, they headed upstream, passing Stadacona without stopping to enquire on the natives' health, and arrived at Charlesbourg-Royal. Much of the original settlement had been dismantled by the Iroquois. With the treachery of Cartier no doubt fresh in his mind, Roberval decided to rename the colony France-Roy. Having heard of Cartier's problems with the local tribes, he and his mixed bag of colonial recruits built a fortified colony on the bluff, near where the explorer had constructed the fortified lookout. Included in it were observation towers, soldiers' barracks and a central building containing a large kitchen, offices and a meeting hall. Outside were mills for grinding corn to make bread, and an oven. Roberval sent two ships home in September, with instructions to return with supplies the following summer. He also wanted to ascertain the quality of the gems and precious metals that Cartier had taken back to France.

The record of Roberval's winter in Canada is more extensive than Cartier's, even if the result was ultimately the same, with hostile Iroquois, brutal weather, and sickness and disease all taking their toll on the settlers. The vegetable garden didn't have time to thrive, and as the long, snowbound winter set in, three days of the week became known as fast days, where the colonists only had dried cod, porpoise meat and beans to eat. On other days, eight people shared two loaves of bread for breakfast, while lunch might include bacon and butter. For dinner there was half a pound of beef and beans.

Disciplinary infractions were met with harsh punishment, perhaps a necessary measure when a population with not enough to eat and partly composed of criminals was forced to endure a blizzarding winter in close confines. Six men were hanged for theft, while both men and women were publicly flogged and clapped in leg irons for breaches of the peace.

Although Cartier's men had escaped the ravages of scurvy by imbibing their concoction prepared from the bark of the white cedar, the remedy was apparently ignored on this occasion, since over the course of the winter more than fifty of Roberval's men died of the disease. By spring, when the Iroquois came with a gift of medicinal leaves (perhaps hoping that Roberval would abandon their turf as his predecessor had), there were only 100 men left.

The odds were already stacked against him, but Roberval remained desperate in his quest for a financial boon. In June 1543, once the snow melt had ended and upstream movements became easier, Roberval took seventy men in eight longboats up the St Lawrence in search of the elusive kingdom of Saguenay. As before, the exploration ended at La Chine: one boat and eight men were lost trying to pass through the fearsome rapids. Some of the other boats explored a number or tributaries, but without a great deal of luck.

For the beleaguered Lieutenant Governor of New France, it was the last straw. Roberval hadn't even lucked upon the mica and iron pyrites that Cartier had, and so, without waiting for his supply boats to return from France, he decided to pull up stumps and abandon his short-lived France-Roy.

Third time lucky

By the end of 1543, Roberval had resumed his career as a privateer, this time in the Caribbean against the Spanish (with whom the French were again at war). The remainder of his life continued its theme of aristocratic penury until he was killed as a Protestant during a religious riot in Paris in 1561.

As for Cartier, his exploring days over, he'd retired to Brittany soon after returning to France in October 1542. Moving between his farm and his townhouse in St Malo, he earned himself a reputation as a bon-vivant, before dying from the plague in 1557, at the age of sixty.

It wouldn't be through this particular Cartier that the name would come to be associated with jewellery, some 300 years later, but history does acknowledge Jacques Cartier's true legacy—that of being the first to explore the area that opened up mainland Canada to its eventual settlement.

After the failure of both Cartier and Roberval to establish a permanent settlement, the French retreated from Canada, leaving European contact to its fishermen for another sixty years. The redoubtable Samuel de Champlain revisited the Gulf of St Lawrence in 1603 and eventually established the first permanent European settlements in North America north of Florida, by founding Port Royal, near the Bay of Fundy, in 1605, and Quebec City, on the site of Stadacona (by then abandoned by the Iroquois), in 1608.

MAROONED FOR LOVE

By all accounts, Jean-François de la Rocque de Roberval was a tough customer, and probably a ruthless one too. A Protestant from a very old noble family, he had only escaped religious persecution through his proximity to the King. His appointment as Lieutenant Governor of New France also entailed religious compromises, as one of his tasks was the dissemination of the Catholic faith on behalf of the King. Yet in many ways he remained the dour Calvinist of his chosen religion.

The French have long been renowned for their sophistication in affairs of the heart— not so Roberval, it seems. While crossing the Atlantic on the way to an unknown future, Marguerite de la Rocque, a young relative of Roberval who had joined his expedition, fell in love with a soldier on board the ship. Despite the best efforts of her old nursemaid, a native of Normandy called Damienne, the affair was discovered. Roberval's reaction was severe. Having arrived off the coast of Canada, he decided to maroon the young woman on the Île des Démons ('island of the demons') in the Gulf of St Lawrence. As was the custom in those days, his decision to maroon Marguerite meant the maid went too.

Roberval gave the two women some provisions and a couple of arquebuses (the predecessor of the musket rifle) and had them rowed ashore. The soldier, meanwhile, was held on board the ship as a prisoner, no doubt because Roberval needed all the manpower he could get if the colony was going to survive. But, as the vessel sailed off, the lovestruck Frenchman jumped ship and swam to join his beloved on the island.

For a while, the happy couple enjoyed a rustic form of wedded bliss. The young soldier built a cabin for his lady and fed her with the fish and wild fowl he trapped and hunted. But the winter was cruel, and by the end of it, Marguerite's protector was dead. Unable to bury him because the ground was frozen solid, and unwilling to leave his body outside to be scavenged by bears, she kept it in the cabin until the arrival of spring finally allowed her to dig a grave.

After nine months on the island, Marguerite gave birth to a baby boy, but she was weak from her poor diet. Neither she nor Damienne were able to adequately suckle the child and he died. The following winter claimed Damienne too. Left alone now, Marguerite was forced to protect herself, and protect herself she did—by shooting three bears, including one that she described as being as white as an egg. Just as daunting were the island's eponymous demons, which shrieked in the wind as it buffeted her meagre cabin. Apparently, they were quietened when she read from the New Testament.

In the early spring of 1544, she was rescued by passing French fishermen, who'd noticed the smoke from her fire. When they found her, she was malnourished and her clothes had fallen to pieces—unsurprising, given that she had subsisted on the island for close to two years. The fishermen gave her a ride back to France.

Marguerite returned to her home town of Picardy in the north of the

Jean-François de la Roque de Roberval

country, where she became a schoolmistress. Her amazing story became well known and may have been influential in the relative decline of Roberval. Back in 1542, the latter's financial problems and capacity to inherit at least part of Marguerite's estate may well have been his unstated motive for setting her ashore and leaving her for dead.

CHAPTER 5

 The defeated colony of France Antarctique, Brazil (1555–67)

While Jacques Cartier's attempts to establish a permanent French presence in North America had failed due to poor commerce, an inhospitable climate and the unfriendliness of the locals, France's colony near present-day Rio de Janeiro appeared to have everything going for it. Led by Nicolas Durand de Villegaignon, the settlement of France Antarctique was commercially successful, benefited from a pleasant coastal climate and enjoyed good relations with the locals, plus there was enough food for all. It almost seemed too good to be true, and it was. The petty arguments of Christian sectarianism destroyed most of its advantages, but France Antarctique's undoing ultimately came about through the agitation of Portuguese Jesuit priests.

Since the end of the fifteenth century, the New World had remained technically (or at least papally) divided between Portugal and Spain under the 1494 Treaty of Tordesillas, which confirmed a papal bull from Alexander VI the previous year. The line of demarcation, a straightforward vertical division of the globe, had shifted slightly to the west in the year-long interim, though, with the consequence that the Portuguese were able to maintain their claim to Brazil, the easternmost protuberance of the South American continent. But by the middle of the sixteenth century, Portugal hadn't scored the same bounty as Spain had in South and Central America and was over-stretched in terms of the deployment of military resources to support its territorial claims. The jewels of its empire remained in Africa, where they were notable for their trafficking in slaves, and the East Indies, with its spices and textiles. It was no surprise, then, that a nation of keen colonists like France was now eyeing Brazil with more than casual interest.

At the time, the main attraction of this South American territory for Europe was brazil wood, which became the timber of choice for the makers of violin bows, but more importantly was the much-prized source of a red dye used in the textile industry. Initially, Portugal had a monopoly over the trade in brazil wood, despite not being a country particularly renowned for its textiles, but the failure to adequately populate Brazil under a scheme whereby the territory had been divided into twelve captaincies, each doled out to a favourite of the King,

meant that there was ample opportunity for other nations to infringe on their trade. As was usual for the period, much of this infringement was performed by piracy, or 'privateering'. Yet some of it occurred under the auspices of traders who set up relations with the native people.

By the early decades of the sixteenth century, the French had established a trading presence in Brazil. The French held several advantages over the Portuguese. To begin with, they didn't have to pay the Portuguese monarch a royal fifth of their cargo; nor did they have to dock at Lisbon, thus eliminating a range of middlemen.

Furthermore, the Frenchmen sailing in search of the dye were more often than not from northern France, and usually the Norman ports of Rouen and Dieppe, where the textile industries that needed the dye wood were based. For a French manufacturer, French-imported dye wood was inevitably cheaper than the Portuguese equivalent, as it also was for the neighbouring textile powerhouses of Flanders and England.

In addition, where the Portuguese were enthusiastic and ruthless traders in human flesh, the French in Brazil didn't go slave hunting and thus enjoyed superior relations with the native tribespeople, who were more willing to trade with them and less likely to rip them off. There is also evidence to suggest that the locals preferred the goods the French used for bartering to those of the Portuguese. In planning their colonial enterprise in Brazil, the French actually believed they were saving the Brazilians from the cruelty and rapacity of the Portuguese.

French ships had been coming to Brazil since 1503, beginning with the *Espoir*, which had returned with reports of the abundance of brazil wood. French trading voyages became more and more frequent as a result. The Portuguese lacked the numbers to prevent this, tempting the French to establish more permanent settlements. In 1531, two French ships arrived containing 120 men, who built a fort and trading factory on the island of Santo Aleixo (near present-day Recife). However, the Portuguese captured the ships on their return voyage to Europe. They subsequently put the fort under siege and then massacred the Frenchmen when they surrendered.

A dashing corsair

Trade between France and Brazil continued in an intermittent fashion until 1553, when colonising the country became the pet scheme of a French vice-admiral named Nicolas Durand de Villegaignon. Austrian author Stefan Zweig famously described Villegaignon as 'half pirate, half scientist, a dubious but attractive figure', who wanted 'to do something big, something different from anyone else, something wild and daring, something romantic and extraordinary'.

In many ways, he was a French precursor to the generation of dashing English privateers that prospered in the Elizabethan era, men such as Sir Francis Drake and Sir

Walter Raleigh. And he certainly intended to do something 'wild and daring': Villegaigon had sought the permission of his superior officer, Admiral Gaspard de Coligny, to establish a French colony there in Brazil.

Villegaignon's venture was supported by Coligny and received the unofficial sanction of the French king. In 1550, a pageant honouring King Henry II and his queen, Catherine de' Medici, had been held in Rouen and featured an exhibition of Brazilian life, including real Tupinamba tribespeople. Apparently, Henry was so impressed, he visited the exhibition twice and his disposition towards the idea of colonisation soon became more favourable. While the opinions of the Tupinamba were unrecorded, they were something of a *cause célèbre* in a nation whose philosopher Jean Jacques Rousseau would become powerfully identified with the concept of 'the noble savage' some two centuries later.

Despite the monarch's enthusiasm for establishing a permanent French presence, open support for a violation of the Treaty of Tordesillas was too risky. It was wiser to sanction private efforts such as Villegaignon's that could be disowned if the diplomatic situation necessitated it. Gaspard de Coligny's reasons for supporting the Brazilian mission were somewhat different from his king's. He had become a Huguenot, a member of the growing Calvinist Protestant sect in France that was gaining a number of influential adherents in the 1550s and would be officially recognised by Regent

Catherine de' Medici in the 1562 Edict of Saint-Germain. As a Protestant, Coligny saw no merit in the papally sanctioned division of the New World between Portugal and Spain. More than anything else, it was yet another example of the corrupt and iniquitous behaviour of the Roman Catholic Church. The Brazil scheme also appealed to Coligny because the Huguenots were often persecuted in France, and although the King was in favour of its spread, religious tolerance was precarious. In allowing Villegaignon (a fellow student of John Calvin at the University of Paris) to settle Brazil, Coligny was envisaging a safe haven for his Protestant brethren, as well as the chance to make France as powerful as Europe's richest nation, Spain.

Tupinamba Indians were included in an exhibition for King Henry II in Rouen in 1550

Promising beginnings

Two years passed before Villegaignon set sail from France, on 14 August 1555, with three ships carrying 600 sailors and colonists. Most of those sailing came from the coastal provinces of Brittany and Normandy. There were a significant number of Protestants, but also Catholics, including the Franciscan friar André Thévet, who was Villegaignon's chaplain on the journey. Thévet's book *Singularities of France Antarctique* would be published in 1558 and remains the most enduring account of the expedition, even though its author only stayed for a couple of months.

In November, the French arrived in Guanabara Bay, one of the most beautiful natural harbours in the world, and the location of Rio de Janeiro today. Amazingly, the Portuguese hadn't established a permanent settlement there by the time Villegaignon's fleet arrived.

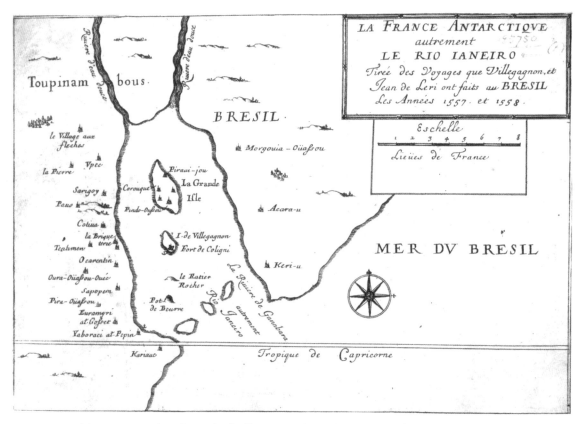

Map of the Rio Janeiro, from the travels of Villegagnon and Jean de Léry in Brazil

It was the perfect place for a colony. The climate was temperate, the harbour exemplary, the brazil wood in abundance, and the 'natives', the French soon discovered, were friendly and willing to trade. Villegaignon, however, was too mad with ambition to be happy running a small show at the end of the world. Having no doubt hoped to conquer a civilisation on the scale of the Inca or the Aztecs, the expedition's leader was not impressed. Writing to his university colleague Calvin, he complained that the country was all wilderness and wasteland, that there were no houses with roofs. The Tupinamba people, he continued, enjoyed a rich subsistence but were too lazy to farm the land; they were without religion (meaning Christianity) or a knowledge of honour or virtue.

For security reasons, Villegaignon decided to build his settlement on the small island located at the mouth of the bay, just off the coast, an island that still bears his name. He built a fort there and called it Fort Coligny after his main patron. The area that is now one of the world's biggest cities, Rio de Janeiro, but was then a few insignificant huts in the wilderness, Villegaignon named Henriville in honour of the King of France.

When Father Thévet sailed back to France and to a notable career of writing about the Americas (without ever again going there), a rich cargo of timber returned with him. Although Villegaignon complained to Calvin about the locals' indolence, relations were so good with the Tupinamba that they often harvested the wood and stacked it on the foreshore of the mainland for the Frenchmen to come and pick up. Ships were soon making the run between France Antarctique and ports such as Rouen on a regular basis.

In fact, things were going so well that Villegaignon decided to expand the size of the colony, and at the same time improve its general moral code. While his own religious beliefs seem to reflect a judicious combination of self-importance and expediency, the vice-admiral's connections in the French Protestant world were impressive. He may not have been a Calvinist, but he shared the same inclination towards repressive disciplinarianism and denial of the pleasures of the flesh. It was an attitude that caused considerable disharmony between himself and his men.

Deprived of French female company, the colonists were constantly tempted by the native women, who wore very little and were equally unburdened by Christian notions of sexual propriety. Villegaignon's zero-tolerance approach to this kind of fraternisation may have been another reason why he chose to build his colony on an otherwise uninhabited island.

His firm stance eventually provoked a rebellion, which was quelled with the aid of some Scotsmen who were loyal to his cause. Sensing perhaps that he might be fighting a losing battle against the sensuality of the tropics, when Villegaignon decided on reinforcements he wrote again to Calvin, requesting a rather more disciplined class of settler.

✳ A CALVINIST CRITIQUE ON WOMEN

'I must respond to those who have written and to those who think that the frequenting of these naked savages, and especially the women, arouses wanton desire and lust. Here, briefly, is what I have to say on this point. While there is ample cause to judge that, beyond the immodesty of it, seeing these women naked would serve as a predictable enticement to concupiscence, yet to report what was commonly perceived at the time, this crude nakedness in a woman is much less alluring than one might expect. And I maintain that the elaborate attire, paint, wigs, curled hair, great ruffs, farthingales, robes upon robes, and all the infinity of trifles with which the women over here [France] disguise themselves and of which they never have enough, are beyond comparison the cause of more ills than the ordinary nakedness of the savage woman—whose natural beauty is by no means inferior to the others. If decorum allowed me to say more, I make bold to say that I could resolve all the objections to the contrary, and I would give reasons so evident that no one could deny them. Without going into it further, I defer concerning the little I have said about this to those who have made the voyage to the land of Brazil, and who, like me have seen both their women and ours.

'I do not mean to contradict what the Holy Scriptures have to say about Adam and Eve, who after their sin, were ashamed when they recognized they were naked, nor do I wish in any way that this nakedness be approved; indeed I detest the heretics who have tried in the past to introduce it over here, against the law of nature (which on this particular point is by no means observed among our poor Americans).

'But what I have said about these savages is to show that, while we condemn them so austerely for going about shamelessly with their bodies entirely uncovered, we ourselves, in the sumptuous display, superfluity and excess of our own costume are hardly more laudable. And to conclude this point, I would to God that each of us dressed modestly, and more for decency and necessity than glory and worldliness.'

Calvinist priest Jean de Léry offering his views on women, nakedness and fashion in his popular book *The Story of a Voyage to the Land of Brazil Otherwise Known as America*. Although he lost the original manuscript, de Léry reconstructed it from memory once back in France. First published in French in 1578, it enjoyed seven more editions before the end of the century, gaining particular fame with an edition featuring works by the Flemish engraver Theodor de Bry. The great twentieth-century anthropologist Claude Lévi-Strauss considered it one of the founding works of anthropology.

Trouble in paradise

In March 1557, three ships under the command of Villegaignon's nephew, Bois le Comte, arrived in Guanabara Bay carrying a further 300 colonists. Many of these newcomers were Calvinists who had followed their leader to his exile in Geneva, although some French Catholics also chose to voyage, giving the lie to the idea that Villegaignon was solely committed to furthering the cause of the Huguenots, as did his subsequent actions.

Almost immediately, the fledgling colony became mired in the intricacies of the same sectarian disputes then running wild in Europe. The Calvinists were renowned for their rigidity in matters of religious doctrine. Furthermore, their belief that entry to the kingdom of heaven was a matter of election rather than good deeds led to an insular arrogance, which was bound to become a source of fractiousness on a small island on which a significant number of people disagreed with their views. Although he had asked for them, Villegaignon soon became ill-disposed towards the Calvinists. Something of a traditionalist in matters of religious ritual, he took particular offence when they advocated suspending the Eucharist, the Christian ritual by which wine and bread are consumed as a symbol of the blood and body of Christ. (The reason, they claimed, was that the Tupinamba were likely to find within it a vindication of their cannibalistic ways.)

It wasn't long before the wrangling between the two Christian sides began to overshadow the many positive aspects of the colony. A frustrated Villegaignon, finding his authority usurped by the religious men, finally decided to forbid the Protestants from celebrating divine service according to Calvinist principles.

As a result, in January 1558 many of them left France Antarctique and returned to Europe. Concern for his own safety led Villegaignon to exile the remaining unrepentant Protestants to the Brazilian mainland. Among them was a Calvinist priest by the name of Jean de Léry, who cohabited for some time with the Tupinamba. De Léry's experiences would lead to his penning *The Story of a Voyage to the Land of Brazil Otherwise Known as America*, a work that is still highly regarded in anthropological circles.

Back on the island, Fort Coligny was now left with a rump of 200 men—far too few for safety, especially given the rumours concerning the aggressive new Portuguese governor, Mem de Sá. He had arrived in Bahia, to the north, in 1557, and it was no secret that he was under constant pressure from the Portuguese Jesuits to expunge the heretical scourge in Guanabara Bay that threatened to sully the New World in the eyes of God.

The end of a dream

With insufficient manpower at his disposal, Villegaignon left Fort Coligny for France early in 1559. Some historians argue that he abandoned his dream of establishing his own empire at this point. Others suggest that he went in search of reinforcements and to take command of a fleet that Coligny had promised him, for the purpose of raiding Spanish treasure ships and destroying the Portuguese settlements along the coast of Brazil. By the time he returned home, however, Villegaignon found himself out favour with the admiral, on account of his harsh treatment of the Protestant refugees he was meant to protect. His reception at court was little better. Although he was not punished, the dashing Villegaignon's career was effectively finished.

Without reinforcements, the Frenchmen Villegaignon had left behind on the island had little hope against attack. On 18 February 1559, a force of 120 Portuguese, augmented by a slightly larger force of baptised Catholic natives, led by Mem de Sá and the warrior priest Manoel da Nóbrega, arrived in a small fleet and overran Fort Coligny, which by then was defended by only seventy-four Frenchmen and their slaves. A Portuguese mass was said and those defenders who hadn't escaped to the mainland were ruthlessly put to the sword.

This wasn't quite the end for the French, however. The Portuguese force wasn't strong enough to pursue the fleeing colonists to the mainland, where the Protestants and their allies, the Tupinamba, constituted a far more potent enemy. After the Portuguese left, it was business as usual on some fronts: French ships came into harbour, loaded their cargoes of dye wood and sailed off to the ports of Normandy as they had before.

The colonists of France Antarctique survived another six years until Father Nóbrega managed to convince the Queen of Portugal to send home-based troops to secure the territory for the Portuguese. She commanded Estacio de Sá, the nephew of Mem, to proceed to Guanabara Bay.

The fleet from Portugal was supplemented with soldiers sent by his uncle from Salvador, and the combined force arrived at Guanabara Bay in March 1565. Estacio founded the city of Rio de Janeiro, under Sugarloaf Mountain, at this point. Ten months later, the Portuguese had built a base on the mainland and their attack began in earnest.

The French were overrun and, as was often the case, those who surrendered were slaughtered. Many of the French retreated into the interior, to live with the naked ladies of the Tupinamba, and were soon incorporated into their culture. There was sporadic guerilla resistance, but by January 1567 it was over. The French had been repulsed and France Antarctique would never be a colony again.

Four years later, it was all over for Nicolas Durand de Villegaignon too. It seems that his patron, Coligny, had deserted him, which may have been why Villegaignon subsequently reaffirmed his commitment to Catholicism. To some of the Protestant groups who had previously supported him, he became known as 'the Cain of America'. Villegaignon died in January 1571 at the age of sixty, having received the last rites from a man of Rome.

Engraving by Theodor de Bry depicting Tupinamba Indians with the French settlers

The French Huguenot colonies of Charlesfort, the Carolinas, and Fort Caroline, Florida (1562—64 and 1564—65)

Despite France's extensive failures in Canada and, most recently, Brazil, Admiral Gaspard de Coligny remained determined. With religious problems ripping his country apart, the committed Huguenot maintained that the answer could well lie in the Americas. And, to a large extent, the ownership of the east coast of America was up for grabs, with Spain's efforts at settlement continually coming up short. The French made two attempts to found a colony on the North American coast within the space of three years. Both failed utterly, through a combination of French stupidity, Spanish ruthlessness, and plain old bad timing.

In 1559, when the Portuguese attacked and destroyed Fort Coligny in Guanabara Bay, Brazil, the promise of France Antarctique as an organised beacon of French glory in the New World was sunk (see page 50). But Admiral Gaspard de Coligny wasn't giving up. If Canada was too inhospitable and Brazil ceded to the Portuguese, why not split the difference and try a colony on the east coast of North America? After all, the Italian navigator Giovanni da Verrazzano had been sailing under the French flag when he became the first European to chart the coast in its entirety—so what right did the Spanish, theologically corrupt, fanatical and vicious, have to monopolise this territory? Besides, all of Spain's previous attempts to settle Florida had ended in disaster and proved fatal for those who'd led them: Ponce de León, Narváez and Soto.

In the same year that the Portuguese had destroyed Fort Coligny, Spain sent six ships and 1500 colonists with considerable pomp and purpose from Vera Cruz, Mexico, with a brief to found a colony that could be used to protect its treasure ships from pirates. The expedition, led by Tristán de Luna y Arellano, was yet another embarrassing failure. His fleet encountered a hurricane on reaching the Florida coast and disintegrated into a shambles, causing the Spanish authorities to abandon the idea of settling Florida.

Another event of 1559 that influenced Coligny's way of thinking was the Peace of Cateau-Cambrésis, signed by France, Spain and England. In this treaty, England renounced its claim to land on the European continent, and France ceded most of its domain in Italy (including Piedmont and Savoy) to Spain. Consolidation was provided through a dynastic marriage between Phillip II of Spain and Elizabeth, the daughter of Henry II, King of France. Within France, however, the peace was perceived as a national humiliation. And given Phillip's zealous hatred of 'Lutheran heretics', it was hardly surprising that the treaty, along with the death of Henry, would soon become a catalyst in the outbreak of religiously inspired civil war. These were desperate times.

Coligny was under no illusion that the Spanish would be content to allow a French settlement prosper so close to the route of the annual treasure fleet, whose riches had made Spain the greatest power in Europe. If he was going to found a successful colony, the Admiral of France needed someone who knew how to command and who had the military skill to fortify the settlement before the Spanish found out about its existence and attacked. His earlier choice as a colonial leader, Nicolas Durand de Villegaignon, had proved a sorry failure at France Antarctique. Despite its economic success, Villegaignon's massive ego and his inability to harmonise the difficult relations between the Protestant and Catholic factions there had probably doomed the colony long before the Portuguese arrived to inflict their Jesuit-inspired violence.

For his second attempt to place his Protestant elect, Coligny chose Jean Ribault, a skilled navigator from the English Channel port of Dieppe. Ribault lacked the social rank of Villegaignon but was seasoned in the ways of men and, Coligny hoped, would display more common sense.

Charlesfort debacle

On 18 February 1562, Jean Ribault sailed from Le Havre with two ships under his command. The crossing took about ten weeks and, having sighted the Florida coast the day before, the Frenchman landed at the mouth of what is today the St Johns River, near Jacksonville, in early May. He called the waterway the River of May, in acknowledgment of the month that had just begun.

From the outset, the signs were positive. Ribault described the land he'd discovered as 'wonderfull fertill, the ground fat so that it is likely that it will bring wheathe and all other corn twice a year'. Fresh water was plentiful, grapes were growing in the wild, and his French nose found the spring aroma of the trees and flowers rather pleasant. He took possession of the land on behalf of Charles IX, France's new boy king, and erected two columns to commemorate this. Next, he set about building a fort on what is now Parris Island (in Port Royal Sound, South Carolina), in order to defend the King's new territories against the Spanish and the local native people, who, as was often the case in these situations, were wary but basically well disposed towards the Europeans. Once the fort was built, Ribault named it Charlesfort, in

honour of the King. Soon afterwards, he left a small detachment of men to maintain the fort, and headed off for France, with the intention of returning with the men and provisions necessary to bolster the fledgling colony.

Ribault left Charlesfort in June and was back in France by the end of July. Unfortunately, by that time France had fallen into civil war and it proved impossible to procure the men and provisions the colony needed. Being a Huguenot, Ribault was forced to seek refuge in England. His initial welcome faded fast and he was soon locked up in the Tower of London, probably for refusing to undertake a colonising mission under the patronage of Queen Elizabeth. It seems his nationalism trumped his religion in matters of loyalty.

Meanwhile, the Spanish had got wind of the new settlement and issued a warning to the French. The Captain-General of the Spanish Indies Fleet, Pedro Menéndez de Avilés, warned King Phillip II of Spain that Spanish shipping routes would be put at risk if the French were allowed to consolidate the colony to the extent where it could harbour ships. Menéndez was also concerned that the French might incite slaves in the Spanish colonies of the Caribbean to rebel against their masters. Since Spain's power was almost entirely contingent on the wealth gleaned from the New World, it was advice that Phillip heeded. In May 1563, he ordered frigate commander Hernando Manrique de Rojas to set sail with his fleet and destroy the French garrison.

The French settlers had already done a pretty good job of destroying Charlesfort themselves, however. The supplies they had been left by Ribault had soon become exhausted. As military men, they no doubt viewed agricultural work as belonging to the realm of peasants, preferring to make themselves parasitically dependent on the Native Americans for food. Although Ribault had praised the abundance of the land, the men he left behind devoted their time to squabbling and dissension. To be fair, it must have been psychologically harrowing to be thus deposited on the other side of the world,

Settlers at Charlesfort seek provisions from friendly Native Americans

especially given that because of the civil war at home, no French ships left Europe.

In the end, there was a mutiny, and the commander whom Ribault had appointed, Captain Albert de la Pierri, was murdered after he had executed a settler and exiled another to a small island. Having waited forlornly for a sign of rescue on the horizon, after little more than a year in the colony the men decided to build their own ship and head back to France. The native tribespeople were eager to be rid of these troublesome interlopers and so helped them out, showing the Frenchmen how to make the hull watertight by using moss and the resin of trees.

Some time after setting out for home in the spring of 1563, the voyagers ran out of food and drinking water. They chose one of their shipmates by lot and ate him. Soon afterwards, the cannibals were rescued off the English coast.

By the time de Rojas arrived with his Spanish warships to destroy the colony, only a single French boy remained. Ribault's two columns, with the French coat of arms inscribed on them, were the only other sign of France's disastrous first settlement in Florida.

Back for more

Although Charlesfort had proved a singular failure, the glowing reports of the land and the military resources made available by the peace with Spain the following year, as well as the worsening domestic situation between the Huguenot and Catholic sections of French society, meant there was considerable incentive to mount a second expedition. Coligny wanted to use Ribault again, but the latter was still out of action in England. He was forced to appoint René de Laudonnière, Ribault's naval second-in-command on the previous mission, in his stead.

With direct funding of 50,000 crowns from King Charles, Laudonnière departed for Florida in the spring of 1564 with three ships. In addition to the 300 mainly Huguenot colonists, there were 110 sailors and 120 soldiers. The colonists included craftsmen (carpenters and apothecaries among them), as well as servants for the soldiers, pages, and four women, one of whom was Laudonnière's chambermaid and housekeeper. There were also several gentlemen volunteers and an artist, Le Moyne de Morgues. Interestingly though, there were no clergymen on the trip. Villegaignon's debacle in France Atlantique had perhaps wised up Coligny to the disruptive role that clergy, with their alternative chain of authority, often played in these circumstances. As the early English colonies in New England and on Providence Island would likewise prove, men of God were not always an advantage when trying to establish footholds in the New World.

Laudonnière was expressly instructed by the Queen Regent, Catherine de' Medici, not to antagonise the Spanish. The peace between the two countries was precarious, as always, but there were also tactical reasons for staying under the radar. Specifically, if the Spanish were unaware of the French presence, then the colony would be well entrenched by the time they could do anything about it. Laudonnière reached the coast of Florida after a fairly uneventful trip, on 22 June 1564. He entered the River of May, was heartened by the friendly greeting he received from the local Native Americans, and began to erect a fort, which he named Caroline (near the present-day city of Jacksonville).

The Frenchman described his new surroundings as a place 'so pleasant, that those which are melancholicke would be enforced to change their humour', yet it increasingly became clear that not all of his fellow colonists shared the sentiment. As was the case with Charlesfort, trouble was not long in the making. The initial problems came from the gentlemen who had volunteered to accompany Laudonnière at their own expense. Like members of the clergy, they were prone to consider themselves above manual labour and separate from the disciplinary regimen often necessary to maximise the chances for the survival of a nascent colony. When commanded by Laudonnière to help build the fortifications to protect the settlement against the Spanish, they complained. Their discontent grew stronger as it became clear that the instant riches that had fuelled their dreams showed no sign of eventuating.

Fort Caroline was built in the shape of a triangle, with a trench and turf battlements on the land side and a bastion made of sand and bundles of sticks to the south, which contained the ammunition magazine. The side facing the river was enclosed by a timber palisade. Within the fort were Laudonnière's lodgings and a main courtyard with covered galleries extending from it. The local Timucua tribespeople helped thatch the roofs with palm leaves. Seven pieces of artillery were transported to the fort and placed to command both sides of the river. A meadow led to a pine forest about a kilometre (half a mile) away, where there was a freshwater spring. Once the fort was finished, a baking oven and storehouse were built in the meadow.

For those tempted to think they had landed in the Garden of Eden, which might be a sign of God's providence, the region was already densely populated by pagans, with a number of tribes existing in close proximity. The closeness of these tribes to one another meant they were frequently at war. Indeed, one of the reasons the Spanish had found it so hard to establish colonies in Florida was that the native peoples of North America were far more formidable warriors than those they had encountered in most of South and Central America.

The River of May marked the centre of the area inhabited by the Timucua people, whose population was concentrated in villages along the river and its tributaries. They were a tall people, tattooed, and many wore dyed fish bladders in their pierced ears. The Frenchmen commented on the strong physiques of both men and women of the Timucua, while an unusual aspect of their society was a large

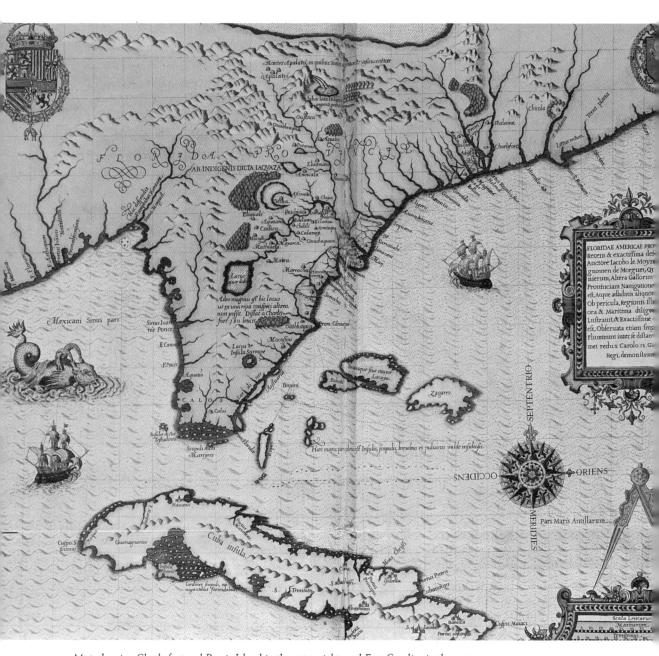

Map showing Charlesfort and Parris Island in the upper right, and Fort Caroline in the centre

proportion of transvestites (who the French believed were hermaphrodites), whose low status meant that they performed much of the heavy and dirty work, including carrying the provisions while the tribe was on the warpath, as well as nursing the contagiously ill and burying the dead.

The tribe was divided into various confederations under a *paracusi*, or chief. The *paracusi* of the area that the Frenchmen settled near the mouth of the river was Saturiba, who had thirty lesser chiefs under his leadership, each of whom ruled a village. A village usually consisted of a few large communal houses, built with stanchions and rafters made out of whole trees, and roofed with palmettos. Up to 100 people lived in the houses. A small room divided off for the chief and his wife was the only private space; in the centre was a hearth where a fire was kept burning day and night, while along the sides of the house were the sleeping quarters. The Timucua slept on their backs, using wooden pillows made with a hollow for the shoulders and a raised part for the head.

The reason Saturiba was so welcoming to Laudonnière and his men, and indeed why he was prepared to share his staple provisions with them, was that he perceived that an alliance would be useful in war against his enemies both within and without the confederation. Laudonnière, who lacked the experience of Jean Ribault, ended up offending Saturiba, however.

The Frenchman had heard that there was gold and silver to be found at Thimagoa,

a village some distance up the river, and sent a lieutenant upstream to ascertain the truth of these rumours. The officer travelled 160 kilometres (100 miles) inland and left a soldier in every village on the way back. A fortnight later, another French officer, Captain Vasseur, took the same route and was delighted to find that one of the men had procured 2.3–2.7 kilograms (5 or 6 pounds) of silver by trading with the local tribespeople. He also heard of a great chief named Outina, whose soldiers covered themselves with gold and silver plate for armour when they went into battle. Laudonnière wanted to trade with Thimagoa. Saturiba, on the other hand, wanted the French to join him on a military sortie against the chief of Thimagoa, an arch rival, and was deeply disappointed when Laudonnière refused to help. Saturiba went into battle anyway, and returned with scalps and prisoners.

The relationship between the two men was further strained when Laudonnière contrived to return some of these prisoners to Thimagoa, hoping to be able to forge an alliance with the precious metal-owning Native Americans. He then bullied Saturiba into trying to achieve peace with Thimagoa, something that insulted the warrior deeply. The insult mightn't have mattered if the French had had any competence at agriculture, fishing or hunting for game.

On 28 July, one of the ships returned to France, carrying presents for the Queen, including fifty pearls, some gold and silver, and alligator hides. A number of the better-

67

off disgruntled colonists returned as well. Given the fate of those who stayed, they would count themselves uncommonly lucky. Two hundred colonists remained: 150 soldiers to man the garrison, the craftsmen, servants and four women.

Reinforcements were not expected until March the following year. The gender imbalance alone was a recipe for discord. But worse still was the fact that while there were soldiers and craftsmen, there weren't any farmers in the group. For food, the French continued to rely on the Timucua, who were increasingly irritated by the presence of these parasitical pale faces who did nothing to advance their cause.

It is a difficult thing to control a hungry, sexually frustrated group of men composed of two religious sects that hate each other; men who have travelled at great risk to themselves because of dreams of gold and silver, only to find that the best chance for their immediate future lies in the backbreaking tedium of subsistence farming. To a certain extent, the leader of the colony, Laudonnière, had to shoulder some of the blame for aiding and abetting these fantasies, just as Ribault had a couple of years before. Ribault had passed on to his men the locals' tales about the fabled Seven Cities of Cibola, mythical cities of unimaginable riches that had already incited several disastrous Spanish ventures into North America. Similarly, Laudonnière shared with his colonists at Fort Caroline a report from one of his scouts, concerning a man who had drunk from the fountain of

youth and lived more than two centuries to tell the tale.

Looking for a way out

At just thirty-five years of age, René de Laudonnière wasn't an inspiring leader, and he certainly wasn't able to prevent a mutiny. During the autumn of 1564, two barques that the French were building were seized by a large group of the colonists, who demanded to go on a privateering mission against the Spanish in the Caribbean.

After leaving the colony, the mutineers captured several ships and conducted onshore raids, on one occasion holding the Governor of Jamaica to ransom. One of the barques seized a Spanish ship and the mutineers murdered a judge who happened to be on board; they in turn were captured by the Spanish, and almost all of the thirty-three Frenchmen were hanged. The other barque made it back to the Florida coast. An attempt to live independently failed, after which they sought the mercy of Laudonnière by asking to rejoin the colony.

In embarking on their escapade, the mutineers effectively destroyed the chance for Fort Caroline to consolidate itself as a colony. Laudonnière's orders not to antagonise the Spanish had been given for good reason. The piratical venture gave Spain both the excuse and the motivation to find Fort Caroline and wipe it off the face of the earth. Realising this, Laudonnière had the ringleaders hanged, although it would make little difference.

Morale wasn't helped by the declining rations over the winter. While the Timucua grew two crops of corn a year, they tended not to store much of it. Instead, over the course of the winter, during the three months when there was no corn, they disappeared into the forests and subsisted by hunting and gathering, eating foods that ranged from tadpoles and spiders to deer. The French were unable to keep up with them and unwilling to emulate some of the Timucua's more unorthodox meals (despite their own fondness for frogs' legs and snails), although they did take to eating snakes. As the colonists' stores began to run out and the food aid the Timucua had so far provided was withdrawn, the disharmony in Fort Caroline got worse. The men took to staring out to sea in the hope of rescue. While their leader had found the surroundings so uplifting at the start of the summer, there was no chance now of the 'melancholicke' changing their humour.

In the spring, the decision was made to abandon the colony, and the men, many of whom had previously resisted the idea of planting crops, started to work on building a ship that would take them home. They were down to their last ten days of rations when four sets of sails were spotted on the horizon. Most likely they were Spanish, thought Laudonnière. But as the ships approached, he realised, to his relief, that they were English. It was a fleet under the command of privateer and slave trader John Hawkins.

Hawkins was generous in sharing his provisions with the Frenchmen and offered to take them back to France. While many of the soldiers welcomed the gesture, honour was at stake and Laudonnière felt unable to accept the offer. He'd been incommunicado for more than six months and was unsure as to whether England and France were at peace or at war now. After all, Ribault had ventured to England for peaceful reasons, and as far as Laudonnière knew, he was still languishing in the Tower of London.

Hawkins seemed to understand the predicament the French commander found himself in. Happy to reach a compromise, he proposed that the colonists name a price and he would sell them one of his ships. It made sense to Hawkins, who had already unloaded his human cargo: an empty ship could only get lost on the Atlantic, whereas money or silver was a far less risky asset. The Frenchmen made him an offer, which included much of their artillery. It must have been a reasonable one, since Hawkins threw in provisions for the crossing, including oil, rice, beans and biscuit, as well as fifty pairs of shoes. Hawkins then sailed off into the Atlantic. Armed with a purpose, the Frenchmen began to ready themselves to sail home.

Back in France, the disenchanted gentlemen who'd returned that summer had given Coligny damning reports on the competence of Laudonnière. As a consequence, while the colonists were preparing to head home, Coligny was putting together a new mission to reinforce the first. By this time, Jean Ribault had been released by the English and he was chosen to lead the fleet and replace

Laudonnière as governor of the colony on his arrival.

On 23 May 1565 Ribault set sail with seven ships and 300 colonists, who included many soldiers and also his son Jacques. On the eve of his departure, Ribault received some disturbing news: the renowned Spanish naval commander, Don Pedro Menéndez de Avilés, was preparing to depart Spain for the coast of New France. In contrast to the orders given to Laudonnière not to upset the Spanish, Ribault was told to resist any attempts by Menéndez to encroach on him or the colony.

Competing colonies

As Coligny knew they would be, the Spanish were particularly concerned by the existence of a base for piracy so close to the route of their slow-moving and vulnerable treasure ships. They might also have been alarmed by Catherine de' Medici's assertion in a letter to the Spanish Ambassador that she wished for all the Huguenots in France to be sent to the Americas. Given that there were at least 40,000 Protestants in France, this throwaway line was probably not the wisest. The Spanish Inquisition was in full swing, after all, and Phillip II enjoyed nothing better than an *auto de fe*, where convicted heretics were burnt at the stake.

The *asiento* (licence) granted to Menéndez by King Phillip was to conquer Florida and establish a colony, but also to exterminate the 'Lutheran heretics' settled there by the French. The rights of all prior adventurers were scratched. In return for funding the mission by himself and through personal subscription, Menéndez and his descendants were to receive trading rights, a pearl fishery and a regular fishery of his choice, as well as all the spoils from any pirate he captured in the next five years. Of course, it was his success as a pillager of pirates that allowed him to stump up the fortune this particular tilt at glory was going to cost.

According to the *asiento*, Menéndez's complement was to consist of 100 soldiers and the same number of sailors, as well as artisans such as stonemasons, carpenters, sawyers, smiths and barbers. Interestingly, the *asiento* required that 200 of the settlers be married, although most of their wives weren't invited on this first fleet. Unlike the French, at least 100 of the settlers were to be farmers, gardeners and labourers.

Menéndez was also ordered to divide the land into *repartimientos*—land to be farmed by tenant Native Americans but granted to the settlers—and to construct at least two towns, each with a fort for protection. Four Jesuit priests and a dozen monks from the order of his choice were to be among the settlers. And filling out the colony's numbers would be 500 African slaves to assist in building and agriculture, including the establishment of sugar plantations to provide an eventual export income. A minimum of one-third of the slaves were to be women. The demographic stipulations of the colony were concluded with a caveat that none of the colonists could be contaminated by heresy (read: Protestant). Nor could they be Moors or Jews. Along with these people, Menéndez was required to provide 100 horses, 200 sheep, 400 swine, 400 lambs, some goats and poultry.

The Spanish admiral went some way beyond the minimum requirements. By the end of June 1565, ten ships with 1500 people, 820 of them soldiers, had assembled in Cádiz ready to sail. Many of the soldiers also had peacetime occupations. Among them were tailors, carpenters, shoemakers, millers, masons, silversmiths, gardeners, barbers, hat-makers, silk weavers and brewers—thirty-eight different trades in all. There were also twenty-seven families and, somewhat more than the number stipulated by the King, seven Jesuit priests. Three of the mutineers from Fort Caroline were also on board, their lives having been spared for their knowledge of the set-up that Menéndez planned to destroy. The admiral was keen to sail, in the hope of beating Ribault's fleet to Florida, but adverse winds forced him to wait another month.

He finally left Cádiz on 29 July and sailed to the Caribbean, where some of his men and three of the priests deserted. His fleet had been dispersed while crossing the Atlantic, and with half the ships yet to arrive in the Americas, Menéndez set sail from Santo Domingo, on Hispaniola. On 28 August, they dropped anchor in an inlet at the mouth of a saltwater estuary the French had named River of the Dolphins, some 80 kilometres (50 miles) south of Fort Caroline. Because

it was the feast day of the patron saint of theologians, Menéndez named the place St Augustine. Seven days later, having allowed his colonists to set up camp, Menéndez sailed up the Florida coast in search of the French.

In the afternoon of 4 September, the Spanish discovered four of Ribault's seven ships anchored outside the bar of the River of May and opened fire on the flagship, *Trinity*. The French fired back but too high to cause any damage to the Spanish vessels, and Menéndez ordered his fleet to move in. According to one of the Spanish chaplains, when Menéndez had drawn within earshot of the French flagship, the following exchanged ensued:

MENÉNDEZ: *Gentleman, from where does this fleet come?*

RIBAULT'S FLAGSHIP: *From France.*

MENÉNDEZ: *What are you doing here?*

RIBAULT'S FLAGSHIP: *Bringing infantry, artillery and supplies for a fort which the King of France has in this country, and for others which he is going to make.*

MENÉNDEZ: *Are you Catholics or Lutherans?*

RIBAULT'S FLAGSHIP: *Lutherans, and our general is Jean Ribault. Who are you?*

MENÉNDEZ: *I am the General, my name is Pedro Menéndez de Avilés. This is the armada of the King of Spain, who has sent me to this coast and country to burn and hang the*

Lutheran French who should be found there,
and in the morning I will board your ships; and
if I find any Catholics they will be well treated.

With the intentions of the Spanish admiral fully expressed, the French decided that discretion was the better part of valour. They weighed anchor and under the cover of darkness slipped out to sea. Once he realised what was happening, Menéndez gave chase but was unable to catch the ships. He returned to the mouth of the river, but seeing Ribault's other three ships still safely anchored behind the bar, and the French soldiers in formation lining the bank of the river, he decided not to attack and returned to St Augustine. When he arrived there, he unloaded his men and supplies and ordered the fortification of one of the natives' communal houses while he considered his options.

Showdown

Having seen the Spanish depart the immediate vicinity, Ribault's other ships, with the exception of the one captained by his son, returned to Fort Caroline, where a war council was held. Ribault was in favour of gathering the best men available, loading them onto the ships and taking the attack to the Spanish, wherever they might have laid up. Laudonnière, perhaps knowing he would be the one left behind with the rump of the

The French settlers at Charlesfort under attack by
Menéndez and his men

men to defend the fort, begged to differ: if adverse winds blew up, then Ribault's ships might be forced out to sea, leaving the fort completely exposed to attack by land. Ribault, a sailor before all else, refused to listen. Taking the best 400 troops available, he set out to attack St Augustine, leaving only 240 men, many of them ill or injured, and no ships, to protect the fort.

Menéndez, a gifted strategist, must have guessed that the doughty sailor from Dieppe would choose his favourite mode of combat to avenge the insults the Spaniard had given to his pride. Using as guides the mutineers and some of the Timucua whom Laudonnière had offended, he marched his troops north through 55 kilometres (35 miles) of swamp and forest towards the Frenchmen. On the morning of 20 September, the force arrived at Fort Caroline.

The French were utterly unprepared. Much of the fortifications had been dismantled and repurposed to build the ships that were supposed to take them home. As dawn arrived, the attackers broke through the flimsy defences and charged into the fort. Most of the Frenchmen were asleep. With no time to don their armour, they emerged bleary-eyed, swords in hand, and were no match for the disciplined Spanish troops. In the space of one hour, 132 Frenchmen were slaughtered, while fifty women and children were captured. The remainder, including René de Laudonnière, fled into the woods, where they were pursued by the Spanish and slain. Only twenty-six men survived.

✳ God standeth in the congregation of the mighty; he judgeth among the gods.

How long will ye judge unjustly, and accept the persons of the wicked? Selah. Defend the poor and fatherless: do justice to the afflicted and needy.

Deliver the poor and needy: rid them out of the hand of the wicked.

They know not, neither will they understand; they walk on in darkness: all the foundations of the earth are out of course.

I have said, Ye are gods; and all of you are children of the most High.

But ye shall die like men, and fall like one of the princes.

Arise, O God, judge the earth: for thou shalt inherit all nations.

Psalm 82, a version of which Jean Ribault was reciting when a Spanish dagger entered his bowels

the Frenchmen had drowned or been killed by the Timucua, 140 remained—hungry, injured, in no state to fight. Menéndez chased them down. Surrounded but having not yet surrendered, the Frenchmen pleaded with him for their lives, asking to be spared until a ship could be found to take them back to France. Their initial appeal fell on deaf ears. The Frenchmen responded with a bribe of 5000 ducats should he let them live. According to some reports, Menéndez then gave his oath that if they surrendered their arms and ammunition without resistance, they would be allowed to return to France. At this point, the Frenchmen surrendered.

The ten Catholics among them were separated from the rest, while the Huguenots were given food and drink. Menéndez then told the larger group that because there were so many of them, he felt obliged to take the precaution of tying their hands behind their backs for the march back to St Augustine. The Huguenots were put into groups of ten and led off over a sand dune. Once they were out of sight, the Spaniards cut them down and decapitated them. The site became known as Las Matanzas, Spanish for 'the massacre', and to this day the estuary on which the town of St Augustine is situated still bears this name.

Menéndez returned to St Augustine but soon hurried back to the coast. He'd heard from his Timucua allies that Jean Ribault and the 200 men who had sailed with him had been shipwrecked on the same sandbar as the prisoners he had recently sent to judgment. Despite his error in abandoning the colony

Having renamed the fort San Mateo, Menéndez marched his men back south to St Augustine. Towards the end of the journey, they passed the area where a couple of the enemy ships had been wrecked. While 200 of

The Spanish settlement of St Augustine

MENÉNDEZ'S ST AUGUSTINE

While Fort Caroline vanished as a French colony, St Augustine, from where Menéndez launched his assault on the French, survived to become the oldest permanent European settlement in North America. But although St Augustine was the first settlement, Port Royal (now in South Carolina), close to where the French had established Charlesfort on Parris Island, became the administrative capital of Spanish Florida. As well as a ruthless mass murderer of defenceless Protestants, Pedro Menéndez de Avilés proved to be an excellent administrator. Within two years of his arrival in Florida in 1565, he had set up a chain of forts along the Atlantic coast as far north as Chesapeake Bay, designed to protect Spanish shipping, maintain Spanish claim to the territory, and serve as bases from which Spanish missionaries could embark on their attempts to convert the native population.

Menéndez was the seventh Spanish conquistador to try to colonise Florida and the first to succeed. It was a formidable achievement, but only a partial success. As was often the case, many of the young men who flocked to the New World with glory and riches in their minds were deeply reluctant to trade in their dreams for the sobering reality of subsistence farming. As a consequence, the settlements dotted along the coast failed to be self-supporting and in the early years of St Augustine, hundreds of people starved to death.

Like the French governors, Menéndez had problems maintaining discipline among his soldiers, who hankered for the glory of plundering ancient civilisations and filling their pockets with gold. In the first precarious years, over 300 men deserted the colony—130 from St Augustine in a single instance, by commandeering a supply ship and sailing away. However, Menéndez was rescued by the arrival of a further 1000 colonists, dedicated farmers among them, who gave the colony the critical mass to survive.

Similar to the French experience again, relations between the Spanish and the Native Americans was a diplomatic minefield. The Calusa tribespeople, for instance, had been using shipwrecked Spanish sailors for ritual sacrifices, a practice which

Menéndez was determined to put to a stop. He established a fort and a mission in their head village of Calos, and a treaty between the Spanish and the Calusa was sealed when Menéndez married the daughter of their chief, Carlos. But Menéndez soon found himself at war with his new father-in-law because of his negotiations with the Calusa's arch enemies, the Tocobago, whom Carlos wanted the Spanish to help him annihilate. It was yet another example of how the Native Americans often saw the Europeans: as a means to achieve pre-existing military and political objectives. The Calusa further clashed with the Spanish over their utter indifference to the Christianity being pushed down their throats. Menéndez eventually authorised the death of both Carlos and his successor, Felipe. After Felipe's death, the Calusa retaliated by burning down the village the Spanish had occupied, and relations between the two peoples were sporadic and usually violent from that point on.

Menéndez left Florida to become Governor of Cuba before returning to Spain. He died in 1574 while fighting against the English in Santander, during the build-up of enmity that led to the Spanish Armada. After the departure of its founder, though, St Augustine faced several more tests of survival.

In 1586, it was attacked and razed to the ground by Sir Francis Drake. In 1668, the colony was raided by the English pirate Robert Searles, who looted the town and sold its mixed-race inhabitants into slavery. A massive stone fortress was then erected and, in 1702 and 1740, St Augustine successfully resisted British incursions from their new colonies in the Carolinas and Georgia. During the Seven Years' War, St Augustine depended on supplies gained by the capture of English ships. However, when the Treaty of Paris ended that war in 1763, Florida was ceded to England and the 1300 Spanish residents were given eighteen months to leave. In 1784 Florida was returned to Spain by the United States following the Revolutionary War. It was only in 1819 that St Augustine finally became part of the United States, when a diminished Spain gave up its claims to the territory.

and leaving it open to attack, Ribault hadn't given up. When Menéndez found him, he and his party were trying to reach Fort Caroline by land. They never did.

Once again Menéndez tricked the Frenchmen into surrender. Their fate became instantly clear when they were marched off to the place where their compatriots lay dismembered in the sand. The men were asked for their religious affiliation. Seventeen of them either were or became Catholics. Their lives were spared. Ribault began reciting Psalm 82. One of Menéndez's officers thrust a dagger into his bowels. The Spaniard's brother-in-law then thrust a pike through Ribault's breast. Just to make sure, another one hacked off his head. The Frenchman's blank eyes watched as his men were cut down to the ground and the colonial ambitions of Admiral Coligny bled into the sand.

Menéndez later wrote to King Phillip, justifying his actions:

> I put Jean Ribault and all the rest of them to the knife, judging it to be necessary to the service of the Lord our God, and of Your Majesty. And I think it a very great fortune that this man be dead ... he could do more in one year than another in ten; for he was the most experienced sailor and corsair known, very skilful in this navigation of the Indies and of the Florida Coast.

The French would get their revenge in 1568, when a force commanded by Dominique de Gourgues joined with Timucua warriors to destroy the Spanish fort at San Mateo. In retaliation for the killing of the French Huguenots at Las Matanzas, De Gourgues decided to hang all of his Spanish captives.

CHAPTER 7

The vanished English colony of Roanoke, the Carolinas (1585–86 and 1587)

Long known as 'the lost colony', Roanoke Island was the first British colony in the New World. Established on the basis of a royal charter granted to Walter Raleigh, the first attempt to settle there lasted just a year. The English were back again in 1587, but only by default—the intended destination being Chesapeake Bay—and a wretched existence ensued. Having reluctantly headed home for more supplies, a desperate John White, the governor of the colony, had to wait out the war with Spain before he was able to return in 1590, only to find the place deserted, with just a cryptic handwritten sign as a clue. Theories abound to this day regarding the settlers' fate. Drought, the Spanish, local tribespeople, sabotage at the highest level of the English royal court—perhaps the answer will only be revealed through the latest techniques in DNA profiling.

When Elizabeth I was crowned Queen of England in 1559, she inherited a drastic imbalance among the European powers. First Portugal and then Spain had grown rich on the profits of the New World. Their ownership of these territories had been assented to by the authority of the Pope in the treaties of Tordesillas (1494) and Zaragoza (1529). The sixteenth-century English delight in products such as cloves and tobacco only enhanced the profits of the Iberian powers, while the precious metals the Spanish were hauling home by the ton from the Americas further increased the envy of the rest of Europe.

On top of his marital troubles, this imbalance had been a further incentive for Henry VIII to declare England Protestant, and in doing so annex the enormous holdings of the Catholic Church in England. He invested some of this booty in ships and in training navigators and sailors, so that they could compete with the Iberians on the open seas. It wasn't a navy as such, since most of England's ships remained in private hands. Still, by the time of Elizabeth's accession to the throne, English ships were cruising the high seas, pillaging Spanish ships for their treasure, frequently with the unofficial sanction of their queen. For England's first great navigators, John Hawkins, Francis Drake, Humphrey Gilbert and Walter Raleigh, the lines between pirate, defender of the realm, war lord, slave trader, privateer, explorer and coloniser were never fully clear.

Initially a moderate Protestant, Queen Elizabeth was radicalised by her 1570 excommunication by Pope Pius V, who gave the Catholic subjects of England permission to rise against her monarchy. There was a gradual build-up to the war with Spain, then in the fanatical throes of the Inquisition, which culminated in the defeat of the Spanish Armada in 1588. Elizabeth's emerging interest in establishing English territories in the New World was a consequence of this geopolitical tension. The first attempt by an Elizabethan Englishman to found a colony in the Americas was in 1578, when Martin Frobisher made his third voyage to the land that Elizabeth called Meta Incognita, on the eastern coast of Baffin Island in the Canadian Arctic. The intention had been to establish a mining colony there, but the venture was soon abandoned when the loss of a supply ship made surviving a winter impossible. It might have been an inauspicious start, but England had caught the colonisation bug.

Gilbert, Raleigh and Roanoke

Next was Humphrey Gilbert, Raleigh's half-brother. Granted a royal patent for six years to settle North America, his initial plan to found a colony of wealthy disenchanted English Catholics near contemporary Massachusetts was foiled by the crown's insistence that the would-be settlers pay their recusancy fines before embarking. The efforts of Catholic interests in England loyal to Spain were another factor undermining the mission.

Eventually, having found an alternate source of funding, Gilbert set off in 1583 with five boats full of criminals and ne'er-do-wells, intending to take possession of the multinational cod-fishing camp at St John's, in Newfoundland. Raleigh sailed with him, but his ship, the *Bark Ralegh*, was forced to turn around early in the expedition due to a lack of supplies. Gilbert's entry to the port was initially blockaded because of a charge of piracy arising from a previous sortie to the New World, and although he made some land grants, actual colonisation didn't really occur. On his way home, the unfortunate Gilbert was lost at sea. In his stead, Walter Raleigh, a favourite of Elizabeth and famous for his dashing wit, strategy and poetry, was granted a royal patent to 'discover, search, finde out, and view such remote, heathen and barbarous lands, countries, and territories, not actually possessed of any Christian Prince, nor inhabited by Christian People ...' The patent was carefully phrased, forbidding the invasion and overrunning of any European colonies already established in the New World, but granting the right to claim land where there was no Christian power in the immediate vicinity.

In 1584, Raleigh sent out a reconnaissance mission under the command of Philip Amadas and Arthur Barlowe. With the failure of his half-brother in mind, Raleigh's primary intention was a pragmatic one: to establish a defendable settlement from which expeditions against the Spanish treasure ships could be launched. Although Florida was closer, Roanoke Island, nestled between the Outer Banks of North Carolina and the mainland in the enormous Pamlico Sound, was decided on because its position gave it a natural defensive advantage.

Barlowe was highly laudatory in his report to Raleigh. He outlined an Arcadian setting, as so many first impressions of these potential New World colonies tended to do. The 'soile', he claimed, was 'the most plentifull, sweete, fruitfull, and wholsome of all the world', while the native people were 'most gentle, loving, and faithfull, void of all guile, and treson, and such as lived after the manner of the golden age'. But Barlowe managed to omit the fact that the channels around the island were extremely shallow, making it difficult for vessels of an ocean-going size to access it. This difficulty of navigation, combined with the fierce storms that frequented this part of the coast, were two of the factors that ultimately doomed the colony of Roanoke Island to fail.

After the anticlimaxes of the Frobisher and Gilbert missions, the return of Amadas and Barlowe with two natives of the region whom they had kidnapped, Manteo and Wanchese, caused considerable excitement in England. Elizabeth was enthusiastic. Not only did she knight Raleigh, but she permitted him to name the new territory (not necessarily accurately) Virginia, in her honour.

The first time for Virginia

The party that Raleigh assembled for the first attempt to settle Roanoke Island was

primarily military. There were no women, no children, no farmers; although there was also a scientific contingent, comprising Thomas Hariot and artist and cartographer John White.

Intriguingly, there was no Sir Walter Raleigh either, who preferred to stay in England. Sir Richard Grenville was appointed general and admiral of the fleet. He would be in command for as long as he remained in the colony. His flagship, the Queen's galleass (three-masted warship) *Tiger*, sailed with Simão Fernandes as master and chief pilot of the expedition.

Like much English shipping at the time, the expedition depended on Iberian pilots with a pre-existing knowledge of the seas around the American coast. Fernandes, a native of the Azores, held a passionate hatred for Spain, possibly because he was from a Jewish family at the time of the Spanish Inquisition. His loyalty was to Sir Francis Walsingham, one of Elizabeth's chief courtiers and a purveyor of intrigue, who had spared his life when the Portuguese sailor was captured as a pirate in the English Channel. Fernandes claimed to have travelled to Chesapeake Bay under the Spanish flag in the 1560s; as the pilot of the previous year's reconnaissance mission, he was responsible for taking the English to the Outer Banks. In the subsequent history of the colony, however, he played an ambivalent role.

The first attempt to found a colony at Roanoke Island in 1587

The second in command was Thomas Cavendish, later the second Englishman to circumnavigate the world (Drake being the first). Captain Ralph Lane was appointed Governor Designate of the settlement. Like Grenville, Raleigh and Gilbert, and many other men of the era, Lane was a veteran of England's violent conquest of Ireland.

After departing England in April 1585, the fleet was scattered by a storm in the Atlantic. By the time the expedition's flagship, the *Tiger*, reached the West Indies, a split in the leadership between Grenville and Lane had arisen, partly because when they captured two Spanish frigates, Grenville ransomed the sailors and then pragmatically used the money to trade with the Spanish for further supplies. Lane's experience in Ireland had taught him to adopt a take-no-prisoners approach. Grenville's career in Ireland was tainted with charges of absenteeism, but he was no shrinking violet either. According to one contemporary: 'He was of so hard a complexion … he would carouse three or four glasses of wine; and, in a bravery, take the glasses between his teeth, and crush them in pieces, and swallow them down, so that oftentimes the blood ran out of his mouth, without any harm at all to him.'

They left the West Indies midway through the year. The delay had already cost the settlement the opportunity of planting its own crops. This predicament was compounded when Fernandes, despite his expertise, ran the *Tiger* aground as he piloted it through the tricky shoals around the Outer Banks. While the ship was saved and no lives were lost, many of the supplies designed to provide for the men over the winter (such as corn, rice, flour and biscuit) were spoiled. The colony would now be overly reliant on trade with the Native Americans in the vicinity to ensure its survival.

There were at least two goals for this initial settlement. First, was to establish a base for English privateers, especially given that in May of that year Spain had declared an embargo on English shipping, seizing all the English merchant ships in Spanish ports and subjecting their crews to the horrors of the Inquisition. Raleigh had also given the expedition orders to explore the area in order to work out how best to utilise the potential riches granted in his royal patent. This purpose became more important given that it was now realised that Roanoke Island was not the ideal place for Raleigh's envisaged colony, with its poor harbour and lack of arable land. Amadas and Barlowe's reconnaissance mission had done few favours for the colonists.

Making new enemies

On 11 July, Grenville took a pinnace, three longboats and sixty men across Pamlico Sound to the mainland. They explored the rivers flowing into the sound and visited several villages to gauge the trading potential of the area. At Aquascogoc, a two-day row inland, they were treated to a feast by the Native Americans. As they rubbed their contented bellies, the English contingent

discovered that a silver cup they had brought with them was missing. Despite having been fed far more than the value of the cup, Grenville ordered that the village and the surrounding crops be razed.

This overreaction was unsurprising for a bunch of soldiers who had served in Ireland, where the locals were extremely hostile towards the English. Grenville's response to this relatively trivial transgression was essentially an Elizabethan version of the shock-and-awe tactics used by the present-day US military.

He believed that since Lane and his soldiers would be dependent on local aid for sustenance during the winter, a disproportionate response was necessary to prevent the native tribespeople from trying to challenge the Englishmen when they became vulnerable. As the colonists discovered, the logic was flawed. It ignored the prestige the most proximate Native Americans derived from having trading access to the range of goods the English had and, in contrast to Ireland, the generosity the English contingent had thus far been shown.

Despite encounters such as this, by the time Grenville set sail for England, at the end of August 1585, there was considerable optimism for the prospects of an English colony in the region. The mainland around Chesapeake Bay, a good way north from Pamlico Sound, had firmed as the best site for such an endeavour, Lane concluding after his explorations that 'It is the goodliest and most pleasing territorie of the world (for the soile is of an huge unknowen greatnesse, and very well peopled and towned, though savagelie) and the climate so wholesome, that we have not had one sicke, since we touched land here.'

After Grenville left and the seasons changed, relations between the English and the native people deteriorated. Villages that had contact with the Englishmen were afflicted by the diseases they brought with them. Healthy men, women and children as well as elders entrusted with the communal memory died at such a rate that the survivors were unable to properly bury them and putrefying corpses became a feature of Barlowe's arcadian idyll. The colonists came to be seen as harbingers of evil tidings, and the tribespeople began to avoid them.

As winter set in, life in the recently built English fort on Roanoke became unpleasant. The Native Americans and their food were now scarce. Discipline among the soldiers started to fray, with the result that at least one man was hanged. Small groups of men were sent out to forage and the tribespeople, beginning to realise the power they had over the English, threatened to withdraw from the island without planting any seed for the following year's crop.

By the end of winter, Wingina, chief of the Roanoke Native Americans, had retired to the mainland, partly to convince other local tribes to combine in an attempt to attack and wipe out the Englishmen. Captain Lane, meanwhile, had no choice but to wait for the arrival of more supplies, which had

been promised by Easter. With no sign of the ships throughout the spring, and with many of his men dispersed in the quest for food, he was aware of the vulnerability of the settlement and began to plan a pre-emptive strike against the native tribes. On 1 June 1586, the English attacked and Wingina was killed. Any hopes of peaceful coexistence were dashed.

Around a week later, the colony's hopes for relief from home seemed to be vindicated when English sails were spotted on the horizon. But instead of the supply ships, it was a privateering fleet under the command of Francis Drake, who had been on a plundering mission against the Spanish in the Caribbean for nearly a year. The Roanoke colony was supposed to help Drake's fleet reprovision, but it turned out to be the other way around.

On 12 June, on being told of Lane's plans to move the colony to Chesapeake Bay, Drake offered to replace some of the unfit men with his own, and to provide a barque, two pinnaces, boats, equipment he'd taken from Spanish outposts that would be useful for agriculture and construction, as well as weapons and ammunition.

Just as the offer was accepted, however, a powerful storm blew up and scattered the fleet—once again revealing the poverty of Roanoke as a harbour. When the barque that Drake had promised the colonists failed to return after the storm, Lane was sufficiently

FOLLOWING PAGES: The arrival of the English in Virginia

85

WEAPEMEOC

Trinety harbor

disheartened to abandon the settlement. He and his men boarded Drake's ships and headed back to England.

A week later, the promised supply ships arrived to find the colony uninhabited. Sir Richard Grenville returned two weeks after that with more supplies and another 400 men, but seeing the fort abandoned, he left fifteen soldiers to look after it and sailed away. With the exception of a bleached skeleton found by the next English contingent to arrive on the island, these men were neither seen nor heard from again.

Take Two

When Ralph Lane and his men arrived back in England, Raleigh weighed up the information they had gathered. It was agreed that Roanoke Island was unsuitable as a place of settlement, since its poor harbour rendered it useless as a drop-off point for English privateers, while Drake's success had proved that such a base was not a naval necessity after all. Nonetheless, there was considerable enthusiasm about the rich lands in the vicinity of Chesapeake Bay. Governor Lane's explorations having provided him with tales of possible gold mines inland from the bay, his report to Raleigh retained an emphasis on privateering and the mining of precious metals as reasons for starting the colony. Yet the report by Raleigh's scientific advisor, Thomas Hariot (subsequently published as *A Briefe and True Report of the New Found Land of Virginia*), advised against taking the plunder

approach to settling the Americas. He emphasised timber products, silk grass, animal furs and medicines as the most likely sources of enrichment from settlement. Hariot also argued that a long-term commitment would be needed to harness the economic potential of the territory.

The form of the second attempt at colonisation showed that Raleigh had listened to Hariot above Lane. A joint-stock company was set up, with long-term intentions based on the economic model of a plantation. Instead of military men, the colonists consisted of families, possibly Separatists— those who argued for the separation of religion from the state. A fervent Protestant, Raleigh had some sympathy for their cause. Despite the fact that Spanish Catholicism was the primary enemy at the time, there was concern at the dangers of defraying the English state's authority over individual souls, and Separatists had been persecuted during Elizabeth's reign, particularly after the 1583 appointment of John Whitgrift as Archbishop of Canterbury, the most senior position in the Church of England. The Separatist families that served as Raleigh's colonists were the religious antecedents of the Puritans who would later sail to New Plymouth on the *Mayflower*.

The colony's governor was John White, Hariot's naturalist colleague from the previous attempt and a veteran of the first reconnaissance mission also. With him were his pregnant daughter, Elizabeth Dare, her husband, and 114 other settlers, among them farmers and the craftsmen necessary for building a permanent colony. Some of these settlers were members of the joint-stock company and were to receive at least 200 hectares (500 acres) of land for the capital they had invested in purchasing their share. Other, less wealthy members of the contingent had volunteered only 'the adventure of their person', in the hope of escaping from the overcrowded conditions of an Elizabethan England afflicted by a population boom.

On 8 May 1587, three ships set out from Plymouth Harbour in the far southwest of England to establish the city of Raleigh in the New World. With White was another veteran, the pilot Simão Fernandes, one of the twelve assistants of the joint-stock company. Unfortunately, the two men soon clashed over the expedition's priorities. When they reached the West Indies, Fernandes, whose idea of profit was inspired by his sea-dog status and pathological hatred of the Spanish, embarked on a privateering spree

The settlement at Roanoke Island

THE PIRATE PILOT

Perhaps the most influential person in the story of Roanoke Island was Simão Fernandes—the ship's pilot who brought the reconnaissance mission to Roanoke in 1584, was responsible for the loss of the supplies while negotiating the shoals during the 1585–86 settlement attempt, and whose priorities so irritated Governor John White on the final expedition.

Fernandes was born in the Azores, the Atlantic archipelago about 1600 kilometres (1000 miles) west of Portugal, their traditional colonial occupier, at a time when the Iberian nation was ruled by King Phillip of Spain. Fernandes trained in Portugal as a pilot before working for the Spanish in that capacity on the Atlantic and the Caribbean.

In about 1570, Fernandes came to England, where he lived in Plymouth and London. It's likely that his moving was a consequence of the Spanish Inquisition, perhaps because he was either Protestant or Jewish and therefore at risk. While describing himself as a merchant, Fernandes was really a pirate. From 1573, he roved the English Channel seeking plunder, and then teamed up with notorious English pilot John Callice on a mission to raid Spanish assets in the Indies. After raiding a Portuguese ship off his old home in the Azores, Fernandes was arrested as a pirate in England. He was saved from hanging by the intervention of Sir Francis Walsingham, who had the charges dropped, despite the fury of the Portuguese Ambassador. While Walsingham had no gripe with the Portuguese, he decided Fernandes was too useful against the Spanish to waste.

After this rescue, Fernandes was known as Walsingham's man, but he sailed with Raleigh and Humphrey Gilbert on their missions to the Americas. Fernandes was entirely unscrupulous, fond of piracy more than anything else. The main reason why he was trusted by his overseers was his pathological hatred of the Spanish.

But antagonising the Spanish was exactly what John White did not require during the voyage to the Carolinas in 1587. Fernandes wanted to profit, as always, through his privateering and so clashed with White, who was loath to put his colonists (his daughter among them) at risk of capture. Pig-headed and hot-blooded, Fernandes exacted a revenge for what he perceived as the governor's interference in his plans.

Fernandes' behaviour on the final Roanoke mission was so counterproductive, in fact, that historian Lee Miller has concluded that Walsingham had instructed his charge to sabotage the colony—the Portuguese pilot deliberately marooned the settlers on Roanoke Island because Walsingham coveted the Americas to help extricate himself from financial difficulties. In addition, Walsingham was known to be envious of Raleigh's favour with the Queen. It's a controversial explanation, but one that adds even more intrigue to the mystery of Roanoke Island. Fernandes' role in the failure there marked the end of his relationship with Raleigh. The Portuguese pilot fought under Martin Frobisher in the battle of the Spanish Armada. In 1590 he sailed with Frobisher to the Azores on a privateering mission. It's possible he was killed on this expedition, since his name fell out of history thereafter.

The Spanish Armada squares up against the English fleet

that depleted essential supplies. It wasn't until late July, therefore, that the colonists arrived at Roanoke Island, where they found the fort had been abandoned.

The original intention had been to sail on to Chesapeake Bay and establish the colony there. But having delayed the fleet for plunder, Fernandes further infuriated White by claiming that it was too late in the season to sail to Chesapeake Bay because he had also to allow sufficient sailing time (and plunder time) for heading back across the Atlantic before autumn set in. They would have to winter at Roanoke Island instead. But having argued this, Fernandes proceeded to linger at the island for another month, repairing his ships, which would have been easily enough time to sail the colonists the 160 kilometres (100 miles) to Chesapeake Bay.

The exact reasons why Fernandes chose to do this remain unknown. Perhaps it was a display of stubbornness as a consequence of his earlier clash with White. Or maybe it had something to do with Fernandes' role as one of the assistants of the joint-stock company. Given his penchant for privateering, it's highly likely he believed that the company's money and time was better spent preparing his ships for another round of plunder on the way home. On the other hand, some historians have suggested that Fernandes may have believed that such a small and ill-defended group of colonists would be safer on Roanoke Island than in Chesapeake Bay, where the locals were more warlike. Theories abound, one even suggesting that

he was acting on the orders of Sir Francis Walsingham, his benefactor.

Whatever the motivation, it is clear that the colonists were not happy with the outcome. And whatever Fernandes might have thought regarding the local Native Americans being less warlike here than further north, the colonists still had much to fear. Governor White was able to establish relations with the neighbouring Croatoans at least, but many of the surrounding tribes were less friendly—unsurprising, given their treatment by Grenville and Lane the previous year. While hunting for crabs to supplement their diet, one of the Englishmen, George Howe, wandered off alone and was slain by Indians. Relations worsened when White and twenty-four colonists carried out reprisal attacks.

Driven to despair by their predicament, the colonists begged White to leave behind his daughter and his newborn granddaughter, Virginia Dare, and return to England to put their case directly to Raleigh. In the meantime the settlers would use the remaining boats to remove themselves to Chesapeake Bay, where they would set up the colony and await the governor's return with further supplies in the spring. At the end of August 1587, piloted by Simão Fernandes, White reluctantly sailed for England.

Vanished

What exactly happened to the colonists at Roanoke remains a mystery. Raleigh's provisioning of a fleet to relieve them in

1588 was undermined by the attempted invasion of the Spanish Armada, when a royal edict was issued that kept all ships capable of defending the realm in English ports. A desperate John White managed to hire two smaller ships and fill them with provisions. They sailed from Devon in April 1588, but came to grief when they were captured by French pirates 240 kilometres (150 miles) from Madeira. The supplies were appropriated and White received head wounds from a pike and sword as well as gunshot in the buttocks.

The travails of the colonists were probably no easier. Roanoke Island was not highly arable, the local tribespeople were ambivalent to their presence at best, and to make things worse the region was experiencing its worst drought in 800 years, according to the record contained in the rings of trees. And that's presuming they stayed on the island and didn't set off for Chesapeake.

Despite his best efforts, White was unable to mount another rescue expedition until 1590. He sailed on a fleet of three ships under the command of privateer John Watt. After sweeping through the Caribbean in search of Spanish booty, they eventually reached Roanoke Island on 18 August. When he raced onto the shore, his heart no doubt pounding with the anticipation of a family reunion, he was devastated to find the colony completely abandoned. The houses were gone, the settlement reduced to a patch of bare earth. It was as if it had never existed. The only sign of the colonists that remained

was the word 'CROATOAN' carved into one of the trees framing the empty place where the settlement had once stood.

If there was a positive, it was that there were no evidence of violence having taken place there. White had arranged for his settlers to leave a sign giving their destination when they eventually abandoned the island. He determined that they must have decamped north to Croatoan Island, near Cape Hatteras, and organised to sail there the following day.

But fate was against him once more. The hurricane season was in full swing by this time and the skies were eerie with an impending storm. When it hit, the ships narrowly avoided running aground on a shoal, before being forced out to sea. The decision was made to head back to England. White never got to check where the lost colonists had travelled to Chesapeake Bay. After writing a report to Raleigh, he headed to Ireland and then vanished from history.

It's unknown whether the Roanoke settlers made it to Croatoan, or indeed if they were referring to the Croatoan tribe instead of the island. Further attempts to find the colonists in 1602–03 also produced no definitive result. In 1607, Roanoke was superseded by the foundation of Jamestown in Chesapeake Bay, Virginia; the following year, one of its settlers, Francis Nelson, reported seeing four men from Roanoke at an Iroquois village to the south, while there were reports of other colonists working copper for the Native Americans.

Archaeological evidence has unearthed English artefacts at the Croatoan tribe's ancient capital, some 80 kilometres (50 miles) from Roanoke Island, at least suggesting that there was contact between them. As with many mysteries, the theories have proliferated over the years.

It's possible that the colonists were scattered due to the drought, with some members being killed and others incorporated into local tribes. It's possible too that the settlers were lost at sea while attempting to move en masse to Croatoan Island or Chesapeake Bay.

Another, less likely theory is that the Spanish massacred the Roanoke settlers, as they did the Frenchmen at Fort Caroline, Florida, in 1565 (see page 60). Anecdotal evidence that the local tribes once had a preponderance of fair-skinned blue-eyed members is currently being tested using DNA profiling. But the mystery remains unsolved.

CHAPTER 8

The abandoned English colony of Sagadahoc, New England (1607–08)

Sagadahoc, also known as the Popham Colony, after Sir John Popham, the Lord Chief Justice of England, was the first English colony in New England, predating the Puritan settlement in Massachusetts by thirteen years. Situated on the banks of the Kennebec River in present-day Maine, the settlement lasted little more than a year from its inception in 1607 until its abandonment. The reasons are unclear since its records have been lost to history, but the possible contributing factors are certainly wide-ranging: kidnapping, internal power struggles, lack of trade opportunities, a massacre and witchcraft.

In 1606, King James created two competing joint-stock company charters to colonise the territory that Walter Raleigh had named Virginia. The London Company was granted a patent to settle land from the 34th parallel to the 41st parallel—Cape Fear to Long Island Sound—while the Plymouth Company received an intersecting permission to settle between the 38th and 45th parallels—northern Chesapeake Bay to Novia Scotia. They were both allowed to build settlements between the 38th and 41st parallels on the condition that competing settlements were no closer than 160 kilometres (100 miles) to one other.

A year before this, a reconnaissance mission under George Weymouth had carried out an exploration of the region now known as Maine, the US state that borders the Canadian provinces of Quebec and New Brunswick. Weymouth's sponsor was Ferdinando Gorges, who was soon to become a key figure in England's colonial enterprise. Satisfied with his man's encouraging report, not to mention the delivery of a group of Indians from the area,

The arrival of the English colonists in the New World

Gorges had no qualms in signing on as one of the Plymouth Company's major investors.

Adding further political clout to the planned venture in Maine was the appointment of George Popham, nephew of Lord Chief Justice John Popham, as governor of the colony, and Raleigh Gilbert, son of the late Sir Humphrey Gilbert, as second in command. It was Sir Humphrey whose ship had sunk (apparently while he was reading Thomas More's *Utopia*) on his return from an unsuccessful attempt to settle Newfoundland in 1583. No such watery grave awaited young Gilbert, although there might have been some concern that the Plymouth Company's first ship, the *Richard*, which had sailed in August 1606, had been captured off the coast of Florida by the Spanish.

On 1 June 1607 two more ships left England with just over 100 settlers on board, bound for the Kennebec River. The *Gift of God* was captained by George Popham, while the *Mary and John* sailed under Raleigh Gilbert. Their intention was to establish a permanent colony there to trade with the native tribes, provide timber for the British shipping industry and set up a base for exploration in search of the northwest passage through to Asia. They also hoped, as colonists of the day invariably did, to source a supply of precious metals.

Poor relations

The colonists disembarked on 8 August 1607 and immediately set about building a fortified village with a storehouse, a chapel and lodges for accommodation. The village was surrounded by a large, roughly star-shaped log palisade, on which cannon were mounted to defend against possible attacks from the locals. It was named Fort St George, after Popham, the first president of the colony's governing council, but was more commonly known as Sagadahoc.

Details of Sagadahoc's short existence remain sketchy, being based partly on what local Indians later related to Pierre Biard, a French Jesuit priest, when he visited in 1612. What is almost certain is that, from the beginning, relations between the Englishmen and the Indians were vexed.

Part of the reason for this was the English practice of kidnapping indigenous people on previous sorties into an area they later planned to colonise, as George Weymouth had done two years earlier. The English were wary of the tribespeople. Unconvinced of the humanity of 'savages', they were prone to taking a heavy-handed approach, an attitude that had been a factor in the failure of the two colonies at Roanoke Island in the 1580s.

Somewhat paradoxically, they also believed that by kidnapping selected Native Americans, removing them to England and 'civilising' them, they would create allies who could then go among their people and inform them about the general superiority of the English. As a result, the thinking went, the tribes would submit to the colonising force for fear of the consequences, then love them as a child loves their parent or a parishioner their

God. Such an approach failed to allow for the independence and sophistication of political and commercial strategy that the English settlers encountered among the Indians.

George Weymouth had kidnapped five Indians during the spring of 1605. One of them, Skidwarres, returned with the Popham expedition, but was reluctant to establish trade, as was Tahenedo, another of the abductees, who had returned to New England on an earlier ship. These men had promised to introduce the Sagadahoc colonists to the chief of the Abenaki tribe, who lived upriver. The colonists were told of the rich resources of the region and the chief's willingness to trade, yet when they arrived at the designated meeting place, there was no one there.

As summer turned to autumn, the limited trade that did occur with the local inhabitants was disappointing, not the least because of the utter lack of precious metals on offer. At the time of sailing, Ferdinando Gorges and other principal backers had been convinced that the Maine tribes were in direct contact with China via the northwest passage. Weymouth had traded in furs and sassafras (a herb believed, erroneously, to cure syphilis), but the Popham colonists only succeeded in trading their goods for second-rate animal skins. The tribespeople already had trading relations with the French and were apparently not interested in dealing with the English. Back across the Atlantic, the investors in the colony were dismayed when the supply ships they sent returned to England virtually empty.

Unable to get on with the native people, the settlers were also unable to get on among themselves. Like many colonies where men stuck in close confines at a far remove from home, the short life of Sagadahoc was marked by fractious internal politics. Based on reports he was given, Gorges would later write that Fort St George was full of 'ignorant, timorous and ambitious persons' who had split into 'childish factions'.

It was pure nepotism that had dictated the choice of leadership, and factionalism that threatened to destroy it. To one group, George Popham was too old and ineffectual to successfully run a colony, while the other faction held that Raleigh Gilbert was equally unsuited. At twenty-five, Gilbert was too young, lacked the respect of many of his fellow colonists, and was impetuous and self-indulgent—a dashing but fairly useless figure in the wilderness.

The last straw

The bitterly cold and miserable winter of 1607–8 awaited Sagadahoc. Half of the settlers had already left for England, since their late summer arrival had drastically restricted the planting season and there simply wouldn't be enough food to go around. The remainder endured a winter far colder and with more snow than they were used to in England, but with the exception of one man they survived.

The honour of having a fortified village named after him hadn't done much good for

George Popham. The governor died in February, probably from illness brought about by the cold. According to what Father Pierre Biard was told four years later, however, the cause of his death was something far more sinister—witchcraft, the native people insisted. Whether that was true or not, for the fifty or more Englishmen present during

those winter months, there certainly appeared to be a curse of some sort on this settlement beside the Kennebec.

Early in the spring, their spirits can't have been lifted by a fire that destroyed much of the village they had laboriously constructed. Many of their stores were also destroyed, and with the need to rebuild diverting crucial

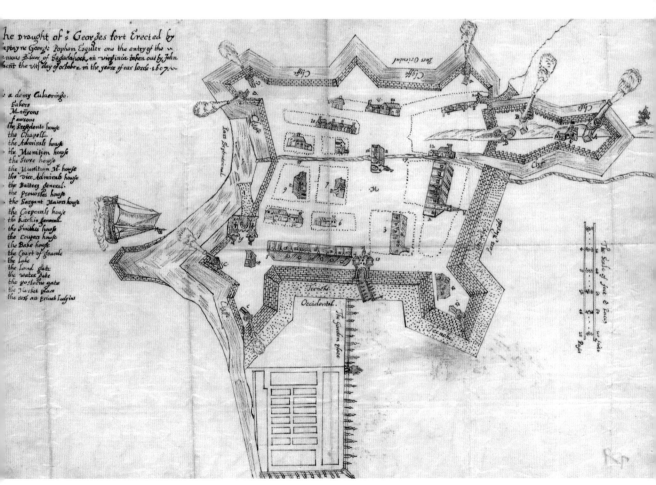

Settlement map of Fort St George

man hours from agriculture, the planting season would again be adversely affected. When the supply ships arrived that spring, they brought the bad tidings that Sir John Popham had also died. With Raleigh Gilbert having already proved unconvincing as a leader, the settlers' morale sank to a new low. When the *Mary and John* returned during the summer, therefore, they may well have been relieved to hear that Gilbert's older brother, John, had died as well, because it forced Gilbert back to England to claim his inheritance. By that stage, life at Fort St George was so wretched, and the profit from trade so minuscule, that they decided to return with him. With the loss of Popham and the departure of Gilbert, the colonists had also lost their connection to England's circles of influence.

In the version of events related to Pierre Biard, however, the decision to leave wasn't entirely their own. The Frenchman was told of a massacre carried out by a native tribe in which eleven of the Englishmen were killed while fishing. Their numbers now severely decimated, and fearing for their lives, the forty or so remaining settlers abandoned the colony soon afterwards. Again, there's little actual evidence to support such a claim, and it's difficult to know whether there was a massacre or not. What is known is that, in August 1608, the surviving colonists split into two parties, between their own domestically made boat, the *Virginia*, and the *Mary and John*, and abandoned Sagadahoc for good.

Aftermath

About the only real success the colony could boast was the construction of the 30-ton pinnace, the *Virginia*. It was the first English ship built on American soil. Made from American timber, the *Virginia* at least proved the potential for shipbuilding of the Maine forests.

The Plymouth Company soon lost its intersecting territory to the London Company, whose Jamestown settlement endured far greater privation than Sagadahoc yet managed to survive. Ferdinando Gorges later made several more unsuccessful attempts to colonise Maine. The Plymouth Company was revived in 1620 and, as head of the new Plymouth Council for New England, Gorges was involved in the establishment of a number of settlements in what is now Massachusetts, including the failed colonies of Merrymount and Wessagusset. Gorges went on to become the founder of the province of Maine, but never set foot in America, and never made any money out of it either.

As for the site of the old settlement at Sagadahoc, a 1680 account of the colony's demise mentions a tribe of Native Americans overrunning the fort once it had been abandoned—and burning it down. It seems the fire was an accident, caused by their ignorance of the gunpowder that had been left behind in barrels. The remains of Sagadahoc were lost until archaeologists uncovered them in the 1990s, a map drawn by one of the colonists proving a useful guide for the excavation team.

CHAPTER 9

Thomas Weston and the English colony of Wessagusset, New England (1622–23 and 1623–30)

With the Plymouth Colony having survived its establishment in 1620, New England began to arouse the interest of parties in search of the profits of the fur trade. One was merchant-adventurer Thomas Weston. Irritated by the Puritans' penchant for putting religious disputation ahead of profit, Weston decided to establish his own colony, populated by sixty men who were most certainly not puritanical. They came to Plymouth, where they offended the Puritans, then settled at Wessagusset (near contemporary Weymouth, Massachusetts) where they offended the native people. Largely incompetent as settlers, Weston's mob were gone by spring, but not before their actions had led to the deaths of a number of Native Americans. Next to arrive was Robert Gorges, as governor-general of the newly patented region of New England, but a single winter was enough for him too. The remnants of Gorges' colony were eventually absorbed into the Massachusetts Bay Colony when it was consolidated in 1630.

When London merchant and ironmonger Thomas Weston approached the English Puritans in their temporary home of Leyden, Holland, about the prospect of forming a partnership to settle and exploit the resources of America, the convergence of interests was not a natural fit. Weston and the backers he represented were looking to make money, while the Puritans, although not averse to money, were looking for a place where they could live undisturbed according to their religious beliefs.

The colony was originally intended to be founded near the Hudson River, in the northern reaches of Virginia, land which was owned by the London Company—the same organisation that had founded the successful colony of Jamestown in May 1607. However, the *Mayflower* sailed off course while crossing the Atlantic in 1620 and the settlement was made instead on the western shore of Cape Cod Bay, in what is now Massachusetts, land that had been granted to the newly formed Plymouth Council for New England.

The tale of the *Mayflower*, its arrival and the terrible first winter the pilgrims faced are well known. Less well known is the fact that their Plymouth Colony, like many of the early English settlements in America, Jamestown included, failed to supply an adequate return on the investments of its backers. With their sober habits, dour temperaments and scorn of physical luxuries, the Pilgrim Fathers, Thomas Weston had supposed, would make an ideal vanguard for the establishment of a colony whose primary economic activity (at least initially) was likely to derive from the lucrative trade in furs. He was dismayed, however, to discover that the Puritans were more concerned with matters of their organisation and survival than they were with rewarding the faith of their investors.

At some point in early 1622, Weston determined that, instead of waiting for the Puritans to turn him a profit, he would take the bull by the horns and found his own colony. His mode of recruitment for this venture was altogether different, and possibly vengeful. He scoured the pubs, streets and brothels of London and assembled a crew of more than sixty men, whom he himself described as 'rude and profane'. Whether he chose them as an affront or an antidote to the Puritans is unknown. Richard Greene, Weston's brother-in-law, was the man he appointed to lead the expedition and act as governor of the settlement.

Doomed to fail

At the start of spring 1622, Weston sent an advance party of eight men in a fishing boat to reconnoitre a suitable location for the establishment of his new colony. After exploring the coast of Maine for some weeks, this reconnaissance team journeyed to the Plymouth Colony, where they were joined by the sixty other settlers in June.

Unlike most colonies the English established, Weston's complement was devoid of women and children. And his venture was ill conceived in almost every aspect. He had failed to adequately provision his settlers when they left from London in April, and on their arrival at Plymouth (that is, New Plymouth), they quickly became dependent on the Puritans for supplies. Some of Greene's men were flogged for stealing corn from the Puritans, while others abused their hosts at the same time as they demanded food from them. These men were not armed with the same wit as the fabled roisterer of Merrymount, Thomas Morton (see page 121), who was philosophically opposed to Puritanism and capable of taking them on in debate. Rather, they were louts.

The relationship between the two parties worsened until Greene's men decided to leave for their own colony as planned. Rather than anywhere in Maine, and at the pilgrims' suggestion, a site was selected at Wessagusset, midway up the coast of the present-day state of Massachusetts. They arrived there in late July, erected blockhouses and started their new life.

With autumn fast approaching, the new arrivals showed themselves to be utterly incompetent settlers. Unlike the Merrymount colonists two years later, the men at Wessagusset soon offended the local Native Americans. Unsurprisingly for a bunch of ne'er-do-well urbanites, they also failed to use the limited time they had to grow food. And even more stupidly, they then ignored the chance to fish before the rivers froze over. By the time winter arrived, the men had completely exhausted their supplies.

Despite their relief at being rid of the offensive Londoners, the Puritans maintained contact with their near neighbours, even occasionally combining with them to trade with a local native tribe. According to the Governor of the Plymouth Colony, William Bradford, one of the chief reasons for Wessagusset's severe food shortage was that the settlers used much of their corn as currency to purchase the favours of Native American women. By the onset of winter, the men were in a pitiful state. It is thought that ten of the sixty died during that first winter, while their leader, Richard Greene, had already met his maker in October. Bradford later gave the following description of the men at Wessagusset:

> ... so many sold their clothes and bed coverings; others (so base were they) became servants to the Indians, and would cut them wood and fetch them water for a cap full of corn; others fell to plain stealing, both night and day from the Indians, of which they grievously complained. In the end, they came to that misery that some starved and died with cold and hunger. One gathering shellfish was so weak as he struck fast in the mud and was found dead in the place. At last most of them left their dwellings and scattered up and down in the wood and by the watersides, where they could find ground nuts and clams, here six and there ten ...

As was usually the way with the establishment of a European colony in the New World, the chief of the local tribe had hoped that an alliance with the Englishmen at Wessagusset would help him against his more powerful enemies. Yet this disordered, starving rabble were unlikely to inspire fear in the heart of any enemy. They were pests. When an English bootprint was found beside a raided granary belonging to his tribe, the chief approached the settlers and demanded justice. Instead of hanging the culprit—who remained in good health and was therefore an asset to the colony—the men chose one of their weaker, older members to fly from the gibbet. The tribespeople were not convinced. Thomas Weston's 'rude and profane' colonists continued to steal corn from them throughout the winter and into the spring, mainly because they had little choice.

Confrontation

Eventually the Indians decided to take action. Rather than kill the men outright, they first complained to the magistrates on Plymouth's governing council. The magistrates replied that the Wessagusset settlers were a distinct body whose behaviour was outside their jurisdiction, and that they couldn't intercede in any way since they had nothing to do with the colony.

Unfortunately for the Massachusetts tribespeople, this wasn't actually the case. After the outrages persisted, and having tried the diplomatic route to no avail, the tribesmen decided to eradicate the settlers at Wessagusset. They made the mistake,

English settlers collecting American corn

however, of informing the Puritans in Plymouth of their plan. Massasoit, the Wampanoag *sachem* (king), who had helped the Plymouth Colony during its first, dire winter, and who was grateful for the medical treatment he had recently received from them, informed the pilgrims that the Massachusett Indians, together with neighbouring tribes such as the Nauset and the Pamut, were going to attack Wessagusset.

William Bradford and his governing council knew that it would set a dangerous precedent if a group of Englishmen were slaughtered by the local native people. Accordingly, on 26 March, they sent Captain Miles Standish, Plymouth's military commander, to seize the angry chiefs. Standish succeeded by using underhanded means: having invited tribal representatives to a supposed meeting, he ambushed and killed two of the chiefs, Witawamut and Pecksuot, when they arrived there, before killing another Native American man and hanging a young boy from a tree. Startled by the ambush, the rest of the warriors scattered while Standish and his men pursued them. Witawamut's severed head was brought back to Plymouth and mounted on a pole, to remind the local indigenous population of the price of aggression against their colonial masters, no matter how righteous the cause.

However undeservedly, and against the Plymouth Colony's claims of separation, Thomas Weston's men were saved. But, with no food available, their colony was doomed. On Standish's advice, Wessagusset was abandoned. Some of the settlers went to Plymouth, others to fishing stations to the north, in Maine. By April 1623, only three men remained. They were all killed by the local tribes. A few months later, Weston finally arrived from London via Maine to take up the leadership of his trading colony—only to find it no longer existed.

Welcome to Weymouth

A second attempt to settle Wessagusset occurred in September 1623, when Robert Gorges, son of Plymouth Council for New England patron Sir Ferdinando Gorges, arrived there with 120 colonists. Gorges junior was Ferdinando's second son and had cut his teeth in the service of the Venetian navy. The reasons for his appointment and this new attempt at settlement were twofold.

Firstly, the Plymouth Council investors needed someone to enforce the trade monopoly that their joint-stock company now enjoyed in New England, thanks to a new charter granted by King James I. It was proposed, for instance, that fishermen using the area should pay a duty of five fish for every hundred they caught. Secondly, Ferdinando Gorges, like many of the West Country adventurers and entrepreneurs, was a gentleman without a significant estate, but he dreamed of being a great feudal lord in the New World. Once his son and the first batch of colonists had settled in, he proposed to follow them with far greater numbers and establish his fiefdom.

The Puritans had a number of reservations about these developments. For a start, they held a grudge against Gorges for his betrayal of Robert Devereux, Earl of Essex, at the end of the Elizabethan era. In addition, the Puritans were somewhat alarmed by the fact that Gorges' son had been appointed governor-general of the entire territory; while their man Bradford would be on New England's governing council, they would no longer be completely free to choose how things were done. Even more alarming perhaps was that the new batch of settlers included two Anglican clergymen, which suggested that their Puritan separation from the Church of England might be under threat.

Gorges' dream crossed over religious boundaries, however, and he was more enthusiastic about the Puritans in Plymouth than they were about him. He had been trying to attract colonists to New England for some time and with little luck, but the survival of the Puritans and the fact that a permanent settlement had been established certainly made the region an easier prospect to sell.

The doubters in the Plymouth Colony had to cede the point that, with relations with the local native tribes currently on a knife edge following Captain Standish's skirmish, there was safety in numbers. And at least the moral quality of the new colonists was far superior to those who'd arrived under Thomas Weston's scheme.

In contrast to Weston, Gorges had chosen his settlers carefully. As well as a number of gentlemen and members of the clergy, there were practical people such as farmers, mechanics, traders and tradesmen. And there was also the moderating influence of women and children. The time of their arrival, however, in early autumn, was less than ideal: it left them little time to prepare for the harsh winter.

It was this state of affairs that finally persuaded Robert Gorges to take possession of the abandoned Wessagusset site, rather than start completely afresh. In this way, Weymouth Colony, as Wessagusset would now be renamed (after the English seaport in the county of Dorset), became the hoped-for 'spiritual and civil' capital settlement of the Plymouth Council's, and Gorges senior's, New England empire.

Governor Gorges

Shortly after Gorges had set his people up at Weymouth that September, he sailed off to perform his first duty as governor-general: ironically enough, the pursuit and detention of Thomas Weston. The London ironmonger's quest for profit had recently landed the Council for New England in hot water at the English court. It seems that Weston had bought some weapons on the premise of taking them to America, but instead had arranged for them to be sold (at a profit) to parties on the Continent who were at war with the King.

Heading south, Gorges met up with his quarry at the Plymouth Colony, where the governor tried to assert his authority over

Miles Standish ambushes and kills the two Indian chiefs Witawamut and Pecksuot

Weston but—somewhat surprisingly, given the events over the previous year or more—was obstructed from doing so by Bradford. Eventually Weston was arrested, and his ship seized and sailed north to Weymouth, where it wintered. However, this came about mainly because Weston decided that, if he were to be detained, then Gorges rather than himself would be responsible for feeding his crew over the winter.

That winter was far fiercer than Gorges and his colonists had expected, so much so that by the end of it most of them were ready to give up. In the spring, news arrived from Sir Ferdinando that he was having trouble raising money from the eminences who constituted the Plymouth Council for New England. His advice to his son was to return to England until a more financially suitable climate for colonisation arose.

Robert Gorges was happy to leave. His ships had arrived too late in the season to allow for planting crops. He had failed to convincingly assert his authority in Plymouth. And the New England winter, far harsher than anything seen at home, had severely dampened his spirits and ruined his health. On the way back to England, in the spring of 1624, he sailed by the fishing stations in Maine, all of which refused to pay the five-fish-per-hundred duty the Plymouth Council had demanded. Gorges lacked both the gravitas and the firepower to enforce the claim.

Some of his disillusioned colonists decided to return with him. Others remained, largely because they thought that Gorges' diversion

to the north posed too many extra risks. If Gorges had sailed directly for home, then Wessagusset might well have been abandoned for the second time in as many years. Those who remained under the leadership of one of the clergymen lasted only one more winter before they too returned to England. A few people drifted into Plymouth or moved to Virginia, and the colony was eventually absorbed into the Massachusetts Bay Colony in 1630.

Puritan delight

After operating as a pilot for Gorges, Thomas Weston had his ship returned to him. He sailed to Virginia and then returned to England, where he eventually died of the plague. As for Robert Gorges, on whom so many expectations and hopes had rested in 1623, his short stay in New England had ruined his health. He would never fully recover and died several years after his return home, still a young man.

For the Puritans at Plymouth, the original Wessagusset settlers had deeply offended their sense of propriety, while the later Weymouth Colony had promised to compromise their right to self-determination and even their religious practice. Both these threats came to nothing after all. The failure of Weymouth left a vacuum to be filled. And to the delight of the Plymouth Colony, in 1630 the foundation of the Puritan colony of Massachusetts Bay ensured that their way of life and religious beliefs would be preserved.

CHAPTER 10

The vanquished Dutch colony of Formosa, East China Sea (1624–62)

The early seventeenth century was a time of great expansion for the Netherlands, mainly at the expense of the Portuguese, and from their base in Batavia the Dutch were able to extend their influence into the Pacific. With foreign traders banned in mainland China, Formosa (or, as we know it today, Taiwan) seemed an ideal place to set up a trading base. In 1624, the Dutch established a colony there and, over the coming decades, having seen the agricultural potential of the land, began to import Chinese labourers from the mainland. However, a heavy taxation regimen and harsh treatment provoked the Chinese to frequent dissension and one serious revolt. The Dutch succeeded in quelling this revolt by playing them off against the island's aborigines, the Tainan. All was well until Lord Koxinga (Zheng Chenggong), a warrior dedicated to the failing Ming dynasty, needed somewhere to fight a rearguard action against the Manchu. His clever strategies and numerical superiority saw him capture Formosa after a nine-month siege.

Unlike most of the tales in this book, the story of the Dutch colony of Formosa is largely one of success undone only by a failure to defend the island against invasion. The rise of the Dutch as an imperial power was rapid. After much fighting, the Seven Provinces of the United Netherlands (meaning 'lowlands') achieved independence from Spain in 1581. In 1602, the Netherlands government granted a 21-year trading monopoly to the Dutch East India Company, or VOC (for Vereenigde Oost-Indische Compagnie). The company was thus granted exclusive rights to trade between the Netherlands and all countries from the Cape of Good Hope to the Straits of Magellan. To facilitate this, the VOC was empowered to carry out war, conduct treaties, take possession of territory and erect fortresses.

Most of the VOC's early successes came from displacing the Portuguese in the Spice Islands, today known as the Maluku Islands, in eastern Indonesia. The first permanent trading post was established in 1603 at Banten in West Java, while Batavia, present-day Jakarta, was settled in 1611 and would eventually became the Asian headquarters of the company. Over the following decade, the Dutch were increasingly eyeing territories such as Portuguese-held Macau, one of a number of failed naval attacks on which occurred in 1622. The following year, Dutch traders stopped by the island of Formosa, 120 kilometres (75 miles) due east of mainland China, to ascertain its suitability as a base for commerce in the region. The Portuguese had discovered Formosa in 1544 and given the island its name, meaning 'beautiful island'. It appears to have been an opinion with which the Dutchmen agreed.

Good business

In 1624, the Dutch established a permanent colony on Formosa, as a base for trade with China and Japan. Over a number of years, the VOC sent 600 officials and 2000 troops to build primary forts on the island's southwest coast. Fort Zeelandia (today the site of Fort Anping) was built on a sandy peninsula off the coast of the main island, Tainan, with direct access to the sea. It was made from bricks imported from Batavia that were bonded together with a local mortar comprising sugar, sand, ground seashells, coral and glutinous rice. Fort Zeelandia was finished in 1634 and served to protect the main harbour the company used, and to defend the territory from attacks by sea. It would come in handy in the decades to follow.

The other main fortress was Provintia, which they built further to the north, on the site of today's Tainan City. Completed in 1650, Fort Provintia was primarily built for the purpose of expanding Dutch control of the southern portion of the island. Having noted its agricultural potential, the company began to import Han Chinese labourers into the region to grow rice and sugar cane. In doing so, they inevitably came into conflict with the local aboriginal people, the Tainan, whose hunting grounds were diminished by the clearing of forest for the purposes of cultivation.

While the Dutch have a somewhat warm and fuzzy reputation these days as a 'nation of tolerant bicycle riders or blissed-out hippies enjoying a joint in an Amsterdam café, their colonising was the most ruthless and vicious of all the Europeans, with the exception perhaps of the Portuguese. When the Tainan people inevitably revolted against the taking of their traditional lands, in the Great Matou resistance of 1635, the Dutch embarked on a punitive campaign that lasted ten years, killing a total of 300,000 and cutting the Tainan population in the southwest by half. Those who refused to accede to Dutch rule were either killed or escaped to the mountainous areas further north. The land there was not so conducive to agriculture and the Dutch didn't bother to try to control it.

One of the great ironies of European colonisation is that when natives weren't being killed or enslaved, they were often being converted to Christianity. In 1627, the Dutch Reformed Church, which espoused a Calvinist Christianity, sent its first missionary to Formosa with the intention of converting the Tainan. By the time the Dutch departed the island, over thirty missionaries had come to Formosa. They established schools and translated the Bible into a Romanised version of the indigenous language, with the result that over 6000 of the Tainan were converted during this period. Despite the fact that the Dutch had eradicated half of their number, the Christianised Tainan came to see them as allies against the increasing numbers of Chinese.

It was VOC policy throughout the East Indies to import as labourers Han Chinese, who were renowned for their work ethic. The land opened for agriculture was designated crown land, thus rendering the Chinese tenant farmers. The conditions in southern China at the time were bleak, especially in Fujian province, where overcrowding and poverty were endemic, and from where most of the farmers were sourced. Many of the Chinese were refugees from the war between the Ming and the Manchu. Migrating to Formosa was an activity that preceded the Dutch, yet it accelerated dramatically during their decades of colonisation. Interestingly, the emigration was usually temporary, since Chinese citizens weren't allowed to leave China for more than three years at a time.

This practice of temporary emigration had actually been started by the pirate, trader and Ming Dynasty warrior Zheng Zhilong. Known as Iquan to the Dutch, he had been christened Nicholas Gaspard in Macao and married a Japanese woman while living in Nagasaki. When the Tokugawa government closed Japan, Zheng had set up a base on an island off the coast of Fujian, with a fleet of 800 ships that alternately plundered and traded with both the Dutch

FOLLOWING PAGES: VOC ships trading in the East in the mid-seventeenth century

and the Chinese. His half-Japanese son, Zheng Chenggong, whose hatred for the Manchu would bring about his father's demise, would later rule the island.

The VOC took a cut from agricultural production primarily through a raft of taxes including a poll tax (where households were taxed by the number of residents), customs duties, commodity taxes, barbarian trade taxes, fishing taxes and hunting taxes.

Traditionally, the trade between Formosa and its Chinese neighbours had mainly been in deer products such as hides, preserved venison and powdered antlers, the last of which was used for medicinal and aphrodisiacal purposes; in exchange, the Tainan aborigines bought mainly rice, salt and textiles from China. A similar trade existed with Japan, although deer hides were by far the most dominant export there. Through its tax

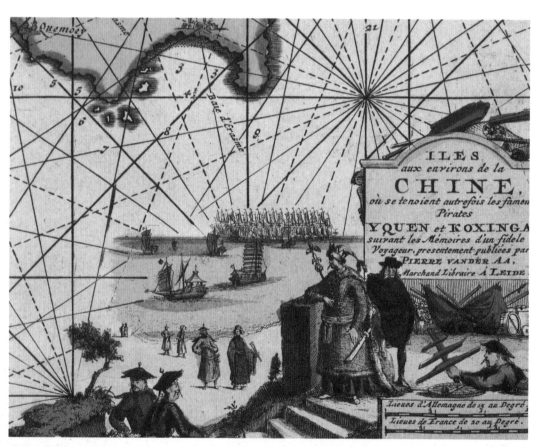

Detail from a Dutch map of southern China showing the islands where Koxinga and other pirates were based

regimen, the VOC took a good slice of this pre-existing business without having to do much at all.

When the crops began to develop, the sugar cane found a ready market in Japan while the rice, in contrast to the previous trade balance, was exported to China. The Dutch also mined sulphur (a key ingredient in the manufacture of gunpowder), which they sold to China and Cambodia. With direct trade with foreigners banned in China, Formosa was also the ideal base from which to trade and transport goods such as silk back to Holland. Zheng Zhilong brought the goods across from the mainland and paid a customs duty to the Dutch colonists on Formosa. The VOC then shipped the goods to Europe, where they were sold at astronomical mark-ups.

The price of success

All in all, Dutch Formosa seemed like a highly successful colony. Perhaps too much so. The first hint that this could become a problem came in 1652, when one of Zheng Zhilong's offsiders, Guo Haiyi, decided the Dutch were onto too much of a good thing. Guo had led more than 2000 Fujians to Formosa to open up more land to cultivation, and he took umbrage at the inflexible, arrogant colonists and their exploitation of his people through heavy taxation.

On 7 September 1652, he invited his allies over and as they got drunker and drunker the genie of antipathy towards the Dutch was let out of the bottle, which is exactly what he intended. With the men full of 'Dutch courage', Guo filled them in. He would invite the Dutch officials to a feast to celebrate the mid-autumn festival; then, in a classic Chinese strategy, once they were comfortably ensconced, Guo's supporters would put the dignitaries to the sword, effectively cutting the head off the colony's government. Meanwhile, Guo would have his army of supporters waiting to storm Fort Provintia, thus enabling the Chinese farmers to gain control of the cultivated plains for themselves.

The next morning was no doubt one of powerful hangovers. At least two of Guo's guests awoke feeling uneasy about what they'd signed up for. Proving that blood can go to water, one of them was Guo's younger brother. Another was a local Chinese heavy, Pu Zai. As the date of the attack grew nearer, they became more and more nervous; where Guo only saw victory, these two doubters became increasingly fixated on the potential cost of defeat. For, although the Dutch were avaricious, life on the whole was better now for the Chinese who had fled the mainland than for those who had stayed behind. Just before the plan went into action, the two men went and visited the VOC governor, Nicolas Verburg. When Guo cottoned on to this, he took 16,000 troops and mounted a lightning attack on Fort Provintia, overrunning the fort and then burning it to the ground. More than 1000 Dutchmen were killed.

GHOST COLONIES

If Guo's plan to kill the colonial dignitaries had succeeded, this victory may well have marked the end for the Dutch occupation of Formosa. The following day, however, Governor Verburg ordered a force of 120 armed troops to face Guo and his men. Two days later, this force grew enormously with the arrival of 2000 Christianised native Tainan troops. Guo's rebels now lacked the advantage of surprise that had been so crucial to their plot. Worse still, the farming hoes and bamboo sticks at their disposal were woefully inadequate against the guns of the Dutch and the Tainan's bows and arrows. Some 1800 Chinese settlers were killed during the ensuing conflict. Guo was one of them, for which he could probably count himself lucky. When the Dutch captured his second-in-command, they roasted him alive before parading the corpse through the streets with his head on a bamboo stick. Two of Guo's generals were drawn and quartered. The leaderless Chinese forces fled for their home turf, with the Tainan army in ruthless pursuit. The fighting was fierce, but the Tainan eventually prevailed. By playing the Chinese off against the Tainan aborigines, the Dutch had managed to survive.

The Zheng factor

Guo Haiyi's attempt to overthrow the Dutch in 1652 might have been a failure, but it wasn't long before the Dutch had a more formidable Chinese opponent to face. Kicked out of home for throwing a stone that knocked the hat off his local mayor, Zheng Zhilong had risen from nothing to become the most powerful single player in the East China Sea. After years of plundering Ming ships, Zhilong had been appointed Admiral of the Coastal Seas by the Ming dynasty, and in that capacity he defeated the forces of the Dutch East Indies in 1633. He continued to fight for the Ming after Beijing fell to the Manchu in 1644 and the Emperor committed suicide. In this, he was greatly helped by his son, Zheng Chenggdong, who became known to the Dutch as Koxinga.

The elder Zheng's work for the Ming had made him an extremely wealthy man and he used that wealth to buy large chunks of Fujian province. As a landowner, however, his assets were geographically fixed and more vulnerable, therefore, to the political situation than those he had invested in piracy and shipping. Sensing a change in the political climate, in 1646, Zhilong defected to the Manchu by withdrawing his defence of the Ming capital, Fuzhou, which effectively sealed its downfall. For this, he was richly rewarded by the Manchu.

If Koxinga had been a good Confucian son who obeyed his father, then Zheng Zhilong might have died rich and happy. But his son refused to abandon the Ming cause. In 1658, he captured Jiangsu, the provincial capital of Zhenjiang province, then surrounded the southern imperial capital, Nanjing. The siege of Nanjing was marred by poor strategy, however, and from a strong position Koxinga's army was forced south.

116

Held responsible for his son's continued resistance, Zheng Zhilong was arrested by the Manchu and deprived of his titles and property. When this failed to bring the young general to heel, the Manchu called Koxinga's bluff and executed his father.

As he moved south, Koxinga was confronted with the need to establish a new base from where he could maintain his resistance against the Manchu. Knowing of the anti-Dutch sentiment that had lingered on the island since the brutal repression of Guo Haiyi's rebellion, Koxinga thought that Formosa might be a good place for such a base. The Dutch had already angered the Ming warlord. In 1655, they sent an ambassador to the Manchu Emperor in Beijing and for two years thereafter, Koxinga, who maintained control of the seas, had enforced a ban on trade between Formosa and China.

VOC governor Frederik Coyett was aware of the attraction that Formosa held to this rump of the Ming dynasty and so requested military reinforcements from his headquarters in Batavia. Headquarters were sceptical about the threat, but nonetheless sent a ship with

VOC trading ships arriving in Fort Zeelandia

✳ THE PEACE TREATY THAT ENDED THE DUTCH PRESENCE IN FORMOSA

A Treaty made and agreed upon this first day of February 1662 by His Highness the Lord Teibingh Tsiante Teysiancon Koxin, who has besieged Castle Zeelandia on Formosa since 1st May 1661; and the Dutch Government, represented by the Governor of the said Castle, Frederik Coyett, and his Council.

Article 1
All hostilities committed on either side to be forgotten.

Article 2
Castle Zeelandia, with its outworks, artillery, remaining war materials, merchandise, money, and other properties belonging to the Honorable Company, to be surrendered to Lord Koxinga.

Article 3
Rice, bread, wine, arrack, meat, pork, oil, vinegar, ropes, canvas, pitch, tar, anchors, gunpowder, bullets, and linen, and other such articles as may be required by the besieged during their voyage to Batavia, to be taken aboard the Company's ships in keeping with instructions from the before-mentioned Governor and Council.

Article 4
All private movable property inside the Castle or elsewhere belonging to officers of the Dutch Government, shall first be inspected by Lord Koxinga's delegates, and then placed on board the said ships.

Article 5
In addition to these goods, each of the twenty-eight Councillors shall be permitted to take with them two hundred rijksdaalders [2.5 gilders], and twenty chosen civilians an aggregate sum of one thousand rijksdaalders.

Article 6
After inspection, the Dutch soldiers may come forth with flying banners, burning fuses, loaded rifles, and beating drums, marching thus for embarkation under command of the Governor.

Article 7
The names of all Chinese debtors or lease-holders in Formosa, with particulars of claims against them, shall be copied out of the company's books, and handed to Lord Koxinga.

Article 8
All the Government archives may be taken to Batavia.

Article 9
Every servant of the Company, now imprisoned by the Chinese in Formosa, shall be liberated within eight or ten days, and those who are in China, as soon as possible. Servants of the Company who are not imprisoned in Formosa shall be granted a free pass to reach the Company's ships in safety.

Article 10

The said Lord Koxinga shall now return to the Company the four captured boats, with all their accessories.

Article 11

He shall also provide a sufficient number of vessels to take the Honorable Company's people and goods to their ships.

Article 12

Vegetables, flesh-meat, and whatever else may be necessary to sustain the Company's people during their stay, shall daily be provided by His Highness's subjects at a reasonable price.

Article 13

So long as the Honorable Company's people remain on land before embarkation, no soldier or other subject of Lord Koxinga shall be permitted to enter the Castle (unless on service for the Company), to approach the outworks nearer than the gabions, or to proceed further than the palisades erected by order of His Highness.

Article 14

No other than a white flag shall float from the Castle until the Honorable Company's people have marched out.

Article 15

Those who guard the stores shall remain in the Castle two or three days after the other people and goods have been taken on board, and thereafter they shall proceed themselves to the vessels.

Article 16

As soon as this agreement is signed, sealed, and sworn to on both sides, each according to his country's customs, Lord Koxinga shall deliver to one of the Dutch ships two hostages, viz. the Mandarin or Captain Moor Ongkun and Pimpan Jamoosje of the political Council. On the other side, and as representing the Company, Lord Koxinga shall receive custody of Mr. Jan Oetgens van Waveren, an official second in rank to the Governor, and Mr. David Harthouwer, also a member of the Formosan Council. Each of these hostages shall remain in a previously fixed place until everything has been carried out in accordance with the terms of this contract.

Article 17

Chinese prisoners at present in the Castle or on the Company's ships shall be exchanged for any Dutch people who have been seized by the subjects of Lord Koxinga.

Article 18

All misunderstandings, and every important matter overlooked in this Agreement, shall immediately be dealt with to the satisfaction of both parties, upon notice having been given on either side.

CH'ENG-KUNG, [L.S.]
FREDERIK COYETT, [L.S.]

soldiers commanded by Jan van der Laan. If he was not needed on Formosa, his orders were to attack the Portuguese colony at Macao instead.

At the same time, He Tingbin, who had earlier served as Governor Coyett's emissary when the trading ban was overturned, helped himself to a lot of money and defected to Koxinga's side. He arrived with a map of Formosa, showing the Dutch defences and the best avenues to attack. But Koxinga realised that it was too risky to launch an assault while the Dutch reinforcements were protecting the island. So, instead of appearing as a threat, he cultivated the Dutch, allaying their suspicions as to his intentions by pointing out the synergies of the business they shared between them. The strategy worked. Van der Laan returned to Batavia, and his contemptuous report on Coyett's apparent misjudgment resulted in VOC headquarters deciding to replace the latter as governor with Herman Klenke van Odessa.

Besieged

On 23 April 1661, Koxinga landed on Formosa with an army of 25,000 men. With the information provided by He Tingbin central to his strategy, he forced the Dutch to surrender Provintia and withdraw to Fort Zeelandia, which Koxinga then cut off from the rest of the island. While Zeelandia had some provisions, its position on a sandy peninsula jutting into the sea meant it had no decent supply of fresh water.

Governor Odessa had left Batavia to take up his new post, but once he'd arrived at Formosa, he discovered he couldn't land and was forced to turn back. When the VOC in Batavia heard of the predicament, they swiftly sent a force led by Jacob Cauw to liberate the colony. Cauw's ships were delayed by a typhoon for a month, and he eventually arrived at the island only to assess that the situation was impossible. Claiming he was sailing for Fujian to enlist the help of the Manchu, Cauw instead headed for Siam, thus abandoning Coyett and his fellow countrymen to their fate.

On 1 February 1662, eight months to the day since the siege of Fort Zeelandia had begun, Governor Coyett's defenders finally capitulated. On their surrender, the Dutch were treated with dignity. When they sailed away from the island shortly afterwards, thousands of ghosts of the VOC's ruthless subjugation of the island and its inhabitants were left behind.

For the next three years, the Dutch allied themselves with the Manchu against Koxinga, in the hope of regaining their profitable base off the coast of mainland China. But while they enjoyed some victories, Koxinga and his descendants ensured that the Ming dynasty's control over Formosa was maintained for a couple of decades to come. It was only in 1683 that their resistance was eventually undone by the Manchu. And unfortunately for the VOC chiefs in Batavia, by then they had no interest in allowing the Dutch into China at all.

CHAPTER 11

The carousing English colony of Merrymount, New England (1625–30)

In the history of the colonisation of America, it was frequently the case that one country would try to undo the colonial efforts of another. Much rarer, however, was when a group of nationals tried to undermine the colony of some of their fellow patriots. Yet this is what happened when Mount Wollaston on Massachusetts Bay, under the leadership of English roisterer and lawyer Thomas Morton, incurred the ire of the Puritans in Plymouth. Morton was arrested for erecting a pagan maypole and embarking on a bacchanalian celebration, and sent to England for trial. On the way there, his ship passed incoming Massachusetts Bay governor John Endecott, a killjoy religious bigot, who removed the maypole completely and renamed the colony. Morton was cleared of his charges in England and returned to Massachusetts, where more charges were concocted against him. His house and those of his supporters were burnt to the ground.

When Thomas Morton arrived with Captain Wollaston in 1625 to establish a colony in Massachusetts Bay, it was his second visit to New England. He had been there three years earlier, probably to visit the failed colony of Wessagusset (see page 101), where he had become convinced of the region's economic potential, fascinated by its nature and natives, and irritated by the sanctimonious behaviour of the Founding Fathers in Plymouth. In their most extreme manifestations, the Puritans weren't unlike the Taliban: they hated music, they hated the remnants of pagan worship in English life, they hated drinking, and they were frightened of being overruled by their passions. Convinced of their moral superiority, they were staunchly conformist. And especially so in Massachusetts, where the chance to form a society in harmony with their own values was fiercely protected, to the extent that people were banished and even executed on religious grounds.

Thomas Morton belonged to a different strand of seventeenth-century English culture. A product of the Devonshire gentry, whose strong tradition of exploration had also produced Sir Humphrey Gilbert and Sir Walter Raleigh, Morton came from a region where the rituals and beliefs of a lively rural folk tradition maintained a connection with England's pagan past. Morton's attitude towards religion was lax and hedonistic. In this he wasn't alone. While the Puritans were clamping down on the pleasures of the world, the Elizabethan era, with its theatre, urban overcrowding, and victory against the Spanish

and their repressive Inquisition, had a reputation for licentiousness. One nineteenth-century historian, Charles Adams, went so far as to say that the period of Elizabeth and James I was 'one of probably as much sexual incontinency as any in English history'.

When studying law at Clifford's Inn during the 1590s, Morton enjoyed the bacchanalian student culture of the London Inns of Court, as well as that of the playhouses. He became close friends with Ben Jonson, one of the great Elizabethan playwrights, and was very much a part of the libertarian milieu. After graduating, Morton worked as a lawyer and often acted on behalf of his fellow Devonshire countrymen who'd ended up dispossessed of their land or in prison because of debt. As a result of the economic upheaval and overcrowding of the time, there were more than enough clients to keep him busy. The same factors were also an incentive for many to seek their fortunes in England's first great wave of colonisation, which had tentatively begun with the punitive occupation of Ireland through plantation colonies, the first being established there in 1556. Although an ardent royalist, Morton was also an advocate for the priority of the Common Law over the increasing power of the monarch and the Star Chamber, a legal position philosophically consistent with the underdog status of many of his clients.

While oscillating between London, Devonshire and Bristol, Morton became close to Sir Ferdinando Gorges, who had backed the failed colony of Sagadahoc in Maine in 1607–08 and would go on to become the absentee founder of two more colonial ventures in Maine (see page 95). By 1620, Gorges was the head of the Plymouth Council for New England, a joint-stock company, and most certainly not to be confused with the Plymouth Colony of the Puritans; his ambition was to initiate a series of feudal plantation colonies in the New England region.

When Morton sailed to Wessagusset (present-day Weymouth, Massachusetts) in 1622, he returned home full of enthusiasm for the new territory. The land was of good quality and there were abundant resources in the form of animal skins, especially beaver furs, for which there was a lucrative market back in England. The local native people had been drastically thinned by a plague in 1617, he noted, and were fairly well disposed towards friendly relations with European colonists.

The merry mount

In the summer of 1625, Morton returned to New England on board the *Unity*, along with a Captain Wollaston, two other gentlemen and around thirty indentured servants. With Sir Ferdinando Gorges' backing, the intention was to start a colony a short distance from the site of the two failed attempts at Wessagussett, first by Weston and then Gorges' son Robert. The new arrivals took possession of land on a hill located at present-day Quincy, just south of Boston.

Much had changed regarding the local Native Americans' disposition towards the English since Morton's visit three years before. The high ground he was to settle had been cleared for agricultural use by the Massachusett Indian chief Chickatawbut, but he no longer had sufficient numbers in his tribe to utilise the land. Not only had many of his people been lost to pestilence, but in 1623 some of his best warriors had been massacred by Captain Miles Standish, Plymouth Colony's military commander, in defence of Thomas Weston's motley crew at Wessagusset.

The new colony was christened Mount Wollaston, after Morton's associate and co-founder. The settlers built a house on the hill, which had commanding views over the bay, and over the next few months got down to planting on the cleared land. For Captain Wollaston, however, one New England winter, with its blizzards, sub-zero temperatures and deep drifts of snow, was enough to convince him that he didn't want to live there. Come spring, he took some of the indentured servants and went south to Virginia, where he effectively sold them into slavery.

While this was happening, Morton, who remained convinced of the colony's potential, took over its management. He warned the remaining servants of the captain's actions and promised them freedom in return for their loyalty. With Wollaston out of favour, the colony was renamed Maremount, from the French *mare*, meaning 'sea'. However, history would remember it as Merrymount, a

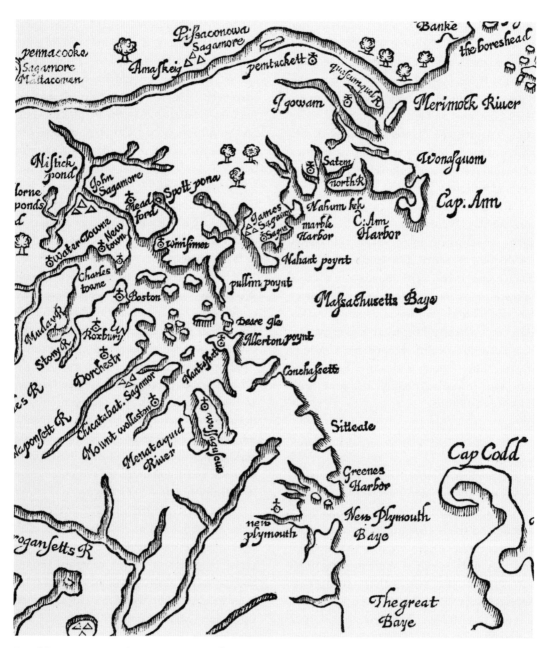

Detail from a 1635 map of North America showing the early settlements of Massachusetts, including Mount Wollaston

nickname at first that derived from the lifestyle there.

Whereas relationships between the local Wampanoag tribes and the Plymouth colonists were severely strained, not least because of the activities of Standish, Morton lacked the Puritans' sense of superiority and developed a good rapport with the Massachusett. He was genuinely interested in the culture of the Native Americans. A large part of the later account of his adventures, published in 1637 as *Revels in New Canaan*, was devoted to the subject. A nascent anthropologist and harbinger of the idea of 'the noble savage', Morton believed that aspects of Native American culture were superior to that of the English:

> ... yet are they supplied with all manner of needefull things for the maintenance of life and lifelyhood. Food and rayment are the cheife of all that we make true use of, and of these they finde no want, but have, and may have, them in a most plentifull manner.

> If our beggars of England should, with so much ease as they, furnish themselves with food at all seasons, there would not be so many starved in the streets, neither would so many gaoles [jails] be stuffed, or gallouses furnished with poore wretches, as I have seen them.

Part of his consideration of the local Indians as people rather than savages was demonstrated in the kinds of goods he was willing to trade with them. Morton was happy to exchange both guns and grog for the beaver skins, and since he enjoyed good relations with the Massachussett, he didn't perceive them as a threat. They coveted the guns and thus were prepared to offer more skins for them than they were for goods of a comparative value at English prices; in addition, the guns made it easier for them to hunt. As far as Morton was concerned, it was a win-win situation.

Down in Plymouth, however, the colonists were losing business to Merrymount and were understandably less sanguine about the idea of native tribesmen with guns. Their views were also somewhat different from Moreton's when it came to the trade of skins for liquor. The Puritans didn't drink alcohol and didn't make liquor. For them, selling alcohol to Native Americans was immoral. While Morton argued that he only ever sold the grog to wealthy chiefs and their traders, this was probably disingenuous, considering that he was happy for his Massachusett neighbours to join in his celebrations. Morton was most interested in trading to make a profit, after all, and in this he was unhindered by Puritan morals.

With a combination of fire water and firearms, Morton and his men were soon getting rich on the beaver trade. One of his servants, he estimated, earned for himself £1000 from the trade—a massive amount of money at the time. This facility for commerce was no doubt the primary concern for the Puritans. Yet Thomas Morton was well connected and it wasn't a simple matter of

125

just arresting him. According to some accounts, the reason he was in America in the first place was because a warrant for his arrest on a murder charge had been issued in England. But the details are vague. If it was true, it's likely that his connections were protecting him on that matter too.

The maypole saga

Having spent close to two years at Merrymount, in the spring of 1627 Morton decided to honour an ancient tradition and erect a maypole to celebrate the arrival of the new season. This was a common English rural tradition, and one that was generally marked with considerable licentiousness. During pagan times, the festival had been known as the Beltane Rites and had often been celebrated with a dedicated bacchanalian frenzy. Dancing around the maypole usually had more to it than just dancing, and it was a celebration that the Puritans, wary even of the residual pagan elements of Christmas (the Winter Solstice Festival), condemned.

The pole was a pine tree some 24 metres (80 feet) tall. According to William Bradford, governor of the Plymouth Colony at the time:

> [The men were] drinking and dancing aboute it many days together, inviting the Indean women, for their comforts, dancing and frisking together (like so many fairies or furies rather) and worse practices. As if they had anew revived the feates of the Roman Goddes Flora, or the beastly practices of the madd

> Bacchanalians. Morton likewise (to shew his poetrie) composed sundry rimes and verses, some tending to lasciviousness, and others to the detraction and scandal of some persons, which he affixed to this idle or idol May-polle.

Not only was Morton out-trading the Puritans, but he was also having fun, and this clearly didn't concur with the puritanical version of godly providence. After the second May Day bacchanalia in 1628, the Plymouth governing councillors (whom Morton referred to as 'Princes of Limbo') were getting worried that Merrymount was becoming a focal point for anyone disenchanted with the Puritan mode of life. If not an actual threat to the Plymouth Colony—which was by far the largest English settlement in New England, with more than 200 people there—then Merrymount was at least capable of proving a thorn in the side of the religious dictatorship they hoped to grow. It was a role that Morton was more than happy to play.

In June 1628 the Puritans sent their enthusiastic law enforcer, Miles Standish, to arrest Morton on a series of trumped-up charges. At the time, Morton was at Weymouth, around 12 kilometres (8 miles) to the south, while most of the other Merrymount colonists were inland collecting furs. The raid had, in fact, been planned so that there would be few people around, thus minimising the chances of a fight, the Massachusetts having gone inland hunting too. When Captain Standish and his eight-man troop arrived, the few men capable of making a defence of the colony were all too drunk. Standish cut down the maypole.

Morton was tracked down and gave in without resistance. He was then taken to Plymouth, where, his guilt assured, a discussion on his fate occurred. Standish, for instance, was all in favour of summary execution, but some of the calmer heads prevailed. Morton still had connections back home, and the hierarchy of authority between New England and the mother country remained unclear. Instead of killing him, they decided to maroon him on an island until a ship could be found to take him back to England to face justice.

Morton was deposited on one of the islands within the Isles of Shoals, approximately 16 kilometres (10 miles) offshore from the coast, and may well have starved to death if it weren't for his Native American friends from the mainland bringing him food. Before long, he was put onto a fishing boat bound for England. Once he'd arrived in London, the charges against him were dismissed.

Puritans from Plymouth witness the Maypole celebrations at Merrymount

✳ The maypole incident of 1628
(as contained in Thomas Moreton's Revels in New Canaan)

The setting up of this Maypole was a lamentable spectacle to the precise seperatists [Puritans]: that lived at Plymouth. They termed it an Idoll; yea they called it the Calf of Horeb: and stood at defiance with the place, naming it Mount Dagon; threatening to make it a woefull mount and not a merry mount ...

There was likewise a merry song made, which (to make their Revells more fashionable) was sung with a chorus, every man bearing his part; which they performed in a dance, hand in hand about the Maypole, whiles one of the Company sung, and filled out the good liquor like gammedes and Jupiter.

THE SONGE

Drinke and be merry, merry, merry boyes,
Let all your delight be in Hymens joyes,
Joy to Hymen now the day is come,
About the merry Maypole take a Roome.

Make greene garlands, bring bottles out;
And fill sweet Nectar, freely about,
Uncover thy head, and feare no harm,
For hers good liquor to keepe it warme.

Drinke and be merry, merry, merry boyes,
Let all your delight be in Hymens joyes,
Joy to Hymen now the day is come,
About the merry Maypole take a Roome.

Nectar is a thing assign'd,
By the Deities owne minde,
To cure the hart opprest with grief,
And of good liquors is the chief,

Drinke and be merry, merry, merry boyes,
Let all your delight be in Hymens joyes,
Joy to Hymen now the day is come,
About the merry Maypole take a Roome.

Give to the Mellancolly man,
A cup or two of't now and than;

This physick' will soone revive his bloud,
And make him be of a merrier mood.

Then drinke, &c.
Joy to Hymen, &c.

Give to the Nymphe thats free from scorne,
No Irish; stuff nor Scotch over worn,
Lasses in beaver coats come away,
Ye shall be welcome to us night and day.

Then drinke, &c.
Joy to Hymen, &c.

This harmless mirth made by young men (that lived in hope to have wives brought over to them, that would save them a labour to make a voyage to fetch any over) was much distasted, of the precise Seperatists: that keep much ado, about the tithe of Muit [mint] and Cunmin [cumin]; troubling their braines more then reason would require about things that are indifferent: and from that time sought occasion against my honest Host of Ma-re Mount to overthrow his undertakings, and to destroy his plantation quite and cleane ...

Endecott and Salem

While Morton was travelling to England in summer 1628, the arrival of the martinet and religious bigot John Endecott drastically changed the political landscape of New England in favour of the Puritans. The grant given to Endecott's backers in the Massachusetts Bay Company effectively placed Merrymount under his control, although there was confusion as to whether this new company had any legal right over the Plymouth Council for New England, a conundrum that would occupy the English courts for some time. A man with a hot temper and a fine line in righteous vengeance, Endecott renamed Merrymount 'Mount Dagon', after the Philistine god of agriculture, and promised that it would become a place of woe. By April 1629, he'd taken up his appointment as Governor of the Massachusetts Bay Colony.

Having escaped his charges in England, Thomas Morton might have been wise to stay there. However, the promise of New England, its revelling and its riches, as well as the chance to rile the Puritans yet again, was too much of a temptation. The Plymouth colonists were not impressed to see him in their midst again midway through 1629, and after a short enforced sojourn in Plymouth, Morton returned to Merrymount to pick up where he had left off. In his absence, the settlement had persisted under its new name, but only just. His fellow colonists were heartened by his return.

The joy was short-lived. In response to the famine of 1629, Endecott tried to assert top-down control over what was grown on the plantations within his sphere of influence. A number of the planters who had preceded him resented this diminution of their autonomy. It seemed that some of Morton's former enemies might become his allies. Eventually, though, they all caved in to the governor's demands—which included both political and religious obedience on pain of banishment, and the diversion of profits from the beaver trade to the building of churches, forts and other public infrastructure.

Only Morton resisted, ignoring the company's claims to a monopoly. He persisted in trading as he had before, although he did stop trading guns for fur. In response, on a number of occasions Endecott sent his troops to raid 'Mount Dagon' for the food stored there. He probably would have arrested Morton immediately had the famine not been such a distraction.

It wasn't until the autumn of 1630 that Endecott decided to deal with Morton decisively, by which time the great Puritan migration to New England had begun. That year, more than twelve ships carrying some 1000 colonists arrived under the leadership of the new Massachusetts Bay Colony governor, John Winthrop. Morton would have seen them enter the bay from his house at Merrymount and may well have guessed that his life as a frontier Puritan baiter was coming to an end. In early September, a warrant was issued for Morton's arrest. Armed emissaries of the Plymouth magistrates court were sent to fetch him.

On 17 September, some two weeks after his arrest, Morton was arraigned. In a trial in which the outcome was determined before it had even begun (his defence being cut short by a disinterested court), Morton was ordered into the stocks until a ship was available to transport him to England. His property and assets were confiscated while the colony at Merrymount was ordered to be burnt to the ground, in order that 'the habitation of the wicked should no more appear in Israel'. He remained in the stocks for four months until the *Handmaid* returned him to England.

Morton in Maine

The year 1630 marked both the last chance for Thomas Morton to run a colony and the consolidation of the Puritan caste of New England. In another sense, however, it marked the tensions between freedom and authority, hedonism and morality that would feature in the history of New England, in the case of Roger Williams and the establishment of Rhode Island, for instance, and more generally in the character of American society.

Although his colonial days were done, Morton refused to give up the fight. Back in England he became the attorney for the Plymouth Council for New England in its battle against the Massachusetts Bay Company. In 1635 he succeeded in having the company's charter revoked, which drastically affected the fortunes of the Plymouth Colony. Two years later, he used his literary connections with Ben Jonson and the like to publish a three-volume tome, *Revels in New Canaan*, whose denunciation of the Puritan cause made him a celebrity. But the tide of history was against him. With the outbreak of the English Civil War in 1642, Morton returned to America.

The temptation to visit Plymouth and gloat over his famous court victory overcame his small supply of good sense, and on his arrival there he was arrested as a Royalist agitator and put in jail while evidence was collected for his trial. By this stage, he was in his late sixties; his health was failing, and so was his capacity to rebel. In the end, he capitulated by asking for clemency on the basis of his health. The Puritans obliged and Morton moved to Maine, where his benefactor, Sir Ferdinando Gorges, had established a plantation colony of West Countrymen. It was in this convivial company that Thomas Morton peaceably spent his remaining years until he died there in 1647, aged seventy-one. It was a fine innings for a man who'd been merry that much.

The legend of Merrymount survived long after Moreton, most notably in American literature. Some of the more famous writers to explore the subject include the author Nathaniel Hawthorne and the poet William Carlos Williams.

CHAPTER 12

The Puritan colony of Providence Island, the Caribbean Sea (1630–41)

In 1630, two colonies in the Americas were founded by Puritan businessmen seeking to combine godliness with profit. One, the Massachusetts Bay Company, survived a harsh climate and a difficult beginning to become the backbone of New England, and the beacon on the hill whose values remain deeply entrenched in the national mythology of the United States. The other was Providence Island. Situated off the Mosquito Coast (now a part of Colombia) in the pleasant climes of the Caribbean, and funded by some of the bigwigs of English Puritan society, it seemed the more attractive option by far. But a combination of inadequate crops, overbearing control from company backers in London and increasingly disgruntled colonists, all set against the backdrop of impending civil war in England, saw it fall to the Spanish after eleven fruitless years of operation.

Setting up colonies by company charter backed by royal patent was the method used for England's first settlements in the New World. It was a risky business, and more often than not, the original investors got burnt. In most cases, the investors were sorely disappointed by the slow prospects for a return on the capital they had outlaid. The first decades of these ventures usually ran at a loss, while the inhabitants frequently faced starvation. In Jamestown, Virginia, a desperate lack of food over the winter of 1609–10 saw only sixty colonists survive out of 241, while the story of the *Mayflower* pilgrims being rescued from starvation by Native Americans is one of America's most famous.

Investors often admonished the settlers for their tardiness in providing a return on investment, while the colonists were not shy in asking for greater and greater injections of capital, in order to keep their settlements afloat as they tried to find crops that could be grown profitably. This tension was another feature of almost all the early English colonies. However, for the 1629-founded Providence Island Company, it would prove particularly troublesome. To begin with, there were fewer shareholders, each with a greater investment, compared to most of the other joint-stock operations. The Providence Island Company was set up with a working capital of £3800 and just twenty investors, or so-called adventurers. Of these, nineteen had put in £200, while the twentieth, Henry Rich, the first Earl of Holland, was given a free share because of his capacity, as a

favourite of King Charles I and his queen, Henrietta Maria of France, to represent the company's interests at court.

The adventurers included some of the foremost Puritans in the country, many of whom would go on to play important roles in the English Parliament during the interregnum years. They were a tight clique and there were many incestuous connections between them. John Pym, treasurer of the Providence Island Company for most of its existence, later became the leader of the Long Parliament in the build-up to the English Civil War. Robert Rich, Earl of Warwick (who, in contrast to his brother, the Earl of Holland, fell out with the court because of his Puritanism) was a noted privateer, Puritan and veteran investor in colonial ventures. He would be appointed commander of the English fleet by Parliament. Their cousin Sir Nathaniel Rich was also an investor, and Henry Montagu, Earl of Manchester, was another. The latter married Warwick's daughter, Anne, fought on the Parliamentary side during the war and became Lord Chamberlain after the Restoration in 1660.

The tightness with which the initial shares were held and the social standing of the members suggested a great degree of confidence in the venture. As was often the case, the initial reports of Providence Island were glowing. Around 180 kilometres (110 miles) to the east of Nicaragua, although now part of contemporary Colombia, the climate was balmy, with sea breezes to mitigate the near-tropical location. The prevailing scientific opinion of the day was that abundant crops and precious minerals were generated by the effects of heat: crops were fertilised by the sun's masculine penetration of the feminine soil, while precious metals were drawn to the surface by its magnetic powers.

Then as now, the landmass of the island was about 17 square kilometres (6½ miles), not a huge amount given that there were three mountain peaks in its centre, each around 340 metres (1115 feet) high. And except for the fertile ground at the base of these peaks, most of the arable land was to be found in the narrow valleys between the spines radiating from them. However, to some extent the Providence Island Company envisaged the island as a launching pad to extract value from the mainland of Central America, rather than an end in itself. It was no coincidence that Robert Rich, Earl of Warwick, maintained the largest privateering fleet of any English aristocrat. Indeed, it was some of Warwick's privateers who had discovered the island for the English in the first place.

When colonists initially complained about the sharecropping system by which the company got half the profit for crops grown, they were assured that the bounty would be so great that half of the profits would make them wealthy men. By contrast, Massachusetts Bay had a larger number of investors drawn mainly from the middling ranks of Puritan society. Importantly, more of the investors actually moved to Massachusetts, while for the most part the high-society Puritans of the Providence Island Company were anticipating making their fortune while pulling the strings from England.

The time was ripe for colonisation. In the 1620s, the English economy had experienced a depression, particularly because the textile industry, which accounted for over 80 per cent of England's exports, had gone into decline as a result of a failure to keep up with technological innovations in mainland European cloth-making centres such as Flanders. Many of the Puritan grandees came from areas dependent on the textile industry, and their desire to set up colonies was partly out of a sense of economic noblesse oblige. England's population had exploded in the sixteenth century and the idea of transplanting struggling Englishmen into the New World seemed a good option. This logic was confirmed by the belief that crops grown in these colonies, such as indigo, cochineal, cotton and silk grass, could provide the raw materials for the resurgence of the English textile industry, in which a number of the Providence Island Company members had a stake.

This sense of wanting to look after lesser Puritans was compounded by the desire to protect Puritans from the campaigns against them, most notably by Archbishop William Laud, whose totalitarian approach to religion would cost him his head in 1645. The forebears of the Puritans, the Separatists, had been involved in Roanoke Island, while the sailing of the *Mayflower* in 1620 to New Plymouth,

ROBERT RICH, SECOND EARL OF WARWICK

When this future leading Providence Island investor inherited his earldom in 1619, he became one of the greatest landowners in England, with large estates in Essex and ownership of chunks of London. Warwick's landholdings in England were never enough, however, and he was a key figure in many of England's early company colonies in the New World. Warwick was an investor in the Bermudas (Somers Isles), Guinea, Amazon River, Virginia and New England companies. His influence could make or break a company, especially in his early years, before his Puritanism alienated him from the court with the accession of Charles I to the throne. Warwick's antipathy towards Edwin Sandys, for instance, was a factor in the dissolution of the Virginia Company's royal charter in 1624. His other hobby seems to have been privateering. It has been estimated that he was responsible for as much as 60 per cent of the privateering funded by English aristocrats during the reign of King Charles I.

With Charles on the throne, Warwick drifted out of favour with the court because of his Puritan sympathies. Much of his energy during this time was devoted to the New World. In 1629, he was instrumental in helping the Puritans gain the patent to set up the Massachusetts Bay Colony, which was settled the same year as Providence Island. In 1632 he was responsible for the conveyance of land that initiated the settlement of Saybrook, Connecticut, three years later. Warwick resigned as president of the New England Company in 1632, as the Massachusetts colonies began their devolution towards self-government. Yet he continued to manage both the Somer Isles Company and the Providence Island Company. While he was unable to make Providence Island profitable, the meetings of the investors became an important assembly, especially with the suspension of Parliament, for influential Puritans who were critical of the King.

During the English Civil War, Warwick was a key player on the Parliamentary side, while his younger brother Henry, the Earl of Holland, remained a Royalist and would later be executed for his sympathies. In 1642, despite the King's veto, the House of

Commons appointed him Admiral of the English Fleet and he was pivotal in bringing the navy over to the Parliamentarians' cause. Two years after this, Warwick was instrumental in the establishment of Rhode Island as a colony practising religious freedom and incorporating dissident New Englanders such as Samuel Gorton, Roger Williams, Anne Hutchinson and John Clark.

In 1649, during the Second Civil War, Warwick retired from public office, after criticism of his cautious behaviour in failing to attack a Royalist fleet moored in the Netherlands saw his naval commission withdrawn. He was suspected of sharing a degree of the Royalist sympathies of his brother. Warwick, however, was a believer in religious freedom to the end. His career took an upturn in 1657 when Cromwell asked him to carry the sword of state during his second inauguration as Lord Protector, and Warwick's grandson married Cromwell's daughter. The resurgence was cut short, however, by his death the following year at the age of seventy-one.

Robert Rich, second Earl of Warwick

Massachusetts, marked the beginnings of the permanent settlement of New England by Puritan refugees. As the population of New England grew, the emigrants were often seen in England as selfish deserters from a worthy cause. Providence Island would be different because the ultimate authority remained in the hands of English-based investors. Unsurprisingly perhaps, the self-focused New Englanders proved better at building their idea of a Puritan society than the Providence Islanders, who remained dependent on the sanction of a distant authority.

Peopling Providence

The first settlers for Providence Island arrived with their governor, Captain Phillip Bell, via Bermuda in 1630. In February the following year, the *Seaflower* left London with just under 100 colonists: men and boys who once they arrived were organised into 'families' of seven.

Each family was given a tract of land to work. Freemen were to keep half of what they harvested, with the rest being returned to the investors. They were encouraged to make individual agreements with indentured servants. The company, meanwhile, had to provide the colony's tradesmen, who proved difficult to procure and often had to be paid in pounds sterling rather than by the products available in the company magazine (store) that reached their captive market at inflated prices. All the colonists were also expected to pitch in for the building of public

infrastructure, most notably the fortifications deemed necessary to protect the fledgling society from Spanish attack.

The initial signs were promising. Lewis Morgan, the first preacher at Providence Island, compared the place to 'the Eden of God'. In a letter home, he wrote of the abundance of 'fish, parrots, tobaccos, cedars, lig vitae [a medicinal plant], fustick [a wood providing a yellow dye], fig trees. Oranges, Lemons, Vines, Figs, Pomegranates, Rhubarb we have planted and they prosper.' The list continued: 'Indigo, Cochineal, Cloves, Pepper, Mace, Nutmegs, Raisins, Currants, and I doubt not but the Land will bear as well as any Land under Heaven.'

While the investors were heartened by the many reports of this cornucopia, the colonists began to get greedy. Having established the colony, the earlier assurance that a 50-percent profit share would yield great riches no longer seemed quite as convincing. After all, why should their hard work be split down the middle with the investors, who were safely at home with their families and only risking their money, not their lives?

Intriguingly enough, it was Lewis Morgan, the preacher who had waxed lyrical about the island, who became the leader for the colonists' resentment towards their bosses. Morgan, who was young, fresh out of college and not the investors' first choice for the job, fought with both Governor Bell and the cantankerous Captain William Rudyard (the brother of investor and MP Sir Benjamin Rudyard). Captain Rudyard generated rancour in the colony from the moment he arrived and seems to have been a prototype for 'the remittance man'—the disgraced sons of the English aristocracy who would later be found throughout the British Empire. In the narrow confines of an island populated by men intent on mimicking the social hierarchies of home, the smallest slights were magnified. Some of the most destabilising conflicts were generated by minor blemishes, such as the failure to return borrowed books in the case of Morgan and Rudyard.

Trouble with clergy

Hearing of the calumny being perpetrated against them by their appointed preacher, the investors convened and decided to extract Morgan from the island. In his place, they sent three preachers, as part of a new batch of colonists in 1632. Along with the clergymen, the ship carried the first real families of Puritans. Among these were some men of substance—Henry Halhead, for one, a former mayor of the northern English town of Bunbury—although none of them rivalled the investors for power and influence. Still, they were of sufficient political gumption to clash with the hierarchy that the company had installed to do its bidding.

Although it was not really his fault, Governor Bell was attacked by the investors for failing to preside over a harmonious Christian colony. As Benjamin Rudyard wrote to Bell in censure:

Wee well hoped (according to our Intentions) that we had planted a Relligious Collonye in the Isle of Providence, instead whearof wee fynde the roote of bitterness plentifullye planted amongst you, an industrious supplanting [by] one of another, and not a man theare of Place (a straunge thing to consider) but hee doth both accuse and is accused; these are uncomfortable fruits of religion.

The situation didn't improve with the arrival of the new ministers. William Rous, a stepbrother of company treasurer John Pym, had sung profane songs on the ship on the way over and regularly beat his servants like a soldier, before dying within a year of his arrival. A second, a Dutchman by the name of Ditloff, had sung the same songs as Rous, but claimed poor English prevented him from knowing what he'd been singing. He earned the ire of governor and company by demanding parochial independence, then refused the sacrament to Henry Halhead because of a dispute over the possession of an apothecary's stone and claims that Halhead had publicly praised somebody whose character he'd attacked in private. Ditloff left Providence Island as soon as possible thereafter, leaving the third minister, Hope Sherrard, as the only official man of God in the colony for the rest of its short existence.

Sherrard was no stranger to controversy either. Although he was initially supposed to reside with Governor Bell, he soon fell out with him. Like Morgan, Sherrard became a locus of resistance to the company, using the weapons of excommunication and refusing the sacraments as a form of spiritual blackmail.

Throughout its history, the colony suffered due to the investors' belief that Providence Island would be best served if the reins of power remained in England. Governor Bell, who had been successful in Bermuda, found to his chagrin that his power to act on the island was limited. Many of the colonists, such as William Rudyard, had influential allies among the investors, and the chains of command were never clearly delineated. If the governor made a decision that adversely affected a well-connected colonist, such decisions were often appealed and frequently overturned following representations by London connections.

Perhaps even more damaging were the delays caused by the deferral of decisions to London. In these early days of the colony, particularly, it could take more than a year before a proposal generated on the island was sent to London, discussed and a final decision made—often for someone on the island to take exception to the decision and start lobbying their London connections all over again. While there was a council of notable citizens designed to help the governor administer the colony, it proved an ineffectual oligarchy. In the power vacuum created while waiting to hear from London, rifts between the planters, preachers, political authorities, company, colonists and military men, as well as those of a more personal kind, were allowed to flourish, thus preventing

the colony from acquiring a sense of its own identity and direction.

Plantation pipe dream

Providence Island's settlers never faced the prospect of starvation to the same extent as their counterparts in Virginia and New England. The climate and soil were good enough to guarantee an adequate subsistence for all. While factors such as the limited supply of land contributed to the colony's failure as an agricultural producer, it was mainly poor management that prevented it from achieving success.

Feeding people, however, was not the same as making a profit. Religious and economic grounds led the company to dissuade the original colonists from planting tobacco. In their initial enthusiasm, the company provided for a wide variety of seeds to be tried on the island: some for growing textiles, some for dying them, others for growing food crops. Yet for most of the colony's existence, tobacco became the staple crop, mainly because it was a known marketable commodity and the settlers—who were constantly under pressure from the company to produce a profit—were not given sufficient opportunity to find a superior money-making commodity. Unfortunately, the tobacco on Providence Island was never first rate and much of it was grown contemporaneous with a glut that drove down the price. The poor price the colonists could get wasn't helped by the investors' demands that they only export it on company ships, which often meant waiting, with the consequence that the tobacco left the island past its prime.

The main attraction of tobacco was that it had been tried elsewhere, namely Virginia, and had succeeded. The colonists' suspicion of outsiders, however, prevented them from learning how best to grow this notoriously finicky crop. While tobacco failed to allow the investors to begin recouping their investment, it nonetheless provided the wherewithal for the settlers to purchase supplies (at high prices) from the company magazine and thereby avoid falling into debt. It was sufficient to put the colony into a holding pattern, but never enough to tip it into prosperity.

The problem of sustainable agriculture was compounded by the failure of the Providence Island Company to attract sufficient migration to properly utilise the land. Indentured servants migrated mainly on the basis that once they had served out their term, they would be given their own plot to farm on a sharecropping basis and the servants to use it. However, from the beginning of the settlement, the company was unable to attract sufficient numbers of servants, and in addition to creating conflict among the freeman colonists, this meant the land was under-utilised. Given that the company didn't permit private ownership of the land (a crucial factor in the eventual success of other company colonies such as Virginia and Massachusetts Bay), the provision of servants was vital, both as a marker of status, and to give the desired

impression that the company was contributing something for its half share of the profits, particularly given that the servants of the colonists also had to work on public projects such as the fortification of the island. The company's failure to supply adequate labour while maintaining ownership of the land contributed greatly to the colony's failure.

Although a Puritan colony, Providence Island's shortfall in servants was increasingly

Cultivating and curing tobacco in the West Indies using slave labour in the seventeenth century

made up through the importation of African slaves. It was one of the many compromises made to the original ideal of building a godly English community in this Edenic New World setting. The justification that African slaves were permitted because they were strangers from Christianity was proved a lie by the fact that conversion did not result in their emancipation.

Puritan pirates and Spanish plunder

Situated in the far southwest of the Caribbean Sea, Providence Island had been chosen partly because of its proximity to Spain's settlements in Central America and the Isthmus of Panama, through which the Spanish treasure ships usually passed on their way to Europe. Given that the Earl of Warwick, with the largest privateering fleet of any English aristocrat, was one of the twenty investors in the Providence Island Company, it seems that motivations for the establishment of the colony were mixed from the very beginning. But equally, its location made the island vulnerable to attack by the Spanish.

Forced by the company, the settlers devoted much energy to the construction of fortifications to defend their island home. The company's stock response to the colonists' complaints was that they were doing it for their own safety. The counter-argument, of course, was that the settlers were donating the labour of themselves and their servants for free to help secure the company's profits.

In July 1635, the island's fortifications were given their first major test. While the Thirty Years' War raged across Europe, England and Spain were at peace. Nonetheless, some of the military men associated with the colony had got around this problem by accepting letters of marque from the Dutch, fellow Protestants who were at war with Spain, which authorised them to plunder Spanish ships. Irritated by the presence of a potential nest of pirates in their midst, the Spanish decided to attack Providence Island.

Captain Gregorio Castellar y Mantilla's ships anchored outside the main harbour of New Westminster and sent a messenger ashore, demanding the surrender of the island. Governor Bell refused. With the fortifications near the harbour too well constructed, the Spanish captain decided to attack from the relatively unprotected eastern side of the island's northern neck, a tricky approach given the prevailing winds. By the time Castellar was able to assemble his forces, the colonists had managed to lug their cannon across and rip through the sails of the Spanish ships as they laboured into the wind. The 'torn and battered' fleet, the company reported to the Earl of Holland, sailed away in 'haste and disorder'.

While this constituted a victory for the colony, it was also the first step towards its extinction. As a consequence of the attack, the Providence Island Company was able to petition King Charles for the right of reprisal against the Spanish. Essentially this was a licence for piracy. The attempted invasion had cost the company little. The letters of reprisal issued by Charles, therefore, were not really connected to the need for financial compensation. As the report of the Secretary of State, Sir John Coke, to the King showed, the reasons for granting the licence had more to do with the fact that the Providence Island Company was unable to sustain itself, and unless his majesty permitted privateering, a valuable strategic asset and source of royal income (the taxes paid on Spanish bounty) was likely to be lost. Strapped for cash, as English monarchs invariably were in those days, and unsure as to what foreign policy to pursue as the chaos of the Thirty Years' War continued over the Channel, Charles issued the letters of reprisal in December 1635, so marking an end to the policy of an honest peace with Spain.

The Providence Island Company's profit-hungry adventurers were delighted. Finally they had found a way to make easy money from the place. From 1636, the island became a haven for English pirates—exactly what the Spanish had initially feared.

Military men

While there were benefits for the company, the situation for the colonists was rather different. To begin with, privateering made the island more of a target for the Spanish. In the remaining five years of the colony's existence, the balance of power was increasingly in favour of the military faction, since their activities were responsible for the company's profits, while high-quality colonists such as Henry Halhead were increasingly marginalised.

Resentment between the settlers and the company continued to grow because the investors expected them to contribute their labour to the increased defence effort, which now included compulsory military exercises once a month. By this point, the preacher Hope Sherrard had become the centrepoint of a group of colonists who were organised against the governor's party and the increasing militarisation of the settlement. Sherrard finished his tenure by being shipped back to England in chains by Deputy Governor Andrew Carter. With Sherrard was stellar import Henry Halhead—a clear indication that whatever the intentions of the Providence Island Company, the results were far from spectacular.

And now, not only was the colony at risk, but the practice of privateering also made emigration to the colony more risky as the Spanish were likely to take the opportunity for revenge on English ships. People voted with their feet, in droves, for the safer situation of New England, which also offered the facility of owning land. On Providence Island, African slaves came to outnumber the colonists.

The Puritan grandees were somewhat confounded by the failure of their colony to deliver the riches they'd envisaged. Men such as John Pym increasingly came to occupy a back seat in company affairs as the conflict between the King and Parliament absorbed more and more of their attention, while the influence of others such as the privateering Earl of Warwick grew. By 1640, the situation on the island had deteriorated to one of constant squabbling, while investment in finding a way to make it agriculturally viable had largely ceased. The shambolic condition of the governing council was shown when the third governor, Captain Nathaniel Butler, abandoned the colony in the hands of his cowardly and incompetent deputy, Andrew Carter, and returned to England on a ship full of plundered Spanish goods, captained by Samuel Axe.

To make things even worse for the colonists, in May that year, soon after Butler had quit, the Spanish were back. Following pleas from the Governor of Cartagena (in modern-day Colombia) that his city was being strangled by the effects of English piracy, a fleet of thirteen ships manned by over 700 men was assembled and sailed to Providence Island. They faced up to the English but were delayed in their attack by unfavourable winds.

When the Spanish were sighted, Governor Carter proved himself a coward as well as an incompetent; instead of manning the ramparts, he promptly fled to Warwick Fort, where the women and children were hiding, as 300 Spaniards landed on the island. Carter's pessimism was misguided, however, and the assault was defeated.

Spanish ships at a port in the Caribbean, protecting a fleet of treasure ships

As the Spanish prisoners were rounded up, pardons were found inside their uniforms. These were dispensations signed by Catholic priests that absolved the sins of conquest. The Spaniards were permitted to 'lie with virgins and women, whom they might slay or keep alive at their pleasure', while the men were all to be put to the sword.

The presence of these pardons was something the Spanish soldiers didn't live to regret. Desperate to resume some semblance of authority, Carter ordered all the Spaniards to be slaughtered, even those who had surrendered on the promise that their lives would be spared. When the investors discovered this, he was ordered home for breaking the codes of civilised warfare.

Andrew Carter was still on the island the following year, however, when the Spanish made a third attempt to conquer the island. This time they sent in the heavy artillery, General Francisco Díaz Pimienta, Admiral of the Plate Fleet, whose main task was the transportation of precious metals from the New World back to Spain.

On 24 May 1641, Pimienta stormed the island via its main harbour with a force of 1400 men in pinnaces and easily overwhelmed the colonists. They found the island well provisioned with food and weapons. The 381 slaves were taken to Cartagena to be sold, while the 350 colonists were fortunate in that their lives were spared. Many of them returned to England to fight in the civil war, while others drifted into the colonies already established on the North American mainland or to other English Caribbean assets such as Bermuda and Barbados.

Downfall

The Providence Island Company persisted until 1650 when it was wound up, still in debt. By then many of the original investors such as John Pym and the Earl of Holland were dead. Against the backdrop of their roles in the English Civil War of 1642–51, Providence Island was reduced to an unfortunate footnote in lives of major achievement. For the colonists, some of whom had toiled for eleven years for no return, the prospects were often much bleaker.

CHAPTER 13

The Dutch colony of Mauritius, western Indian Ocean (1638–58 and 1664–1710)

It was only the threat of the English or the French colonising the island of Mauritius that provoked the Dutch into establishing a permanent base there. During their first attempt, in 1638, slaves were imported from Madagascar to help harvest ebony and grow crops, but cultivation was repeatedly thwarted by cyclones and plagues of rats. Twenty years later, with the venture losing money, settlers eking out a mere subsistence and successive colonial governors having been driven to drink, the order was given to abandon Mauritius. During the next attempt, plantation agriculture proved successful, mainly because of the arrival of settlers who had their own farms, but a major hurricane in 1695 devastated much of the colony. A long period of decline ensued, and by 1710 the island had been abandoned once again. Five years later, just as the Dutch had feared, the French arrived.

Located east of the African mainland, and separated from it by the vast landmass of Madagascar about 800 kilometres (500 miles) away, Mauritius had been visited by sailors since the times of the ancient Phoenicians, and while some were undoubtedly shipwrecked there, none had ever decided to settle. When the Dutch first visited the island during their second expedition to the East Indies, in 1598, they found a terrain uninhabited by humans, which nonetheless was fertile, had supplies of fresh water and was rich in animal and marine life. In addition to the many unique species that had evolved in isolation from the rest of the world over millions of years, such as the dodo, the Portuguese had left pigs and goats behind for the benefit of future shipwrecked sailors, while the monkeys and rats that had escaped from the Iberians' ships had also prospered.

The Portuguese had never erected permanent settlements on the island but they had named it Ilha do Cerne, meaning 'island of swans', which may have been an approximate reference to the dodo. When Vice-Admiral Wybrant van Warwijck became the first Dutchman ashore in September 1598, he renamed it Maurits, after the stadholder, or leader, of the Netherlands. This first visit lasted little more than a fortnight. However, as the frequency of Dutch expeditions expanded greatly with the formation of the Dutch East India Company, the VOC, in 1602, Mauritius became a frequent refreshment station for Dutch ships, a stopover point where they could get fresh food and water either on the way out to Asia or on the way back home.

The lush fertility of Mauritius, its stands of valuable ebony and the large chunks of ambergris (a secretion from the abdomens of sperm whales used for making fragrances) that washed up on its beaches led to proposals to colonise the island as far back as 1604. The VOC preferred to trade with and/or conquer already extant societies, though, and was resistant to the idea of settling Mauritius, but at the same time it was very keen to preserve the monopoly granted to it by the Netherlands government.

By the late 1630s, the threat of either the English or the French taking possession of the island as a result of Dutch inaction was enough for the VOC to overcome its reluctance and found a permanent settlement there. On 31 December 1637, a fleet sailed from the Netherlands for the Indies. On board was Cornelis Gooyer, the first Dutch commander of Mauritius.

The first settlement

Gooyer and his twenty-four men arrived in Mauritius on 6 May 1638 and proceeded to build a fort named in honour of Maurit's successor as stadholder, Frederik Hendrik. The fort would become the administrative focus of the colony. The site he chose was on the southeast coast, where the Dutch ships were used to harbouring and where the city of Mahébourg can be found today. Having built the fort, Gooyer's instructions were then to start harvesting ebony and exploring the agricultural potential of the island.

Within a year, successive visits by Dutch ships had resulted in the population of the garrison growing to eighty people. The VOC chiefs were dissatisfied with Gooyer's performance, however. Apparently he spent too much time dealing with the French ships that pulled into Mauritius, rather than developing the settlement, and there were accusations of his trading in ambergris behind the company's back. In October 1639, he was transferred to VOC headquarters in Batavia (present-day Jakarta), where he died soon

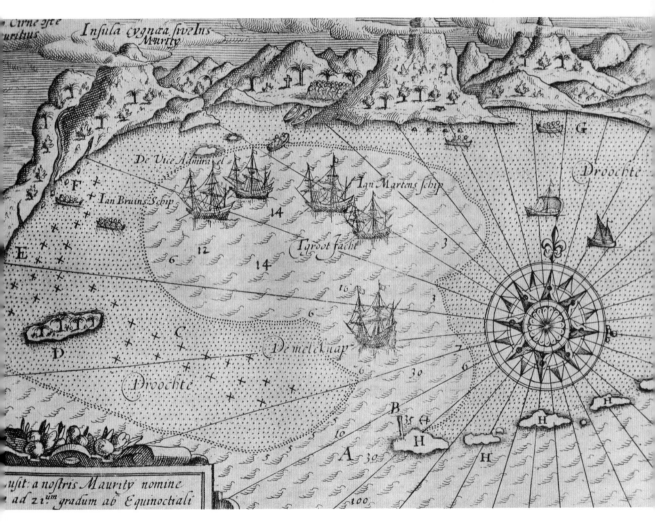

Arrival in Mauritius. Dutch map from 1595

after arrival. His replacement as Governor of Mauritius was Adriaan van der Stel.

Under Van der Stel, the colony showed signs of improvement. The new governor put some discipline into the isolated rabble that was the garrison he'd inherited, and with the help of carts imported from Batavia, he began to exploit the island's ebony. His task wasn't helped by the fact that the Governor-General of the VOC, Antonio Van Diemen, viewed the settlement as a mistake. When

a shipwreck hoped to be a Portuguese treasure ship turned out to be Dutch, and a mineralogical survey showed it to be carrying no precious metals, Van Diemen's enthusiasm dwindled even further, as he didn't consider Mauritian ebony and ambergris sufficiently lucrative trading items to justify the expense of maintaining the colony. As a consequence, the men sent to Mauritius were quite often invalids from other areas under the company's control. They certainly weren't best suited

Engraving by Theodor de Bry of the Dutch in Mauritius

to arduous work such as logging, and even the healthy ones bitterly resented the work, arguing that it was not what they'd signed up for.

There were frequent desertions during this period, mainly aboard visiting English ships, which didn't carry the risk of getting caught up with the sectarian violence plaguing Europe at the time. Van der Stel had started with eighty men, but illness and desertion soon brought that number down to fifty. The governor's requests for more men were refused by Van Diemen, who had his own personnel shortage in Batavia.

Outside help

The problem of labour was solved, as it usually was in those days, by the purchasing of slaves. In November 1641, Van der Stel sailed to Madagascar, with instructions to form a relationship with the Malagasy kings in order to procure slaves in exchange for goods such as linen, combs, mirrors and iron cookware. He signed a memorandum of understanding with the king of Antongil, an area with a large harbour on the northeast coast of the island. On this first trip, Van der Stel returned to the colony with 105 slaves, mainly tribal enemies captured during the region's frequent wars. In doing so, he effectively tripled the population of Mauritius. However, more than half of them soon escaped to the centre of the island, where they established a series of alternate settlements that would ultimately outlast the Dutch.

Van der Stel now wrote to Van Diemen asking for twenty or thirty Chinese agriculturalists, whose skills were valued in other Dutch settlements such as Batavia and Formosa. The request was denied, and he was ordered instead to educate the Madagascans in cultivation.

The success of agriculture in Dutch Mauritius was patchy at best. Crops grown included rice, sugar cane, indigo and several kinds of fruit and vegetable, but they were rarely successful enough to make the colony self-sufficient in terms of food. This wasn't so much the fault of the workforce as the island's plague populations of rats, which managed to eat entire crops. While the climate was generally conducive to agriculture, crops were also destroyed on a regular basis as a result of hurricanes.

In 1645, Van der Stel resigned and was posted to Ceylon (now Sri Lanka), where he was captured there and beheaded by the Sinhalese. The governors who came after him faced much the same problems as he'd done in their quest to make a success of Dutch Mauritius; and after their initial enthusiasm was exhausted, a number of them lapsed into alcoholism, petty tyranny and general torpor. Slaves from Madagascar were augmented with convicts from Batavia. These two categories of inhabitant tended to outnumber the company employees, who were also hardly the cream of the crop, since the VOC often sent employees to Mauritius for disciplinary reasons as well as poor health.

Perhaps the greatest blow to the settlement of Mauritius came in 1652 when the VOC founded a colony on the Cape of Good Hope, in southern Africa. It rapidly established itself as the reprovisioning stop of choice for all VOC ships, meaning that Mauritius became even more peripheral in the company's thinking. This marginalisation wasn't helped by the state of the ebony trade. The rampant logging of the first years of Dutch settlement had resulted in diminishing returns, since the loggers had to travel increasingly further to find the resource. At the same time, there was a glut of ebony in Europe that threatened to send prices crashing. The colony became even less profitable and the VOC ordered it scaled down. This state of affairs persisted for a few more years until 1657, when the company finally ordered the abandonment of Mauritius. The garrison left the island in mid July the following year and the fort was destroyed.

Second time around

Between 1658 and 1664, Mauritius remained officially unoccupied, although some runaway slaves most likely remained in the interior. They were added to by a group of castaways from the VOC ship *Arnhem*, which was wrecked during a storm and sunk in February 1662. The fact that some of the crew had made it to Mauritius and were able to survive for some time until their rescue caused the company to rethink its abandonment of the

island. As before, it was the threat of French or English occupation that motivated the bosses of the VOC. They wrote to the commander of the Cape Colony in 1664, ordering that a small party be dispatched to take back Mauritius for the Dutch.

A dozen men were sent, under the command of Jacobus van Niewlandt. Included among them, for their experience of local conditions, were some of the *Arnhem* survivors, although it's hard to know exactly what they thought about this. Not long after they had arrived on the island at Grand Port, more than half the men deserted their commander for a life of hunting goats and drinking palm wine. Unable to fulfil his instructions from the VOC, Van Niewandt retreated to a hut and wrote his daily journal until he died there from a stroke in May 1665.

His replacement, George Wreede, was made of sterner stuff. Having arrived with eighteen men extra only to find Van Niewlandt dead, he apprehended the deserters and sent them in chains to the Cape Colony, then set about resuming the collection of ebony. However, his men complained so much about his leadership that he was forced to spend two years in the Cape himself, defending his actions to his superiors, during which time things reverted to their usual lackadaisical state. After being acquitted of any wrongdoing in 1667, Wreede returned to Mauritius to continue his command. But by this time, his energy for gleaning a profit for the VOC had dissipated. He neglected the stocks of ebony and started drinking heavily, and in that way at least improved his relations with his underlings.

Wreede drowned while hunting turtles and sea-cows on a small island off Mauritius in early 1672. His replacement as commander, Hubert Hugo, was an intriguing choice, since he was in his second career with the VOC and had been a pirate sailing under French letters of marque in the interim. Hugo sailed with his wife and children, but his wife died on the way over. When he arrived, he was confronted with a shambles. The cannon had rusted and couldn't be fired. The timber of his house had rotted and it was infested with rats. There were next to no supplies, and the settlement's garden had been destroyed by insects and locusts. Wild dogs and pigs had the run of the colony.

Lovers and despots

Like many of the governors before him, Hugo set about reinvigorating the colony. He built a stone house for himself, as well as a church, sawmill, arrack distillery, tannery and 16 kilometres (10 miles) of road to help get the ebony out of the forest. The gardens were refurbished and the slackers who had taken advantage of Wreede's turpitude were put back to work. All of this made Hugo unpopular with his charges, of course, something that was exacerbated by his cruel and whimsical administration of justice.

When his teenage daughter, Maria, fell in love with one of Hugo's subordinates, Pieter Col, the governor reacted disproportionately.

At first he banished Col to a remote place on the island and forbade them to meet. When the two young lovers contrived to meet behind the colony's garden and were reported by Maria's brother, Hugo reacted strongly. He clapped Col in irons and imprisoned him on half rations for several months in the hold of one of the company's yachts, where the Dutchman's skin was afflicted with disfiguring and unpleasant infections. Even this failed to quell Maria and Pieter's ardour for each another. Sometime later, Hugo intercepted a secret wedding vow between the two that was written in blood. Once again, his paternalistic impulses went out of control. Hugo sentenced Col to be flogged, branded and then made to serve five years' hard labour on Robben Island (the same place where, 300 years later, Nelson Mandela would be imprisoned by South Africa's apartheid regime for eighteen years).

Disgusted by her father's cruelty, Maria later abandoned him and moved to Batavia. After a number of other complaints about Hubert Hugo's style of justice, he was officially forbidden from trying serious cases as the colony's chief magistrate. This offended him so greatly that he resigned.

Hugo's replacement, Isaac Lamotius, arrived in 1677 and remained governor of Mauritius until 1692, by far the longest tenure of any of the Dutch commanders. He arrived to find the colony in better condition than Hugo had, but the population drunk and fractious. At first Lamotius tried to befriend the *vrijburgers*, the freemen who

A DODO'S LIFE

Not all the ghosts to be found in these failed colonies are human. Indeed, over the course of colonisation, many native animals too have suffered from the arrival in their territory of rapacious, hungry humans and the dogs, cats, rats and the like that accompanied them. Few animals suffered as completely as the dodo, however. A relative of the pigeon, it's not known how long the dodo was on Mauritius before the Dutch established their settlement, but the island has only been there since a volcanic eruption formed it some 8 million years ago. Whether the first dodos flew there or hitched a ride on floating debris, such as tree trunks, remains a mystery. In its isolated existence, the dodo grew big. Scientists have argued that its loss of flight was a trade-off for the more important ability to store large amounts of fat to get the bird through times of scarcity, especially as there

The dodo became extinct during the period of Dutch colonialism in Mauritius.

were no natural predators on the island. It was an omnivorous animal that fed on fruit and seeds that dropped to the ground. It also waded into marshes, where with its sharp beak it was adept at spearing fish. A curious detail about the dodo's diet was its penchant for eating small stones; it is claimed that this helped with the digestive process.

As with many things about the dodo, the origin of the name remains unknown. Explanations from the Dutch language variously suggest that the name comes from dodoor meaning 'sluggard' or dodaers meaning 'plump bum'. The other common explanation is that the word is derived from the Portuguese doudo, meaning 'fool' or 'crazy'—a reference perhaps to the bird's seeming indifference to its fate.

By the time that the Portuguese and then the Dutch began appearing on Mauritius, the dodo had lost the ability to recognise a potential predator when it saw one. Dodos sometimes even approached the men who were preparing to club them into oblivion. However, the big birds were protected to some extent by the poor taste of their meat, which was so bad that another Dutch name for the bird was walghvogel—literally, 'nauseating bird'. Only when nothing else was available would a dodo be used as a source of food.

Nonetheless, by 1680, around 100 years after the first contact between the dodo and the Dutch, the bird became extinct. The main problem wasn't the humans but the animals they brought with them. The worst of these were the crab-eating macaques, which soon discovered that dodo eggs were an easy meal. Rats also ate the eggs, while dogs and cats fed on the young. The Dutchmen abetted this process by cutting down the forests that were the birds' natural habitat. Before long the dodo bird was done.

ran the farms. However, this only created contempt for his authority, and his reign was marked by conflict between himself and the settlers, especially after the arrival in 1685 of Jean Dubertin, a former lieutenant from the Cape Colony who had been banished to Mauritius for embezzling from the VOC.

In his twenty-five years ruling the island, Lamotius fought a losing battle to keep the colony afloat. Rats once again destroyed the crops, and most of the ebony had already been felled. The free settlers frequently engaged in illegal trade with the English ships that called into the northern part of the island. They also allied with the escaped slaves in the centre to establish conspiracies against Lamotius. In 1679, his pregnant wife and daughter were burnt to death in a fire started by a drunk and incompetent employee. By that time, he had already had to hang a slave and put one of the settlers in chains for their part in a plot against him. It is no surprise that a man who had lost his family and was faced with VOC indifference on the one hand, and active hostility from his charges on the other, became paranoid, mean and vindictive. Lamotius made several attempts to resign but was unsuccessful each time. Frustrated, he retreated into despotism.

His tenure eventually came to an inglorious end, when he was arrested for the cruel treatment of the Dubertin family and shipped back to the Cape for trial. He was found guilty and sentenced to six years' hard labour on the nutmeg plantations of the Banda Islands, in contemporary Indonesia.

Pirates and cyclones

Lamotius was replaced by Roelof Diodati, a Dutchman of Swiss–Italian descent. In his eleven years as governor between 1692 and 1703, Diodati encountered many of the problems of his predecessors. Despite the best efforts of the settlers and the promise of the land, Dutch Mauritius still hadn't managed to become self-sufficient in terms of food. Runaway slaves rampaged through the interior and often raided settlers' farms, while a number of the other slaves were plotting to kill the Dutch and take control of the island for themselves. Plus, the colony was constantly being put on the back foot by natural disasters such as cyclones and floods. The worst of them, in 1695, destroyed entire farms to the extent that many of the *vrijburgers* decided to leave. This was arguably the tipping point for the colony's eventual demise.

Unlike many of his predecessors, Diodati showed diplomacy in his relations with the settlers, and even married one of their daughters. Yet by the time he became governor, the northern part of the island was increasingly coming under the control of English pirates, who had chosen to use it as a base and continued to trade illicitly with the settlers. With only a couple of dozen men under his command, there was little Diodati could do about this, except protest.

In 1703, after asking to be relieved of his command, Diodati was replaced by his deputy, Abraham Momber van der Velder, who had also asked to be relieved, only to find himself promoted instead. Despite being a competent man, the situation under Momber's leadership deteriorated remarkably. His assistant died of tetanus after fighting a duel (unwisely against the colony's only surgeon), while in 1706 all of the company's buildings and stores were burnt to the ground by slaves. The food situation also worsened. There was an increasing number of cyclones, and crops failed more and more. Meanwhile, hunters sent into the interior to supplement the settlement's diet were finding less and less game in the forests, perhaps because the pursuit of ebony had resulted in so much of the forests being destroyed. Momber made the decision that the convergence of bad luck amounted to a message from God and tendered his resignation.

In 1707, the VOC decided to again abandon Mauritius. The settlers were given the choice of moving to the Cape or to Batavia. At that time there were 244 people on the island—48 VOC employees and 32 farmers, with 24 wives, 69 children and 71 slaves. The numerous runaway convicts and slaves were not included in this offer. The gradual evacuation of the settlers began that same year and went on until 1710, when the island was officially abandoned, although a remnant population of ex-slaves and deserters remained. Having heeded the message from God, Momber died destitute in Batavia, a month after his arrival there.

Missed opportunities

Within a 72-year period from 1638, the Dutch made two attempts to establish a settlement in Mauritius and failed miserably. The conditions were against them, as was the VOC for much of the time. Yet it's hard to be too generous to the colonists. A mere five years later, the island was settled by the French, who renamed it Île de France and managed to establish a thriving plantation economy based on sugar cane. Under its new colonial interlopers, Mauritius became an asset, fought over and later won by the English. It would never be abandoned again.

CHAPTER 14

The forsaken French colony of Fort Dauphin, Madagascar (1642–74)

Intended as a base from which the French hoped to expand their nascent influence in the Indian Ocean, Fort Dauphin was first settled under Jacques Pronis in 1642. As if leading by example, the governor contributed to initial good relations with the locals by marrying the daughter of a powerful chief and offering men to fight his battles. Subsequent governors took a distinctly unsympathetic approach with the Madagascan tribespeople, however, and the island became a war zone after the first six years of settlement. With the colony's economic returns never more than marginal, tropical diseases eroding the settlers' health, and the spectre of mutiny ever present, Fort Dauphin's days were numbered. The final blow came with the accidental arrival of twelve French women, who soon snared potential husbands among the many colonists who, like Pronis, had intermarried. In response to this outrage, the local tribes attacked and massacred half of the remaining settlers. Of the 4500 people who migrated to Fort Dauphin over its 32-year existence, there were just over sixty left when the colony was finally abandoned.

As Portugal's maritime power began to wane in the early seventeenth century, first the Dutch and then the English began to eye the opportunities for exploiting some of the spice trade with the Indies themselves. The French, whose colonial energies were absorbed by New France (Quebec), were slower than their neighbours to investigate this potential. However, under powerful politician Cardinal Richelieu in 1642, the first Compagnie Française des Indes Orientales, or the French East India Company, was formed. Before the company had even been ratified by the king, its first ship, the *Saint Louis*, had been dispatched under Commander-Governor Jacques Pronis to establish a colony on Madagascar, from where it was hoped France could extend its influence throughout the Indian Ocean.

Disenchanted island

The initial site chosen for the colony was on the bay of St Luce, in the southeast of the island. However, after their arrival there in the southern autumn of 1642, twenty-six of the forty passengers died from fever, the locals were hostile and the topography was found to be unsuitable for the construction of defences. It was abandoned some months later and Pronis took his depleted complement south to a nearby headland on the Taolagnaro Peninsula that looked more defendable and benefited from sea breezes. The native people there appeared to be somewhat more amenable to the presence of strangers in their midst than those to the north. Founded on 24 September 1642, Pronis named the colony Fort Dauphin in honour of the future 'Sun King', Louis XIV, who at the time was five.

The chief of the local native people, Dian Ramaka, was familiar with Europeans. A number of his subjects were the descendants of shipwrecked Portuguese sailors, while Ramaka himself had spent three years in Goa and been baptised a Christian. In imitation of the conduct of European royalty in concluding alliances, Pronis married one of Ramaka's daughters, which helped maintain the peace—except for the fact that many of his fellow Frenchmen were scandalised by the idea. In 1646 they mutinied when, during a food shortage, Pronis's wife and family asserted their status and commandeered the colony's stores. Already unpopular with his men by virtue of being Protestant while they were Catholic, Pronis was held captive by his countrymen for six months until he was released following the arrival of a company ship. Twelve of the mutineers were exiled to Île de Bourbon (now known as Réunion), an island to the east of Madagascar and the first permanent French colony in the Indian Ocean.

As the English were also discovering at their settlement in the west of Madagascar, St Augustine Bay, the political situation between the surrounding tribes was a complex web of shifting allegiances in an environment of continual small-scale warfare. Chiefs fell in and out of alliance with each other at a rapid rate, while there were frequently traitors within tribes. The usefulness of the French to Dian Ramaka was not so much the increased firepower as the symbolic status he gained by having Europeans and their guns in his army.

While Pronis gained some local cachet by marrying the daughter of Ramaka, it didn't earn him the friendship of the other tribes. When he heard that one of the other local *roandria* (chiefs) had slept with his wife, he planned an elaborate and lucrative revenge. Inviting the chief and his relatives to visit him in the fort, Pronis then kidnapped seventy-three of them and sold them as slaves to a Dutch ship that stopped in on its way to the colony at Mauritius.

If the relationship between the colonists and the Madagascans had begun to sour under Pronis, they rapidly worsened with the arrival in 1648 of his superior, Étienne de Flacourt, who relegated Pronis to second-in-command. While Pronis's behaviour was comprehensible to the Madagascans as the behaviour of a chief, the new governor pursued a ruthless campaign of subjugation designed to reduce all the Madagascan *roandria* to vassals of the French.

In his first two years, Flacourt adopted a tactic of dawn raids, in which more than fifty villages were razed to the ground. In establishing the clear potential of the French to destroy their fields and food supplies, he hoped the native people would be forced to come to Fort Dauphin, surrender, and ask for protection in order to survive.

Not surprisingly, the Madagascans resented this, but their weapons were no match for the colonists'. In 1651, after Dian Ramaka had maintained a brief siege of Fort Dauphin, Flacourt ordered an attack on the chief's own seat of power, about a day's walk inland. Forced to flee by the organised savagery of the assault, Ramaka and his son were both shot in the back and killed by the French forces as they tried to escape across a river.

Colonial tribalism

Flacourt's reign as governor coincided with a long period of isolation for the colony. Following his arrival in 1648, no other European ship was sighted until 1654. The main reason for this appears to have been that Fort Dauphin had little in the way of exports to warrant the company sending regular ships.

The quality of the land that the French had occupied was insufficient to guarantee a subsistence for the colonists, especially since few of them had the know-how to create successful tropical gardens. This had several major consequences. Firstly, the settlers were usually hungry, a situation that was capable of increasing internal dissension, as Pronis's imprisonment back in 1646 had demonstrated. Secondly, it meant that in order for the colonists to survive, they had to effectively take food, usually cattle, by force from the local tribes. This, of

Detail from a seventeenth-century French map showing Fort Dauphin

158

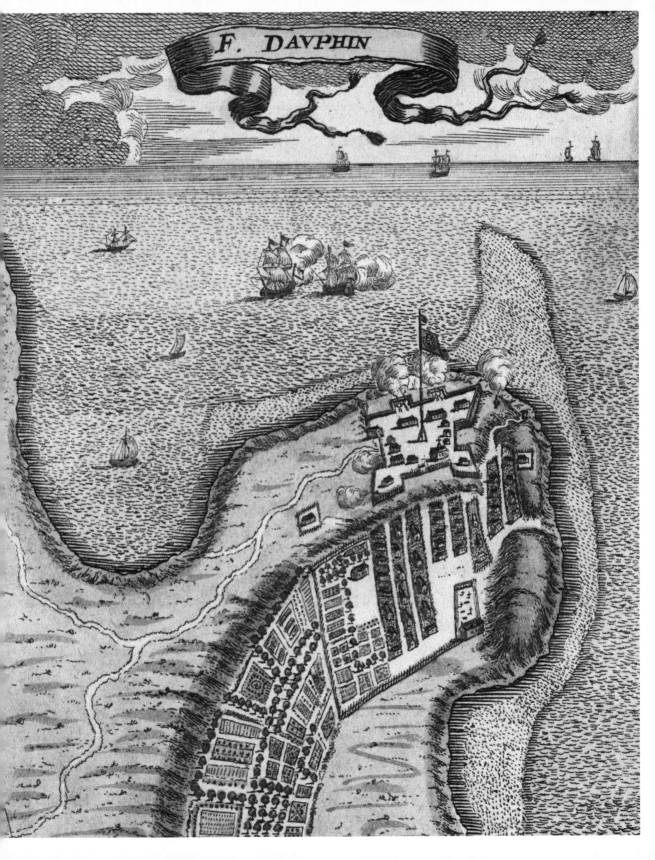

F. DAVPHIN

course, exacerbated the enmity between the French and the locals. However, this enmity was rendered complex by the increasing frequency of intermarriage between colonists and native women, something that Pronis had pioneered. The advantage was that any man who married a tribal woman was no longer constrained to live in close proximity to Fort Dauphin, as he usually had the protection of his wife's tribe and was able to farm inland, where crops tended to be easier to grow than directly on the coast, where the vegetation was stunted by the salt air and wind.

For most of the colonists, living in Fort Dauphin would have been a fairly miserable life. On the promise of rich soil and precious metals, they had travelled thousands of miles on risky seas, yet their expectations were sorely disappointed. Even when the company ships came, the colony had trouble providing enough exports to vindicate their visits. Ebony, leather, beeswax, aloe, wild pepper and benzoin (the perfumed wood resin) were not the most lucrative of crops. It would be another 200 years before Madagascar's main contemporary export, vanilla, originally a Central American plant, was successfully grown. Perhaps the only export of any great value was slaves, but Madagascan slaves acquired a sensible reputation for being lazy and recalcitrant.

Just as bad was the fact that when the ships arrived, it was often the Madagascans who had first dibs on the products, since the settlers were usually in debt to those who had supplied them with cattle and rice. The

colonists might have benefited from having a ship permanently stationed there, so they could have sent it out for supplies when necessary. Indeed, after no ship arrived for almost six years, Flacourt became so desperate that he built a boat of his own and set to sea in search of supplies; the small ship nearly sank in a storm, and limped back to Fort Dauphin ten days later with nothing to show for the effort.

This was perhaps the last throw of the dice for Étienne de Flacourt, who caught the scent of mutiny on his return and was probably lucky that a ship arrived in 1655 to take him back to France. It seems strange that Flacourt would ever try to return to Madagascar, but having written an account of his experiences (published as *History of the Great Isle of Madagascar and Relations*, in 1658), that's just what he did. One misfortune was anticipated by another, however, and during the trip out from France his ship was attacked by Barbary corsairs off the north coast of Africa and he drowned.

Flacourt's replacement as governor was a man called Champmargou, who arrived in Fort Dauphin in 1556 to find Pronis dead and the fort burnt to the ground. His response was to embark on an even more punitive regimen than Flacourt had. But the consequence of this live-by-the-sword arrogance was that life in the colony became even more precarious: the Frenchmen's enemies multiplied as Champmargou never quite had the numbers to assert military supremacy over the native tribes.

In a pattern that bore a resemblance to the contrasting strategies of Flacourt and his deputy, Jacques Pronis, the harshness of Champmargou was offset by his second-in-command, Le Rochalais de la Vacher, also known as La Case. Like Pronis, the latter effectively became a local chief by marrying the daughter of a *roandria*. An inspiring leader in battle, he raised an army of mainly natives that successfully prosecuted wars against two other tribes.

In 1664, La Case's indigenous troops were called on to save Champmargou. From 1663, a number of Catholic priests had arrived in Madagascar and begun to evangelise aggressively among the native tribespeople. One particularly arrogant priest, by the name of Etienne, decided to insult a powerful chief, Dian Manangue, by ripping off the pagan charms that were hanging around his neck. The outraged Manangue reacted by putting the priest and his party to the sword. In response, Champmargou embarked on a rampage of vengeance during which, according to one account, 150 villages were razed to the ground, 1000 natives killed (including women and children) and 4000 cattle taken. This overreaction in turn outraged the Madagascans, who decided to obliterate the angry canker of Frenchmen who had installed themselves on their land. After a series of battles, Champmargou was reduced to defending a besieged Fort Dauphin with only eighty able men. In desperation he applied to La Case for assistance. Although he was no great friend of the governor, La

Case probably saw the perpetuation of the French presence on the island as helpful to his cause. The potentially decisive battle was defused by his native army, and Champmargou remained on the island until 1668.

Company rules and jealous wifes

The period from 1664 onwards saw several thousand Frenchmen arrive in Madagascar as the restructured French East India Company underwent an expansionary phase, backed by Louis XIV and funded by his courtiers, who saw it as a means of obtaining the Sun King's favour. Yet, for all the investment, there was little improvement in the conditions of those sequestered at Fort Dauphin. Many of these new arrivals quickly succumbed to the trifecta of malaria, dysentery and malnutrition, while others became the casualties of the constant warfare.

Along with this wave of settlers came potentates representing the authority of the new company over the old. In 1665, a ship arrived carrying a new governor, Pierre de Bausse, who immediately appointed Champmargou his deputy. Champmargou, however, resented the dimunition of his authority, and began to surreptitiously militate against company policy. Meanwhile, La Case, who had fallen out with Champmargou since rescuing him the previous year, was indifferent to the company and more concerned with maintaining his power base, which at one time was supported by over 3000 Madagascan warriors. In this way, the

MIXING IT WITH THE LOCALS

One of the questions faced by many colonists was whether or not to get into bed, quite literally, with the locals. In terms of the European colonising powers, generally speaking, it could be said that the practice was encouraged by the Spanish and Portuguese and viewed with ambivalence by the French and Dutch. The English, a mongrel composition in terms of their own history, were at the other end of the spectrum. Going native was actively frowned upon, and the inevitable expressions of sexual curiosity were usually restricted to prostitutes and mistresses, rather than wives.

Miscegenation between colonisers and colonised was no guarantee of success. But it's highly likely that the French colony of Fort Dauphin—where men were dispatched without wives in the expectation that they would marry native women—lasted longer than its English

The natives of Madagascar, engraving from 1653, based on a description by the West Indies Company

equivalent on the island, St Augustine Bay, precisely because intermarriage incorporated the French into the intricacies of Madagascan allegiances and also expanded their ability to feed themselves.

A major advantage of miscegenation was that it gave colonists access to the store of local knowledge, particularly agricultural techniques, that could prove essential to survival. One of the reasons why the Viking colony in Greenland eventually failed was their failure to learn from the Inuit how to adapt to changing conditions. And a reason for this was that intermarriage between the two peoples hardly occurred at all.

The most successful colonial cultures where miscegenation was encouraged were in South America under the Spanish and the Portuguese. And this established a precedent. When colonies such as Nueva Germania and New Australia (see pages 249 and 271) were founded in Paraguay, with the intention of maintaining racial purity, it wasn't long before settlers were marrying into the local population after all.

Even in successful colonies, a lack of intermarriage between the original inhabitants and the new settlers could cause tensions that could pervade a society for centuries. One only has to think of absurdities like apartheid in South Africa (which was first colonised by the Dutch, at roughly the same time that the English and the French formed their abortive Madagascan colonies) to realise the folly of attempting to maintain cultural or racial purity in places inhabited by more than one group of people.

politics among the French leaders came to resemble the internecine antipathy of their Madagascan counterparts.

With Madagascar as the intended jewel in its crown, it wasn't long before the 1664 incarnation of the French East India Company collapsed and its assets reverted to the Crown. In 1671, Admiral Blanquet de la Haye advised Louis XIV to abandon the colony of Fort Dauphin. By that time,

Illustration from an early 1800s book showing French colonists and Madagascan natives

despite all the effort invested, only 200 settlers remained, surrounded by a constant war zone, and most of them had stayed only because they'd married native women or had nowhere else to go. The colony sputtered on for another three years.

When the end finally came, it was as a consequence of these intermarriages. In August 1674, a dozen young French women bound for the settlement on Îl de Bourbon (now Réunion) were wrecked on Madagascar's southeastern coast, near Fort Dauphin. Without the wherewithal to make their own living, the women convinced some of the colonists who rescued them to marry them. However, these men were already married to natives. The first wives were furious when they heard of their usurpation by these women, who had no status in Madagascan terms. Indeed, had they not been rescued by the French, the survivors would probably have been slaughtered or enslaved. The Madagascan women therefore withdrew the support that their kinship afforded the Frenchmen.

During the marriage festivities, the native armies attacked, killing more than 100 of the settlers and all the new brides. When the forces of long-time enemy Dian Manangue then converged on Fort Dauphin, only sixty-three French colonists remained alive. Faced with almost certain death if they stayed, the colonists were lucky that a small ship, the *Blanc-Pignon*, was moored in the harbour. Under cover of night, the Frenchmen snuck away from the fort and boarded the boat. As they sailed away from the island, they brought to an end more than three decades of French effort to create a permanent colony on Madagascar.

Not quite the end

The failure of Fort Dauphin rankled the French, although it would be another 200 years before they could do anything conclusive about it. While pirates used Madagascar as a base for much of the seventeenth and eighteenth centuries, colonising the huge island proved difficult. Still, a French trading presence grew there, and it was apparently in response to violations of assets held by French citizens on Madagascar that France invaded in 1883, in what became known as the First France–Hova War. This conflict resulted in the island's Merina rulers ceding the north-coast province of Antsiranana to France.

But it wasn't enough to satisfy the French, caught up as they were in the late nineteenth-century European greed for colonies. In 1885, they mounted a surprise attack on Antananarivo, the Merina capital, and established Madagascar as a French protectorate. When Queen Ranavalona III showed signs of resisting, the French annexed the island in 1896 and forced her into exile. This time, Madagascar remained a French colony, until its independence in 1958.

CHAPTER 15

The lost English colony of St Augustine Bay, Madagascar (1645–46)

In the days before the British Empire was born, there was consternation among the English that, thanks to their colonisation-shy East India Company, they were losing out on a wealth of trading opportunities to the Dutch. In 1635, the Courteen's Association was formed, with the aim of building trade through colonisation. Its first planned ventures failed to get off the ground but by March 1645, 140 men, women and children under Captain John Smart had arrived to settle St Augustine Bay, on the southwest coast of Madagascar. And that was all they achieved. The land was barren, the native people treacherous and hostile, while dysentery and malaria were endemic. After just a year, the sixty surviving members abandoned the settlement—their antipathy toward the locals so powerful that they burnt down their own huts rather than leave them behind for the tribespeople. Unable or unwilling to re-establish the colony on the Comoros Islands, Smart's fellow survivors were left scanning the horizon, in the hope of finding a passing ship and a ride home.

By the 1630s there was considerable opinion in circles at the court of Charles I that the English East India Company was failing to serve the national interest through its refusal to establish colonies. Many of the American colonies had survived the critical years of their foundation and had started to flourish, and some influential figures at the court believed that the same thing should be happening in more exotic climes. The company's preferred modus operandi was to set up trading posts rather than colonies. However, the success of the Dutch in establishing profitable and prestigious colonies, particularly in the Spice Islands (today's Maluku Islands, an archipelago in eastern Indonesia), meant that there was growing criticism of this policy, particularly as the East India Company held a monopoly and actively resisted the entry of any competitors to its business.

In 1635, to considerable protest from the company, the Crown violated this monopoly by issuing royal assent to the Courteen's Association to trade in the Indies. The reason behind the move was reported at the time to be a need to 'settle factories and plant collonies after the Dutch manner'. Sir William Courteen had financed the colonisation of Barbados during the previous decade, but under this new joint-stock operation such colonies on the East Indies trade route were not quick to emerge. In the early years of the Courteen's Association, during which Sir William died and was replaced by his son, all available capital was needed to procure and outfit a fleet to make the annual trading trips between England and the Indies. One of the key features on this trade route, and therefore a prime candidate for settlement, was the vast island of Madagascar, to the east of Africa. Back in 1615, the English East India Company had reached a trading agreement with Mughal emperor Jahangir, as a result of which English ships often plied the eastern coast of Africa and frequently used St Augustine Bay, in the southwest of the island, as a stopping-off point to replenish their water and trade with the locals for livestock.

Rather than an initiative from the Courteen's Association, the first tangible scheme to settle Madagascar involved King Charles's nephew, Prince Rupert of the Rhine. A series of reports from those who had visited Madagascar (or in some cases merely pretended to have done) surfaced in England, praising the island for its fertility and abundance of resources, which included spices, cotton, indigo, silver, pearls, ambergris and slaves; the climate was pleasant, while the locals were presumed to be pliable, and thus easy to exploit. Prince Rupert's scheme, like that two years later of Thomas Howard, Earl of Arundel, a noted diplomat, traveller and art collector in the court of King Charles, received royal support on the one hand, but intense obstruction from the East India Company's lobbyists on the other. Neither venture got off the ground, due to a combination of lack of funding and the company's threats to abandon the Indies trade altogether. Charles was forced to withdraw his support for both schemes and

167

for a similar scheme on Mauritius proposed by Lord Southampton.

Political machinations in the lead-up to civil war absorbed the attentions of the King and his courtiers thereafter. And the climate of domestic upheaval likewise put paid to the hopes of Captain John Bond, the man Prince Rupert and Arundel had intended would found their colonies. At the end of 1642, with the Civil War having broken out the previous January, Bond signalled his intent to take 300 settlers and start a plantation colony in Madagascar. This time, the East India Company took its appeal to the Parliament, where it fell on deaf ears. Bond was permitted to sail, but the scheme failed to find enough people who were interested in becoming settlers there.

Enthusiasm for colonising the island was rekindled in 1643, however, with the publication of two books declaring the amenity of Madagascar. Both were written by former East India Company employees. One was penned by surgeon Walter Hammond, who had spent three months there, and was grandiosely titled *Madagascar, the Richest and most Fruitfull Island in the World*. If Hammond was alive today, he might easily have found work writing brochures for unscrupulous property developers. The publication was synchronous with another plan to post a colony there, this time by the Courteen's Association, which now had access to ships, as well as the requisite political clout to get the job done. And this time, something actually happened.

Not a smart choice

In August 1644, three Courteen's Association ships—*Sun, Hester* and *James*—departed on the annual trading voyage to India and the Orient. On board were 140 men, women and children under the command of Captain John Smart, bound for a colony to be situated on either Madagascar or a small island off its northwest coast, Assada. They arrived at St Augustine Bay in March the following year, after an easy trip. The only person who died en route, in fact, was the colony's doctor, while the population was bolstered by the birth at sea of four baby boys.

Liking what they saw at St Augustine Bay, it seems, the decision was made to locate the settlement there. Having unloaded their cargo, the three ships reconnoitred other areas of Madagascar, only to find that the most attractive alternative destinations had already been commandeered by the French and the Dutch. They then sailed off to fulfil their trading commitments for William Courteen junior, leaving the colonists to fend for themselves.

Meanwhile, the new arrivals set about establishing themselves. They sowed corn and constructed the buildings necessary for the colony. When trying to establish trade with the locals, however, the settlers soon discovered that there was much to be desired in the expedition's planning. For some time, visiting European ships had only been able to conduct trade with the Madagascan tribes at St Augustine's Bay by using *vacca* (red

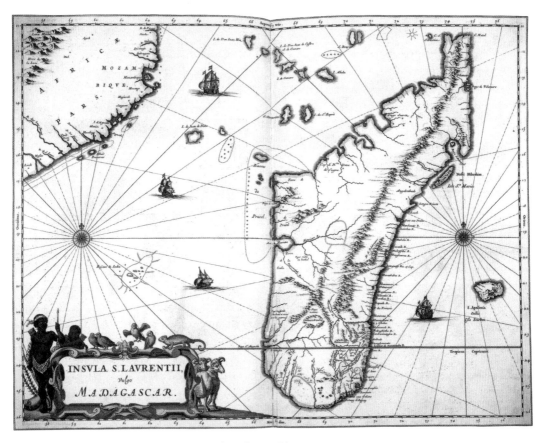

A mid-seventeenth century map of Madagascar by Johannes Blaeu

beads made of carnelian stone) and brass wire as currency. According to a sailor who had visited the bay in 1638, a cow could be bought for seven or eight beads, while brass wire was exchanged for smaller animals such as sheep and chickens. Smart's colonists, however, had arrived without stocks of either item and found that the local people, in addition to resenting a long-term foreign presence on their territory, were reluctant to trade.

As winter in the southern hemisphere passed, it became apparent that the glowing literature about Madagascar had been deceptive. Far from being fertile, the land around the settlement was barren. All the crops the colonists planted had failed, while the pasture was so poor that native farmers of that region would later import the prickly pear to use as feed-stuff for their cattle. Nor was the climate as healthy as the surgeon-authored book had supposed. Malaria was endemic to the region. Many of the colonists were weakened by fever, while a number of others were laid low by dysentery.

The situation wasn't helped by the arrival of two ships, the *Rebecca* and the *Friendship*, which had left England in February 1645 bearing more colonists. They too had banked on the fertility of the land and arrived almost entirely without their own provisions for food.

Instead, they brought with them a gardener with a supply of vines and English roses, most of which had perished on the way over. He was most probably shocked to discover that surgeon Hammond's 'most fruitfull island in the world' had more in common with a desert than the lush English landscape they'd left behind. These ships had also omitted to bring any of the brass wire or beads that would have enabled them to trade for food with the locals. The bare subsistence that the original colonists were surviving on now became even less.

No doubt the local tribes were confused by these English settlers, who had arrived in their midst with neither anything worthwhile to trade nor the wherewithal to feed themselves. Passing traders knew what goods the native people valued, and they were also useful as a slave market for enemies captured in the region's frequent inter-tribal wars. Yet the value of these English colonists with their intentions to make a permanent settlement was far more uncertain. The only thing the locals really wanted from the English at St Augustine were their guns and capacity to use them.

Seeing that the colonists were in desperate need of food, Dian Brindah, the local chief, came up with the idea of employing them as mercenaries against another chief who was threatening to invade his patch. The few Englishmen who were fit for conflict agreed to help and soon had the battle won in Brindah's favour. But seeing the vulnerability of the English, the victorious chief decided that he could get away with reneging on the cattle he had promised as a fee for the fight. Although he was right, it was a decision that showed a lack of foresight. Before too long, Dian Brindah and his tribe had become involved in another war, and so he sent a messenger to ask whether the English might again join him in his campaign.

Captain Smart must have been puzzled by the request. Having just deceived the colonists, why would Brindah so shamelessly repeat his request for mercenary assistance? Would he try the same tactic twice? It was something of a dilemma. If Smart refused, he would be denying his charges the chance of a decent meal, and enmity between the English and the locals would be aggravated. But if he allowed himself to be tricked again, Brindah and his warriors would gain the psychological advantage and might become dangerous. They had already been guilty of rustling the scant herd of cattle the colonists had brought with them, and if the chief failed to cough up the promised cattle a second time, it could well result in open season against the colonists, whose enigmatic presence was one of their main sources of defence.

The decision that Smart made was probably the best one, even though it would adversely affect relations between the colonists and the neighbouring tribe. The Englishman agreed to help and sent forty armed men in boats some 100 kilometres (60 miles) north to Dian Brindah's town. When they arrived, they were greeted with great joy, as an auspicious sign of impending victory. Smart had other ideas, however. When Brindah and three of his sons came to visit the Englishmen's camp at the beach, they were plied with grog until they were legless, then carried onto the boats. Eventually a ransom of 200 head of cattle was agreed on for their safe return. The tribesmen diverted from their battle preparations to deliver the cattle to the English, and Brindah and his sons were returned, unharmed.

Smart was understandably cock-a-hoop at his success. He had turned the tables on Brindah at the same time as putting much-needed food on his own. There was enough meat to feed the colony and to provision one of the ships for a voyage to the Courteen's Association factory in Achin (now Aceh), in northern Sumatra. But while Brindah had pretended good humour on his release, a pattern of treachery between the two parties had been consolidated. More than a few of the cattle paid as the ransom were soon rustled back.

The boon of the cattle gambit was short-lived for the English anyway. As the end of the year and the summer approached, the colonists had no bread, no corn and no food, except for a few skinny cows. The summer rains arrived and the ensuing emergence of mosquitoes led to an outbreak of malaria. There was no medicine to treat the sick (not that the medicines of the time were particularly effective), while the only doctor remaining after the first one had died en route was described by one settler as 'the most unworthy that ever came amongst men'.

On the move

Before long, the situation was desperate. Many of the colonists were dying, and if they remained there, they would all be dead. Smart resolved to take the *Friendship* north to Assada, in the hope of finding a superior site to which the settlement could be transferred. He also hoped to buy slaves to send to Achin and trade for provisions. Things didn't go according to plan.

Not knowing the Madagascan coast, the ship's master refused to risk the boat and insisted on putting well out to sea, where slaves were unlikely to be found. Instead of heading to Assada, they found themselves in the Comoros Islands; after stopping at Mayotte, an island they found lush in comparison to St Augustine Bay, they were at least able to purchase provisions. From there, Smart ordered the master to sail for Assada. However, soon after setting off, the *Friendship* hit a reef. It didn't sink the ship but the master refused to take any further risks, and with most of the crew in agreement, Smart had no choice but to return to St Augustine Bay.

When he arrived there on 12 March, the colony was in even worse shape than before. Because of the barrenness of the land around the settlement, the settlers had been forced to agist most of their few remaining cattle in pasture under the control of the locals. Given the prior history between the two peoples, it was unsurprising that the situation reverted to one resembling the old adage where possession is nine-tenths of the law.

Worse still, the native people had taken to killing off any colonist who happened to stray too far from the settlement. Two colonists sent to trade cattle with them were ambushed and killed; the settlers killed two Madagascans as a reprisal. In return, another two Englishmen were murdered. With a clear numerical superiority, the tribespeople began to attack more frequently. A vital

An idyllic illustration of the inhabitants of Madagascar

boat was cut from its mooring. Another one on the beach was burnt, as was the blacksmith's forge. A colonist who wandered into nearby forest in search of watermelons was found the following day with his throat cut. When Smart had left on the *Friendship*, the population of the colony was 100. By the time he returned, only sixty-three remained, and of those, only twenty were able-bodied men. In all, they now had just four days of salt-beef provisions left.

The obvious decision was to abandon the colony. With a few vital *vacca* beads that had been brought by a visiting ship, the colonists were able to procure supplies from the locals, enough to salt some meat to take with them. Letters were buried, explaining the reasons for the desertion of the colony, and the huts were all burnt to prevent the locals from enjoying them. On 19 May 1646, the sixty remaining colonists left St Augustine Bay. Their intention was to sail north for the Comoros and possibly re-establish the settlement on Mayotte.

When they arrived, a landing party was greeted by the island's king, who gifted them provisions and stated his willingness to become a subject of Charles I. The landing party returned to the ship, but the *Friendship* was then blown out to sea by a storm and subsequently docked at Johanna, an island frequented by English ships plying the Indies trade. Faced with the chance of re-establishing the colony in a new location or being repatriated, Captain Smart's settlers voted overwhelmingly for the latter.

Setting the story straight

It is estimated that of the sixty colonists who left St Augustine Bay, only about a dozen ever saw England again. Rather than a ride heading west towards home, it was an outbound ship that picked up the bedraggled colonists. After some weeks, they were deposited at Rajapur, in India.

One of men who did return home was John Smart, who soon set about defending his damaged reputation. He published a corrective to the glowing accounts of Madagascar that had led to him becoming engaged in such a tragic folly in the first place.

CHAPTER 16

De la Salle and the misplaced colony of Fort St Louis, Texas (1685–88)

When French explorer René-Robert Cavelier, Sieur de La Salle, successfully canoed down from Montreal and followed the Mississippi to the Gulf of Mexico, the immensity of his achievement, and of the river and the land that unfolded before him, filled an already vainglorious man with even more grandiose ideas—dreams of establishing a colony at the mouth of the Mississippi filled his head. Later, in the outrageous opulence of Versailles, the Sun King, Louis XIV, despite his initial scepticism, was persuaded to see sense in La Salle's plan to establish a settlement as a beachhead for the eventual conquest of Spanish mines in Mexico. The dream and the reality couldn't have been more different. The expedition missed the Mississippi, ended up in Texas and was set upon by Indians. When La Salle headed north to Illinois in search of help, he was murdered by one of his own men. Of the 320 colonists who sailed, 180 landed. Only fourteen survived.

In the last few years of the 1660s, rumours were doing the rounds in Montreal of a great river that flowed all the way to the Gulf of California, the wide, finger-like body of water sitting between the Baja California Peninsula and the Mexican mainland. If it could be found and navigated, then the French would have solved the problem of the passage to Cathay (China), which remained one of the imperatives of European exploration in the American continent. Furthermore, if a navigable path to the ocean could be found downriver from the interior of New France (around today's Québec and Ontario), it would make the fur trade more lucrative, since the furs would not have to be hauled overland or paddled upstream in canoes to Montreal.

Such a challenge, and the associated prestige that would surely be afforded the person who succeeded, very much caught the imagination of a young man named René-Robert Cavelier—or La Salle, as history remembers him. As a youth La Salle had endured the bad luck of having his inheritance voided because his wealthy haberdasher father died while La Salle was in training to become a Jesuit, which demanded the forfeiture of one's worldly assets. When he later left the order because of moral weaknesses (what exactly remained undisclosed), he was penniless. In 1666 he followed his Jesuit brother to Canada, where strings were pulled and he was granted an estate on Montreal Island. It was perhaps hoped that he would stay put. However, watching the grass grow and the sheep and cows bending their heads to eat it while gathering hay for the long winter ahead was not the kind of life for someone afflicted with the ambition and restlessness of La Salle. Sometime during 1667, La Salle was soon petitioning the Governor of New France for permission to explore the region and discover the mystery river. His commitment couldn't be doubted, surely; he even sold his farm in order to fund the sortie.

In July 1669, he set off up the St Lawrence River, heading southwest towards the Great Lakes, with a flotilla of nine canoes. On board, the personnel included missionaries eager to convert the natives. The exploration proved to be hard going, not least because La Salle's claims to aptitude were vastly inflated. His co-expedition leader, Bréhant de Galinée, commented that:

> M. de La Salle, who said that he understood the Iroquois perfectly, and had learned all these things from them as a result of the perfect knowledge that he had of their language, did not know it at all, and was undertaking this voyage almost blindly, without knowing where he was going.

After a month of travelling, the party reached Lake Ontario, where the priests heard of a tribe whose language one of them understood—a useful thing when having to explain such abstract concepts as the Holy Trinity and the Resurrection. La Salle was not at all interested in having his authority diminished, nor was he particularly interested in saving souls. His idea of glory had a more materialistic base. When the priests asked him to go with them to find the tribe, he feigned illness, telling them he would spend the winter recuperating before returning to Montreal in the spring. Once the priests had departed, La Salle's party continued their explorations down the Ohio River, possibly as far as Louisville, Kentucky. Most of his men deserted him, and in late 1670 he returned to Montreal flat broke and full of stories that few were prepared to believe.

Fortunately for La Salle, one person who did listen was the new Governor-General of New France, Count Louis de Buade de Frontenac. He wrote to Louis XIV, saying that La Salle was 'a man of intelligence and ability, more capable than anybody else I know here to accomplish every kind of enterprise and discovery'. Armed with this glowing reference, La Salle sailed off to Paris in 1674, where he impressed the Sun King with his talk of a French empire stretching all the way from Canada down to Mexico, with the Mississippi River as its spine. In return for all the fancy talk, Louis ennobled La Salle, granted him Fort Cataracoui (on the site of Kingston, Ontario), which he renamed Fort Frontenac, and a monopoly on buffalo hides (but not the more lucrative beaver furs) to cover his expenses.

Attempts at empire building

On a further trip to France in 1677, Louis rewarded him with a royal licence to build two more trading forts, which were effectively small colonies: one at the entrance to Lake Erie, the other at the southern end of Lake Michigan (near contemporary Chicago). He also licensed him to become seigneur of any lands he might discover and populate in exploring the region between New France and Florida and Mexico.

La Salle set out for the wilderness again in 1679. On this trip his party of thirty men discovered Niagara Falls, and built a 45-tonne boat, the *Griffon*, which they sailed south to Lake Michigan and filled with a cargo of beaver furs. La Salle sent the *Griffon* back to Niagara, then continued with fourteen men in four canoes to what is now the St Joseph River, where another fort was built in January 1680.

From that point on, things started to go pear-shaped. When the *Griffon* failed to return with provisions, the party had to carry all their equipment to the Illinois River. One member of the expedition, a priest by the name of Hennepin, discovered the confluence of the Illinois and Mississippi rivers, but was captured by a native tribe in the process.

La Salle's character proved to be excessive, obsessive, ruthless and autocratic. Stuck in the wilderness together, without necessarily knowing where they were going, tempers began to fray, and his men began to desert him, so much so that La Salle was forced to backtrack to Fort Frontenac. On the way, he discovered that the *Griffon* had sunk with its valuable cargo of furs and that the fort at Niagara Falls had been sacked and burnt by native warriors.

It was now early 1681 and the empire he had promised the Sun King was looking particularly flimsy. And even more so once he eventually returned to Montreal—where there were people who wanted to destroy him, either because he owed them money or because they were incensed at his interference in the lucrative beaver trade.

However, rather than capitulate to social opprobrium, La Salle put together a new team of twenty-three Frenchmen and eighteen Indians. He travelled back the way he had come, en route encountering deserters from his previous mission who wanted to kill him. It was hard work. With most of the lakes and rivers frozen, they were forced to haul their canoes and food across the snow until they came to the banks of the Mississippi, which they reached in February 1682. They waited there for the ice to thaw so they could begin

Construction of the Griffon *on the shore of Lake Erie*

paddling in the spring. This expedition was more successful. They passed the mouths of the Missouri and Ohio rivers, erected a fort at Memphis, then passed the mouth of the Arkansas River, the limit of Marquette and Joliet's famous expedition down the Mississippi in 1673. On 9 April, they reached the Gulf of Mexico.

Dressed in a scarlet outfit with gold trimmings, a jacket he'd squeezed into his canoe since leaving Montreal, La Salle proclaimed the territory they had traversed for France, and named it Louisiana. It was the first non-Spanish claim to territory bordering the Gulf of Mexico. Included in this possession were all the 'seas, harbours, ports, bays, adjacent straits, and all the nations, peoples, provinces, cities, towns, villages, mines, minerals, fisheries, streams and rivers' contained within a territory that spanned the Mississippi and its tributaries, from its source to the Gulf, and the gulf coast as far as the River of Palms (discovered by Cabeza de Vaca, and most likely the Rio Grande). La Salle then buried a cross in the ground, with a lead plate bearing the king's coat of arms at its foot, and embarked on a celebration that fittingly blended the music of hymns with musket fire.

On the way back, La Salle built a fort at Starved Rock, 120 kilometres (75 miles) west of present-day Chicago. After christening the new construction Fort St-Louis-des-Illinois, he granted land to his men and exacted tribute in the form of buffalo skins from the locals. Yet when he returned to Montreal,

instead of a hero's welcome, he was greeted with contempt by La Fèvre de la Barre, Frontenac's replacement as governor-general, who saw La Salle as a rival and was eager for his schemes to fail.

Given the enmity La Salle had already generated in the colony, there were plenty of people prepared to help La Barre bring the explorer down. Rather than deal with the antagonistic governor, who had already dispossessed him of Fort Frontenac, La Salle returned to France at the end of 1683 to try his luck directly with the king. By this time, however, Louis was somewhat sceptical of his subject's grand ambition. In 1682 he had written to La Barre: 'I am convinced that the discovery of the Sieur de la Salle is very useless and that such discoveries ought to be prevented in the future'.

Moving the Mississippi

The king's dismissal of the enterprise may well have brought an end to La Salle's adventures if not for the scheming, Spain-hating priest Abbé Claude Bernou and the fortunate outbreak of war with Spain. In January 1682, Bernou had proposed establishing a colony at the mouth of the Rio Bravo (Rio Grande), with the express goal of conquering the mines of New Biscay in northern New Spain (what is now the Mexican states of Chihuahua and Durango). The linchpin for Bernou's scheme was the former governor of New Mexico, Comte Diego de Peñalossa. He had fled his post out of fear of being persecuted by the

Spanish Inquisition on trumped-up charges and, in revenge, had placed his knowledge and sword at the disposal of Louis XIV. Plans to attack Spain's assets in the New World received a fillip when the short-lived War of the Reunions broke out in the Netherlands between France and Spain on 26 October 1683. Suddenly Louis XIV had a use for the discovery of Sieur de la Salle.

Bernou was attracted to La Salle's claim that he would be able to mobilise up to 15,000 Indians as an army to travel down the Mississippi and fight the Spanish. The Indians bore considerable antipathy towards the Spanish mainly because of their penchant for slave raiding, but it was extravagant on the part of La Salle to think they might be interested in marching thousands of miles to help the French eradicate Spanish holdings in Mexico. If some historians are to be believed, Bernou and La Salle were so keen to get their respective projects up and running that they decided to join forces and hoodwink the Sun King—by moving La Salle's estimated location of the Mississippi more than 645 kilometres (400 miles) to the west, thus creating the impression that the Rio Bravo and the river that La Salle had reached were one and the same.

However, it is more likely that the delusion of the two rivers being one was unwitting due to the lack of a reliable method for fixing longitude at the time, and at worst the product of erroneous wishful thinking. Nonetheless, La Salle's penchant for gilding the lily was at work in his estimate

of the navigability of the Mississippi and the suitability of its mouth as a harbour, given he had elsewhere argued that settlement should be at least 60 leagues (290 kilometres/ 180 miles) inland, given the propensity of the delta to flood.

Such misapprehensions, however they arose, were central to Louis XIV changing his mind about La Salle and his discovery. Instead of dismissing him as a madman, Louis had all the explorer's debts forgiven. He also ordered Governor La Barre to restore Fort Frontenac to La Salle, much to La Barre's chagrin. Louis then gave La Salle command of all the territory between Fort St-Louis-des-Illinois at Starved Rock and the Spanish mines in New Biscay. Finally, the Sun King was generous enough to supply the mission with 100 soldiers maintained at royal expense, commanded by eight officers. He also provided two ships: the *Joly*, a warship carrying thirty-six cannons and a crew of approximately seventy; and the *Belle*, a barque of 60 tonnes armed with four small cannons. These were supplemented with the *Aimable*, a 180-tonne flute provided by a wealthy merchant, and a ketch called the *Saint-François*. With this complement La Salle planned to sail directly to the mouth of the Mississippi and start a colony that could be used to further his king's ambitions against the Spanish.

The mission was to be top secret. La Salle was only permitted to tell his mother where he was going on the eve of his departure. At the end of July 1684, La Salle and his four ships set off from France under the cover of a larger convoy bound for Canada. On board were 320 people, among whom, besides the military contingent, and the forty or so indentured workers and servants, were six missionaries, including Abbé Jean Cavalier (La Salle's brother), and nine volunteers, two of whom were La Salle's nephews. About eight merchants joined the expedition in the hope of making a profit, while those who hoped to settle and make a living in the new territory included more than a dozen women and children, one of them the pregnant wife of a carpenter.

By that time, there was already dissension in the ranks, namely between La Salle and Taneguy Le Gallois de Beaujeu, the naval officer the King had provided to command the sea-going part of the expedition. Given their characters, it was almost inevitable that the two would clash. Captain Beaujeu was old gentry, a military man hardened by war with the experience of commanding men on the high seas. La Salle, on the other hand, was a parvenu, only recently elevated to the nobility and lacking all the decorum and sense of honour that emanated from Beaujeu. The explorer was domineering, yet unschooled in the arts of leadership and dogmatically inconsistent in his decisions.

He first offended the captain by refusing to tell him where they were going and by assuming command of the ship without actually knowing how to sail it. At one point, Beaujeu drily observed, 'There are very few who do not believe he is crazy. I have spoken

of it to people who have known him for twenty years. Everyone says that he has always been something of a visionary'. Yet as a soldier, Beaujeu had his orders to obey, even if he questioned the predicament into which his king had put him: 'I am going into an unknown country to seek something almost as difficult to find as the philosopher's stone, late in the season, laden above the water-line, and with an irritable man', he wrote nine days after the expedition had put to sea.

The situation worsened when La Salle, perhaps paranoid that details of his secret mission would somehow be leaked, refused to stop to take on fresh water at Madeira. When they arrived at the Caribbean territory of Haiti, more than five weeks later, bad water, a slow crossing in tropical heat and overcrowding on the ships (to the extent that the soldiers were forced to sleep on deck, rain, hail or shine) meant that more than a fifth of the complement had fallen ill. La Salle was one of them, and he spent his first week on dry land in a state of utter delirium. It soon became apparent that the mission had suffered a further blow when the fourth ship, *Saint-François*, which had been carrying much of their supplies, was captured by pirates. Having usurped his authority in the crossing, La Salle now turned to blaming Beaujeu.

Missing the Mississippi

Help in reprovisioning came from the Governor of Tortuga, the French-held island off the north coast of Haiti that had long been a nest for pirates. La Salle was also forced to borrow from two of the merchants who had accompanied him on the mission, the brothers Pierre and Dominique Duhaut. The pirates in port warned many of the prospective colonists of the difficulties they faced: Spanish pirates, dangerous shoals, difficult winds and ferocious natives combined to paint a risky picture, especially given the rifts already developing in the fleet. Many of the original party decided to leave the expedition and La Salle was forced to seek replacements from among the ranks of failed pirates and desperados, lowering the tone of the colony's personnel considerably.

On 25 November, they set sail with their remaining three boats in the direction of the North American mainland. With the help of a navigator whose sailing in the region was as a pirate, they charted a course to the Baye du Saint-Esprit, where La Salle believed the mouth of the Mississippi was to be found. For this part of the voyage, La Salle had his possessions transferred from the *Joly* to the *Aimable* (the merchant-donated flute), a sign of the continuing deterioration in relations between Beaujeu and the explorer. The convoy hugged the coast of Cuba until they entered the Gulf of Mexico towards the middle of December.

By this time, the war between France and Spain had ended. La Salle and his fleet had thus unwittingly become invaders of a territory under the authority of a country with which France was now at peace. Of course, given the Spanish and French rivalry in the region, dating as far back as Fort Caroline the century before (see page 60), they were far from the first to make this error. Besides, with the excuse of ignorance to back them up, the mission was unlikely to have caused anyone in France too great an alarm—if the French were found out, their presence could plausibly be passed off as an unfortunate mistake.

Ten days after entering the Gulf of Mexico, they noticed the white colour of the sea. Depth soundings brought up a 'fine, grayish, muddy sand'. La Salle had brought his ships to the point where the Mississippi enters into the Gulf. Unfortunately he didn't realise this, mainly because his latitudinal calculations from his previous expedition had been out by 2 degrees. Given that he hoped for his river to be as far west as possible, La Salle erroneously assumed that the Gulf Stream had taken him east, and that he was in the vicinity of Apalachee Bay, near where the Florida peninsula connects with the North American mainland, and where in 1528 the Spanish explorer Panfilo de Narváez met his fate.

Having sailed to the mouth of the Mississippi, La Salle then proceeded to sail away from it. On the evening of 3 January 1685, despite the ships being isolated from each other by thick fog, he gave the signal for departure. The *Joly* was further out to sea and didn't get the message. It is tempting to think that La Salle preferred to lose Beaujeu rather than have to admit to not really

knowing where he was. Despite realising that Beaujeu wasn't with him, he sailed west until he reached a sort of bay, which was probably Atchafalaya Bay, 240 kilometres (150 miles) west of the mouth of the Mississippi. If the *Aimable* and the *Belle* had turned in here and travelled up what is now the Atchafalaya River, they eventually would have rejoined the Mississippi near its confluence with the Red River. La Salle's ships, however, continued to sail west, passing from Louisiana into Texas.

It was more than a fortnight before the *Joly* caught up with them near Matagorda Bay, which La Salle named Espiritu Santo Bay. Relations between the two French leaders now reached their lowest ebb. La Salle, growing more and more paranoid as his own incompetence in matters navigational became increasingly apparent, decided the best course of action was to unload the colonists and provisions, send Beaufeu packing to France, and then work out the problem of where he was later. To this end, he asserted that Matagorda Bay was one of the lesser mouths of the Mississippi and made plans to bring the supplies ashore. In fact, the only major river emptying into the Gulf at this point is the Texan Colorado River.

The channel that La Salle chose to bring the ships through at Matagorda Bay was narrow and shallow. While the smaller *Belle* would not be a problem, Beaujeu advised

La Salle disembarks his colonists in modern-day Texas, believing he has arrived at the Mississippi

La Salle not to try it with the *Aimable*. La Salle, of course, insisted. The ship was caught on the bar, and despite days spent trying to salvage it, storms and winds meant that most of its cargo was lost. The grave situation was compounded when La Salle's arrogant nephew, Lieutenant Moranget, took an aggressive approach to retrieving the goods that the local Karankawa Indians had taken when they were washed ashore. He and ten soldiers cleared their village with gunfire and gathered their possessions, before stealing the tribespeoples' animal skins and some canoes. In the evening, the Indians counter-attacked and two of the Frenchmen were killed.

For all his disapproval of the expedition, Beaujeu was a man of some honour. Although his orders permitted him to leave once La Salle and his colonists had disembarked, he nonetheless volunteered to reconnoitre Matagorda Bay for a better site to settle. He also offered to sail to Martinique and get provisions for the colony. La Salle was too proud to accept, and in refusing this help he effectively signed the death warrant of most of those who stayed.

Texan misery

When the *Joly* sailed for France in March 1685, many of the intended colonists sailed with it. About 180 people remained, and they could hardly have been sanguine about their predicament. They were lost in the wilderness with a man who was becoming more and more mentally unstable. Their number diminished by the day as a consequence of malnutrition and disease, especially dysentery. One man died from a rattlesnake bite, while native warriors often surrounded the camp at night, howling. Several men tried to desert, but there was nowhere to go. When one party did escape for a time before returning, La Salle had the ringleader executed.

Although they didn't know where they were, the colonists set about building a fort on Matagorda Island. Taking over fifty men in five large canoes, La Salle embarked on his first major reconnaissance. He travelled up Lavaca Bay, a westward extension of the bay, and discovered Garcitas Creek, which had abundant fresh water and fish, while herds of deer and buffalo were seen nearby. This then would be the site for the French colony of Fort St Louis (located near current-day Victoria in east Texas).

He sent for the one remaining ship, the *Belle*, which sailed to within 30 kilometres (18 miles) of the proposed settlement before the water became too shallow and the ship had to be unloaded. The supplies were taken upriver in canoes, but the colonists who had been toiling away on Matagorda Island were not so lucky. Despite their weakness, La Salle ordered them to march the 80 kilometres (50 miles) overland between the island fort and the new site through deep sands and marshland.

When they arrived at Fort St Louis in June, La Salle worked his colonists so hard on the construction of the place that by the time they had been there a month, half of them had died. He kept tight control over the supplies while never letting up on the exertions he demanded from his charges. The result was that more than a few starving men died after trying their luck with the native berries that grew in abundance around the settlement and turned out to be poisonous. Others simply fell down from sheer exhaustion and never got up again. La Salle's capacity for excessive exertion may well have been the result of bipolar disorder. There was little to show for the effort. One two-storey building was constructed from the timbers of the wrecked *Aimable*, but no palisades were built to defend the colonists and most of them were doomed to subsist in roughly constructed huts, whose thatched roofs offered little respite against the elements.

During the autumn, La Salle continued to look for his river in the vicinity of where they had landed. Unsurprisingly, it wasn't to be found. In October, he took the *Belle* and fifty men, leaving thirty-seven men, women and children in Fort St Louis. While the *Belle* stood off the coast, La Salle and some of his men explored in canoes. Their expedition eventually reached east to the Rio Grande, which La Salle again confused with the Mississippi. And once again, it proved a disastrous mission in terms of human resources. A number of men died from eating poisonous fruit, while others murdered each other.

Even more disastrously, as La Salle returned from a sortie inland, the *Belle* was no longer to be seen. Whether it had

sunk or the others had simply deserted was unknown, although a paranoid La Salle assumed the latter. It was a massive blow. Without the barque, the option of sailing to the West Indies either for supplies or to abandon the colony was gone. They were suddenly landbound, with the nearest French settlement more than 1600 kilometres (1000 miles) to the north, at Starved Rock, across uncharted territory that was most likely full of hostile natives.

He arrived back at Fort St Louis in March 1686, suddenly aware of the predicament his insanity had placed him and the rump of the colonists in. Most attempts to grow crops had failed and the produce of the seeds that did sprout—chicory, beetroot, celery, asparagus, melons, and pumpkin—was doomed by the absence of fences and the presence of hungry pigs. The hunting was more successful though it was hazardous. Colonists were killed and maimed as a result of being charged by buffalo, and in one case a wild boar, while another man died from gangrene caused by an infected snakebite. Hunters were at constant risk also from attack by the Karankawa.

In April, knowing he no longer had enough men to run a colony, La Salle decided to head north with a party of twenty men in the direction of Fort St-Louis-des-Illinois, at Starved Rock. Not long after he left, six of the people from the *Belle* returned to Fort

FOLLOWING PAGES: La Salle's map, with Fort St Louis located on Matagorda Bay

185

Chomans 1. Village

Nihata 1. Village

Les Hainsjou 4. Villages

Coloa 1. Village

Les Cadodaqis 6. Villages

Les Tonica 3. Villages

Laensa 1. Village

Seroco Goula R.

Chelod 1. Village

Les Lomia 1. Village

Vispe 1. Vill. 1. Vill.

Ires Auma 1. Village

Opocoula 1. Vill.

Chaque Soma 1. V.

Senis 1. Village

Le Sieur de la Salle est venu de la Baye de St. Loüis jusque a ce Village

Toutes ces Nations ont un langages diferent et ne s'entendent presque point

Bujogoula 1. Vill.

Majoutncha 1. Villa.

Ouacha 1. Village

Missipi R.

Fort

Ria Boho

Laune R.

Masceane R.

Desaguaderos

Lac de l'Ascension

des Fleurs R.

tiennent pour St. Loüis

Caouils 1. Village

Brano ou del nord R.

Chemin que les Epagnol venir a la Baye de

Baye de St. Loüis ou Mr. de la Salle a mis pied a Terre en prenant la Riviere de Laune pour le Misisipi et bati ce Fort 1685.

Embouchures du

Les Gros Bas

Baye de St. Ioseph

Rinconada

Polosy 1. Village

GOLFE DE

Laguna dimas

Ligne du Tropique

Tanipa R.

Echelle

10. 20. 30. 40. 50. 60.

cent dix lieues a 20

Tampique

LES COSTES AUX ENVIRONS
DE LA RIVIERE DE
MISISIPI.
Decouvertes par M.ʳ de la Salle
en 1683.
et reconnues par M.ʳ le Chevallier
d'Iberville en 1698. et 1699.
par N. de Fer, Geographe de
Monseigneur le Dauphin

1701.

COSTE DE LA FLORIDE

Nord

a 1. Village

Chicaca 3. Villages

Quimpis a 6. Villages

Moctoby 1 Village

Biloxi 1. Village

le Fort a eté
bati par M.ʳ le
Chevallier
d'Iberville
en 1699

R. S.ᵗ Roch
Apallachicoly
Bellannes R.
Bacaharde

Pascoboula R.
Village

n'approche pas la coste ny ayant de fond que

Jusque a ces points

Palache R.
de Heahille R.
S.ᵗ Pierre
Diamabula R.
Matanse
Domina de Parabi
Masqui

S.ᵗ Georges
Tour dain R.

Baye de S.ᵗᵉ Caterine

Baye de Bahama

Baye de S.ᵗ Ius

Baye de S.ᵗ Augustin

Cap de Canaveral

S.ᵗ Helene
S.ᵗ André
Cap
S.ᵗ Roman

Baye
du S.ᵗ
Esprit

S.ᵗ Luce

Cap
Misapa
Cap Biscain

Cap de la Floride

Tortuga

Marquet

Caye
Caye large

les Martirs

MEXIQVE

Isles
de
Bahama

Bagama

La Grande
Providence

Caye Nette

I. Sainte

Canal de Bahama

Isles
des
Anguilles

I. Norogne

I. du
S.ᵗ
Esprit

I. Seul

Baye de S.ᵗᵉ Elisabeth

Cap Fromento

Isle
de La Havana

Montavana

S.ᵗ Michel

Caye Romaines

Cuba

90. 100. 110.
Degré

St Louis, with the story that the ship had run aground and that all the other people on it were dead. To compound the situation, rumours had reached the Spanish of the presence of a French colony, which would be confirmed by the sight of the abandoned *Belle* on the coastline.

Oblivious to these developments, La Salle's party continued their march north. The Indians were friendlier than anticipated, and La Salle was impressed by the extent of their civilisation. It was illness that prevented him from travelling any further. With half his men dead and the rest in very poor condition, La Salle was forced to return to Fort St Louis. They reached the colony in August, after more than four months of gruelling travel and without having achieved any real goal. Only eight of the original party of twenty were still with La Salle. Some had died from disease, others had deserted or simply been separated from the main party and got lost. One unfortunate man had been pulled off a raft by an alligator while fording the Brazos River.

One of the men who was lost was Dominique Duhaut, the merchant who, with his brother Pierre, had loaned La Salle the money to reprovision the expedition in Haiti. Pierre now held La Salle responsible for his brother's death and reacted to it by inciting mutiny.

When La Salle returned to Fort St Louis, he found himself in the middle of a soap opera. One of his officers, Barbier, had made a maid pregnant, resulting in a shotgun marriage. A second officer was intending to marry another maid (a union that La Salle would not permit, since she was too far below his social class—many of the young women in the colony had been lifted from the brothels of Paris). In the meantime, La Salle began planning another mission to Starving Rock.

Leaving the women, children, priests and injured, twenty in all, under the command of Barbier, La Salle set out a few months later with seventeen men, in the hope of reaching the Illinois River. The travelling was hard and La Salle, driven by his demons, maintained an exhausting pace. Morale wasn't helped by the fact that La Salle, together with his brother and his nephews, in typical parvenu fashion, monopolised the horses to carry the precious items gifted to them by Louis, while leaving the others to slog their way across swamps, creeks and rivers burdened with the rest of the equipment. This self-importance and exaggerated attention to social status eventually proved fatal.

The embittered Pierre Duhaut was one of a handful of men ordered to stay behind by La Salle for the purpose of shooting bison. Duhaut still harboured a grudge towards La Salle because of his brother's death. When La Salle sent his nephew, Lieutenant Crevel de Moranget, on horseback to collect the meat that Duhaut had hunted, the haughty young officer apparently became angry that the men had reserved the prized marrow from the bones for themselves. The men pretended to accede to his order to hand over the marrow, but murdered Moranget and his two servants with axes that evening while they slept.

When La Salle rode back two days later, on 19 March, to find out what had happened, Pierre Duhaut had little option but to kill him. The former merchant shot him in the head at point-blank range with an arquebus. For the sake of the colony, somebody should have done it much sooner.

The men stripped his body and left it to be devoured by wild animals. They then headed off in the direction of the Mississippi. Having established a precedent by assassinating his leader, some months later Duhaut became a victim of the same tactics, when one of his colleagues was angered by his indecisiveness. Of the seventeen men, only seven made it to the Mississippi, which they followed to salvation at Fort St-Louis-des-Illinois.

The fate of the colonists left behind at Fort St Louis itself was even worse. Disease continued to kill them off and most of the rest were massacred by a Karankawa tribe sometime in 1688. When the fort was later found by a Spanish captain, it had been abandoned. Only a couple of deserters and five children adopted by the Karankawa had survived.

CHAPTER 17

The stymied Scottish colony at Darién, Panama (1698–99 and 1699–1700)

This scheme by Scottish patriot and financial whiz William Paterson was designed to raise Scotland's status in the world and redress the inequity of its relationship with England. In anticipation of the Panama Canal, Paterson proposed to create a colony at Darién, on the narrow isthmus of Central America. He envisaged it would become wealthy through ferrying goods overland between the Pacific and Atlantic oceans, thus eliminating the often precarious voyage around the tip of South America. It was a brilliant idea, but its execution was an utter disaster. Internal politics, poor preparation, the climate, diseases and varying degrees of obstruction from the English and Spanish ensured its failure almost from the outset. And the failure proved catastrophic for Scotland's hopes of independence too. For those colonists who survived, their return home was shrouded in disgrace.

It's hard to imagine a nation renowned for its thriftiness putting so many eggs into the basket of such a dangerous speculation as the Darién Venture. But at the end of the seventeenth century, things in Scotland were looking pretty bleak. Its economy had been ravaged by nearly a century of wars that had badly damaged its traditional trading relations, such as exporting grain to Norway. Adding salt to the wound, England's Navigation Acts of the 1660s prevented Scottish merchants from intermediary trading between England and other nations or territories. Worse still, Scotland's major export earner, cereals, had been severely affected by seven years of famine and drought. Hordes of Scots had abandoned the countryside for the cities, where people were starving to death on the streets. Some pundits believed that the best chance for Scotland, galling as it might have been, was a union with England, on whose larger economy it had become increasingly dependent. But the optimists and dreamers had another idea: to grow the homeland by becoming a colonial power.

Judging by Scotland's previous experiments in colonialism, this optimism was misplaced. Early attempts by Sir William Alexander to establish settlements in Nova Scotia came to an end with the surrender of the claim to France as part of the Treaty of Suza in 1632, leaving the fledgling Scottish colony there in the lurch. A 1684 settlement at Stuarts Town in the Carolinas lasted just two years before it was attacked and destroyed by the Spanish. Only the predominantly Quaker settlement

in East Jersey, established in 1683, survived, although it would merge with West Jersey to become an English-controlled 'royal colony' in 1702.

The Darién Venture in Panama, the Central American territory bordered today by Costa Rica, in the north, and Colombia, was the brainchild of Scottish expat William Paterson, a creative capitalist, most famous for the idea behind the foundation of the Bank of England in 1694. As a young man, Paterson had lived in the Bahamas, where he became acquainted with the surgeon-buccaneer Lionel Wafer, who had spent four years marooned in the jungles of the Darién Peninsula. Wafer was captured by the local Cuna tribespeople, and after narrowly escaping being burnt to death lived among them, acquiring a solid knowledge of their customs and the terrain. As was so often the case, Darién was presented to Paterson as a place where fruit and vegetables just grew in the ground without any help.

In 1510, the Spanish conquistador Vasco Núñez de Balboa had founded Spain's first successful mainland American colony there and crossed the isthmus to the Pacific Ocean (although his father-in-law, Pedrarias Dávila, subsequently moved the colony to the site of Panama City, on the Pacific coast). In 1524, Darién was then razed to the ground by the Cuna. One sixteenth-century explorer described the area as an 'abyss', a 'horror of mountains, rivers, and marshes'. It seems most likely that Paterson never visited Darién before embarking on his venture. However, he was certainly charmed by Wafer's sanguine account, which contained incitements such as the claim, 'I believe we have nothing that grows in Jamaica, but what would thrive here also, and grow very luxuriantly', and talked of stands of precious timber alone capable of paying for the settlement.

Paterson's primary aim, however, was not agricultural. He envisaged the colony providing a direct link between the Atlantic and the Pacific, enabling ships to avoid the precarious voyage around the tip of South America. As the eventual construction of the Panama Canal would show, it was an idea far from absurd. In selling his grand ambition, Paterson claimed the following:

> *The time and expense of navigation to China, Japan and the Spice Islands, and the far greatest part of the East Indies will be lessened by more than half, and the consumption of European commodities and manufactories will soon be more than doubled. Trade will increase trade, and money will beget money, and the trading world shall need no more to want work for their hands, but will rather want hands for their work. Thus this door of the seas, and the key of the universe, with anything of a sort of reasonable management, will of course enable its proprietors to give laws to both oceans, without being liable to the fatigues, expenses and dangers, or contracting the guilt and blood of Alexander and Caesar.*

Rather than doing the trading, Paterson proposed to set up a route between the oceans and profit by charging for the privilege of using it. For the purpose at hand, Panama was the only possible place, and Darién, in the far east of the territory, held several advantages over other sites. To begin with, there were only 80 kilometres (50 miles) between the two coasts; moreover, much of this territory could be traversed along two rivers: the Atrato, which empties into the Caribbean, and the San Juan, which flows into the Pacific. These rivers were not only mostly navigable, but they came within 8 kilometres (5 miles) of each other. It has even been suggested that there was a canal known as the Raspadura Canal between them prior to the arrival of the Spanish. Part of Paterson's enthusiasm for the scheme, therefore, may have rested on his belief that the Atrato and the San Juan could be linked to eliminate the need for portaging commodities altogether.

Keen Scots

William Paterson was an internationalist rather than a patriot, and hadn't lived in Scotland for years. When it was first suggested to him that Scotland might fund his project, he didn't believe it possible. At first, he tried to garner enthusiasm for the idea in a number of port cities in the Netherlands and northern Germany, but to no avail. It was when he moved to London that the idea began to attract backers. In June 1695, the Company of Scotland Trading to Africa and the Indies was founded, with Paterson among its board of directors, and soon proved extremely popular with English investors. Once it attracted English investment, it also brought in money from the Netherlands, since William of Orange, who had become William III of England, was a Dutchman.

However, the English East India Company was most protective of its monopoly over English trade with the East Indies. It petitioned Parliament, who then threatened the new company with impeachment. In addition to this pressure, King William didn't want to risk ruining the peace he had recently signed with Spain, to whom Panama technically belonged. The Dutch and English investors were forced to withdraw, as was the English proportion (about half) of the first fleet of colonists.

Left to re-finance the whole expedition, Paterson remained deeply sceptical that Scotland could adequately fund the Darién Venture. But then he hadn't expected it to become a last-gasp emblem of Scottish nationalism. The scheme drew investment, not just from the purses of Scotland's commercial elite, but also from the squirrelled-away savings of many struggling Scottish families. Given the high-risk nature of establishing colonies and the fact that few actually ever made a profit for their investors, the exposure throughout Scotland was immense.

Thousands of Scots rushed to invest in the Darién Venture in February 1696, and within six months a colossal £400,000 had been raised. Paterson and several members of the company then returned to the Netherlands and Germany to raise more

money and find ships. But, as before, they were sabotaged in their efforts by the East India Company. The English ambassador to Holland even threatened an embargo on any merchants who conducted business with the Company of Scotland—a kind of secondary boycott, similar to that long used by the United States in recent times against those who trade with Cuba.

The most damaging sabotage was internal, however. While the directors were in northern Europe, it was discovered that one of the company's employees, James Smith, had embezzled thousands of pounds from the funds already released for the procurement and fitting out of ships. Some of the stain of this crime attached itself to Paterson. When he returned to Scotland in September 1697, the company held an inquiry, in which Paterson was soon exonerated of everything other than stupidity. But although the report recommended that no action be taken against him, the Council General of Scotland chose to expel Paterson from the Court of Directors, withdrew his share, and initially banned him from sailing on the venture's first fleet. When he travelled to Central America in the summer of the following year, it would be as a private citizen.

New Edinburgh

Five ships had been procured in all for Scotland's brave gamble into the unknown: *Unicorn, St Andrew, Caledonia, Endeavour* and *Dolphin*. Some 1200 people were chosen as colonists, and given the conditions in Scotland at the time, it was no surprise that the number of applications was such that the company could have filled this first contingent several times over. Before the ships left Leith, the main port access to Edinburgh, their crews had to extricate many stowaways, as well as surplus sailors who were offering to work for free in exchange for the chance to be a part of this great Scottish moment.

To prevent interference from the English and the Spanish, only Captain Robert Pennecuik and Paterson were aware of the fleet's precise destination before its departure, on 4 July 1698. As was common at the time, the captains of the other boats carried their instructions in sealed envelopes, which would remain closed until after they had put to sea.

Despite the festive send-off at Leith, problems emerged shortly after the voyage got under way. Forced to travel around the north of Scotland, the fleet encountered fog and the Orkney gales. The sailing was so rough that the colonists were kept below decks. Above them, rifts and mutual suspicion were developing among their leaders. Pennecuik was of a mind to court-martial two of his captains, brothers by the name of Drummond, for rumoured sleights and transgressions.

At the same time, the non-nautical members of the venture's council were hampered by the absurd situation of the presidency rotating on a weekly basis. Despite his fall from grace, Paterson was re-elected to the council at Madeira and was troubled 'exceedingly' to witness important matters regarding the expedition 'thus turmoiled and disordered by tempers and dispositions as boisterous and turbulent as the elements they are used to struggle with'.

Conditions improved with favourable winds across the Atlantic, and the islands of the Caribbean were sighted on 28 September. The fleet stopped at the Danish colony of St Thomas, then at Crab Island, before arriving at Darién on 2 November. Only seventy people had died on the voyage across, which in those days made it a success. The colonists were immediately greeted by the Cuna tribespeople, whose overtures of friendship were reciprocated, and who had no exception to the Scots establishing their settlement.

The harbour that the colonists had arrived at appeared to be a good one, and with Scottish pride they named it the Bay of Caledonia. An escarpment offered excellent positions for the building of defensive batteries, while a number of streams coming down from the escarpment provided fresh water. Pennecuik was moved to grandiosely claim that the harbour was 'capable of containing a thousand sail of the best ships in the world'; and not just that, but 'without great trouble wharves may be run out, to which ships of the greatest burthen may lay their sides and unload'. In other words, it seemed like an ideal place to establish a port to facilitate the transfer of goods from the Pacific Ocean to the Atlantic via the Caribbean Sea.

Darién Indians negotiating with the settlers

The Scots went about building a fortified village. Paterson's optimism was dimmed by his wife's death from dysentery soon after arriving, then dimmed again by the realisation that the colonists had been building their fort in the wrong place. The original site, he wrote, was:

> A mere morass, neither fit to be fortified nor planted, nor indeed for men to lie upon …
> We were clearing and making huts upon this improper place near two months, in which time experience, the schoolmaster of fools, convinced our masters that the place now called Fort St Andrew was a more proper place for us.

A superior site was chosen, on a bluff jutting out into the east of the bay, and south of which the settlement of New Edinburgh was established. But it wasn't long before Darién began to lose its Edenic tinge in the colonists' eyes. An immediate problem was the conflict between the sea-based authority of Captain Pennecuik and that of the land-based settlers. Few men are able to let go of power easily and Pennecuik attempted to maintain his by hoarding the colony's provisions on the ships and releasing them only when he thought it necessary.

This might not have mattered so much if it weren't for the surrounding land being so unsuitable for the kind of agriculture the Scots were used to. The problem of food was compounded by the fact that the Cuna were not interested in trading for the trinkets the Scots had brought with them. Fishing and hunting helped supplement the colonists' diet to a small degree, but most subsisted on Pennecuik's measly ration of a pound of mouldy flour a week, from which they had to remove the maggots and worms by boiling it.

Unsurprisingly, the colonists began to die, a process exacerbated by the arrival of the rainy season in spring, with all its attendant diseases. By March, 200 of the settlers were dead, and on average ten more were dying every day. Except for William Paterson, the councillors had kept quarters on the ship. They had done little to contribute to the construction of the colony, instead continuing to bicker among themselves while those on land died.

The threat of invasion also weighed heavily on the minds of the colonists. In the Colombian port of Cartagena, Spain's South American viceroy had heard rumours that 4000 Scots were already ensconced in Darién, with another 6000 on the way— greatly exaggerating the situation, in other words—and had decided to destroy the colony. In February 1699, the *Dolphin* set sail for the Antilles isle of Curaçao to trade but was captured by the Spanish with all its supplies. The Scotsmen were clapped in irons and gaoled.

Back in Darién, the council members were losing the plot. The illness, bickering, clan politics and incompetence fused into a series of poor decisions, while some of the seamen began to plot their escape. Pennecuik still refused to bring the remaining provisions ashore, claiming there was at best one month's worth of food remaining, yet he also refused to provide the inventory. Suspicions were raised when his sailors were seen filling water casks, and the rumour swept through New Edinburgh that Captain Pennecuik was about to abandon them to starve.

As the polity began to dissolve and the rainy season returned, the colonists held an election. Pennecuik was outraged when the newly elected representatives ordered a search of the ships and discovered them to be well supplied. By now, though, most of the provisions were rotten, and the rest weren't going to last long. A ship was sent to procure supplies and never heard from again. Another sailed for Jamaica and found that trade with the Scottish colony had been black-banned by King William. Morale eroded even further.

One-third of the original contingent were now dead. Any chance of getting sufficient provisions to tide the others over until they'd worked out how to utilise the land had been cut off. The talk turned to abandoning Darién. When a French vessel arrived with news that the Spanish were putting together a powerful force to destroy the colony, the ensuing panic to get on board the ships prefaced any rational decision. What was left of the Scottish fleet departed from the Bay of Caledonia on 18 June, leaving six men lying among the decaying huts of Scotland's dream of financial rescue, too sick to move. Weeks later, a Spanish brigantine pulled into the abandoned settlement and destroyed it.

The colonists might have believed that once they'd boarded the ships they were

saved. If so, they were in for a rude shock. The *Endeavour* sank. The *St Andrew* festered in Jamaica Harbour, throwing its dead over the side daily, as the governor's obedience to the king overrode his compassion for the Scots. The *Caledonia* and the *Unicorn*, captained by the two Drummond brothers, both made it to New York, where the English authorities were undercut by sympathetic Scottish merchants. But only the *Caledonia*, which left New York on 12 October 1699, made it back to Scotland— where the couple of hundred survivors were received as cowards and villains.

Take 2

The news of the Darién disaster would be a long time in reaching Scotland. In the meantime, the nation was again in the grip of famine, and with Wafer's account newly published, there was a sense that the colonists would be enjoying a better standard of living than those they'd left behind.

This opinion was confirmed by the arrival in Scotland in March 1699 of Alexander Hamilton, the accountant with the Darién Venture. A French ship, the *Maurepas*, had visited Darién in the early days when, despite the onset of disease, hope still outweighed despair. Because of his neutrality in the constant squabbling among the councillors, Hamilton had been chosen as the one to return to Edinburgh with their reports and the colonists' mail, in which optimism, combined with the desire to put on a brave face, prevailed. As a consequence of these

C. Allard ex. cum Pr. ord. Holl. et Westfr.

rose-coloured missives, a public celebration was ordered. Cannon were fired in triumph, and in the ensuing drunken riot, the king's representatives were disturbed by the Scots' antipathy towards him.

Three weeks after the accountant's arrival, the brigantine *Dispatch* was sent to Panama with provisions, only to sink off the coast of Scotland. Three weeks after that, two more ships sailed with a further 300 colonists, as well as stores and provisions. On 18 August 1699, a fleet led by the company's flagship— the 150-foot, 38-gun *Rising Sun*—departed from Glasgow with over 1000 colonists on board. The second stage of the Darién Venture was well and truly under way.

It was only while the four ships lay over in Rothesay Bay, waiting for a favourable wind to take them around the Mull of Kintyre, that rumours reached Scotland of Darién's abandonment. The directors of the company simply dismissed them as gossip, concluding:

> *We can believe no set of men in the world of any reasonable measures of discretion and resolution and much less those in whose fidelity and courage we have placed such an entire confidence, could be guilty of so much groundless cowardice, folly, and treachery.*

The second venture consisted of 1300 colonists, among whom were several Presbyterian priests and more than

The colony of New Edinburgh at Darién on the Panama coast, 1698

100 women. They arrived at Darién on 30 November 1699, after losing 160 people on the voyage over, to find the settlement abandoned and destroyed. Also in the bay was Thomas Drummond, who had hired a ship in New York and returned to Darién with provisions. He had been attacked by a Spanish ship a day's sailing away from the colony and had been lucky to escape.

The new arrivals were horrified by what they found. 'Expecting to meet with our friends and countrymen, we found nothing but a vast howling wilderness', said one. Many of them, including some of the new councillors, were of the opinion that they should turn for home. In retrospect, it might have been a good idea.

Having made the decision to stay and rebuild the settlement, they compounded their folly by contemptuously destroying the good relations the first fleet had enjoyed with the Cuna Indians. Despite that, the Cuna informed Captain Drummond, whom they respected from the previous mission, that the Spanish were preparing to attack the colony again. Drummond offered to put together a guerilla force to join the Indians in fighting the Spanish. But as before, the council chose to concentrate on threats to its own authority rather than the greater problems facing the expedition.

This time the governing council was under the sway of James Byres, a particularly inept former merchant with an extremely inflated sense of his own importance in the scheme of things. The councillors refused Drummond's offer, then set about finding a scapegoat for the internal dissent that had understandably become prevalent. On 20 December, a carpenter, Alexander Campbell, was hanged for treason against the council. Soon afterwards, Drummond was arrested. Five hundred colonists were chosen to head to Jamaica, but the wind prevented them from leaving the Bay of Caledonia, while every day, victims of the tropical diseases rife among the colonists were thrown over the side.

When it became definite that a Spanish force had assembled to attack Darién, Byres snuck away on a ship during the night, under the thin pretence of heading to Jamaica for supplies. With Byres out of the way, Drummond was released. A plan was hatched to surprise-attack the advance party of Spanish soldiers, whom the Cuna had spotted approaching the colony on foot. After Drummond's combined force had trudged through the thick jungle, the Spanish were located and engaged in battle on 13 February. Helped by the Cuna, the Scots prevailed, although seven men were lost. When the force returned victorious to the settlement, there were riotous, drunken celebrations that appalled the wowserish Presbyterian priests.

The joy wasn't long in lasting, however. On 23 February the first of a fleet of Spanish ships were spotted heading towards Darién. There were twelve of them in all—far too great a force for the colonists to be able to repel. For the next month they resisted the Spanish invitation to surrender, but on

31 March, on the face of overwhelming force, the Scots eventually submitted to the inevitable. The Spanish permitted them to sail away in the remaining ships.

On 12 April 1700, the last of the Scottish settlers left the colony and the Spanish took possession. The Darién Venture was finished.

Long-term repercussions

Of the 2500 Scots who went to Darién, only a few hundred made it back to Scotland, where they were treated as pariahs. The country, in dire financial straits already, had lost around a quarter of its liquid assets in the venture, and the dream of Scotland as an imperial power had been destroyed. Seven years later, Scotland accepted union with England. Part of the inducement was England's offer to pay off the £230,000 debt amassed by the Company of Scotland Trading to Africa and the Indies. It might be said that the United Kingdom was the product of a failed dream in the Panamanian jungle. Certainly, Scottish resentment towards their neighbours, for what they perceived as England's sabotaging of their chance at independence, would persist for centuries.

William Paterson, having lost his wife and son during the first settlement attempt, made it to New York, arriving there extremely ill. His Darién dream, like a Shakespearean fatal flaw, had come to an end. After a period of recuperation, he returned to England a bitter man, having lost not just his family, but most of his assets too.

Paterson's intellect was irrepressible, however. He continued to advocate for new expeditions to the West Indies, and in 1707 he was an advisor to William III in the unification of England and Scotland. Among his final achievements was laying the groundwork for the Royal Bank of Scotland, which was founded in 1725, six years after his death. The financial strictures of his last years were eased when the English Parliament granted him an indemnity of £18,000, which allowed him to leave the world in relative comfort.

Lionel Wafer, Paterson's inspiration behind the Darién scheme, had waxed lyrical that any crop there would 'thrive … and grow very luxuriantly'; the problem was, so did everything else. The Darién region is one of the most biodiverse ecosystems on the planet with over 2400 plant species and more than 900 species of mammals and birds. It is also one of the wettest places in the world with up to an inch of rain a day falling in the rainy season. Even today, this area of Panama remains such dense jungle that it constitutes the only interuption to the inter-American highway, which runs from the foot of South America up to the limits of accessibility in eastern Canada.

A HEAD FOR FIGURES

William Paterson emerged from obscure beginnings to become one of the key players in British finance at the end of the seventeenth century. Born to small-time farmers outside Tinwald in Dumfriesshire, in the very south of Scotland, he left home at seventeen for Bristol in England. Details of his youthful career remain sketchy, but it seems likely he stayed with a widowed female relative in Bristol, whose death provided him with the wherewithal to pay for his passage to the Bahamas in the Caribbean.

While in the Bahamas, Paterson became a merchant. Yet it was the tales of the Caribbean buccaneers that fuelled his imagination, particularly the story of Lionel Wafer, a former ship's surgeon and privateer who had been marooned on the Darién Peninsula for a number of years. Although it's unlikely that Paterson travelled there during this period, he returned to Europe in the 1680s with the Darién Venture very much on his mind.

While attempting to find funding for the scheme in northern Europe, he amassed a small personal fortune through his business activities, so much so that by the time he set himself up as a merchant in London, in 1687, he was a man of means and influence. In London, Paterson proved himself to be a great capitalist innovator. He founded a company that piped water from the Hampstead Hills down to the rest of

William Paterson

north London and was associated in the property development of west London, between Lincoln's Inn Fields and Kensington.

William Paterson is best known for his role in the founding of the Bank of England. It opened in 1694 as a commercial bank with a capital of £1.2 million, a sum that the directors of the bank advanced to the government, in return for financial privileges such as the right to issue notes up to the amount of its capital. Paterson resigned as one of the bank's directors in 1695, after clashes with fellow board members over the direction it was taking. But his brainchild was a runaway success. In 1709, the capital was doubled, while the charter was renewed in 1742, 1764 and 1781. The bank remained privately owned until its nationalisation by an Act of Parliament in 1946.

The Bank of England helped stabilise the English financial system and granted it independence from the caprices of the monarch. This was one reason why England experienced the Industrial Revolution ahead of continental Europe. It proved invaluable in establishing the conditions whereby capital became available to fund the expansion of the British Empire and the Industrial Revolution. The Darién debacle aside, William Paterson's achievement in this regard cannot be underestimated.

CHAPTER 18

The convict colony of Sullivan Bay, Port Phillip Bay, New South Wales (1803–04)

With one eye on the French and the other on the lucrative sealing and whaling industries, in 1802 the British government decided to found a settlement in the Bass Strait area in order to consolidate its territorial claims in Australia—or New South Wales, as most of it was known then. Early explorers of Port Phillip Bay and the south coast of present-day Victoria had been positive about the bay's agricultural potential and Lieutenant David Collins was given the job of leading over 600 souls, mainly convicts, to settle there. When he arrived in October 1803, the Lieutenant chose Sullivan Bay, on Mornington Peninsula—and immediately regretted his decision. Good fresh water proved scarce, his ships were unable to get close to shore, the soil was far too sandy, and the supply of timber was poor. Within weeks, Collins was looking for better alternatives; within two months, he was waiting for the okay from Sydney to move out. By May 1804, the colonists had abandoned the settlement for Van Diemen's Land, where Collins founded Hobart, on the Derwent River.

Until George Bass made his brave and epic exploration in 1797, it was unclear whether there was a strait in the far southeast of the Australian continent, dividing Van Diemen's Land (now Tasmania) from the mainland. Bass suspected that there was but was only able to prove it definitively on his next expedition in 1798, this time with Matthew Flinders. The discovery of the strait meant that ships sailing to and from Australia could save considerable time by sailing above Tasmania, rather than around it. In 1800, Lieutenant James Grant did just that: sailing from Cape Town, South Africa, to Sydney in the *Lady Nelson* via the newly discovered Bass Strait. When he reached Sydney, Governor King sent him back to explore the coast of what would later be called Victoria.

Grant entered Western Port, to the east of Port Phillip Bay, where he built a rudimentary cottage and planted wheat and other crops on Churchill Island. However, poor weather and approaching winter forced him to return without venturing further west. When Grant returned to England, the job of exploring the coast on the *Lady Nelson* fell to Acting Lieutenant Murray, who had been Grant's first mate. In November 1801, he sailed south from Sydney, eventually encountering Grant's wheat growing 1.8 metres (6 feet) tall and nearly ready for harvest, which increased his optimistic attitude towards the area.

Continuing west, Murray arrived at the entrance to Port Phillip Bay, a short distance from Western Port. But the tip of Mornington Peninsula meant that the entrance was precarious because of the currents caused by a large body of water having such a narrow aperture to the ocean; bad weather made it too difficult to enter. Nonetheless, Murray's curiosity was piqued. After sailing south to King Island, he returned for another look.

This time he made his way through the rip at the entrance to the bay and explored it for a month, later describing it as a most noble sheet of water, larger even than Western Port. Murray named it Port King after the Governor of New South Wales, Philip Gidley King, but when he returned to Sydney, the governor modestly exercised his prerogative and renamed it after his predecessor, the founder of New South Wales, Captain Arthur Phillip.

The journey of Matthew Flinders at the end of 1802, which also explored the inlet, appeared to confirm Murray's sense of the bay's potential. In *A Voyage to Terra Australis*, Flinders wrote:

> *The country surrounding Port Phillip has a pleasing and in many parts, a fertile appearance; and the sides of some of the hills and several of the valleys are fit for agricultural purposes. It is, in great measure, a grassy country and capable of supporting much cattle, though better calculated for sheep ... Indented Head, at the northern part of the western peninsula, had an appearance particularly agreeable. The grass had been burnt not long before, and had sprung up green and tender. The wood was so thinly scattered that one might see to a considerable*

distance; and the hills rose one over the other to a moderate elevation, but so gently that a plough might everywhere be used. The vegetable soil is a little mixed with sand and probably not deep, as I judged from the small size of the trees.

The combined reports of Grant, Murray and Flinders were received with enthusiasm by Governor King. This enthusiasm was shortly expedited into action by the presence of two French ships and a rumour that they planned to establish a settlement on Van Diemen's Land, on the basis that the English had no right of sovereignty because the island had been discovered by the Dutch.

On the basis of hearsay alone, King thought that Port Phillip Bay might be a superior place to live than Sydney, which, like many successful colonies elsewhere, had faced a stark struggle for survival in its early years. King wrote an urgent dispatch to the Duke of Portland, William Cavendish-Bentinck, who at the time was Lord President of the Privy Council in London and shared King's concerns about the activities of the French.

From the account given by Acting-Lieutenant Murray and Captain Flinders of the soil and the natural advantage of Port Phillip in Bass's Straits, I beg leave to suggest the propriety of a settlement being made at that place ... Nor can there be a doubt from the account I have received from these officers, of its being a much more eligible climate for raising wheat than this is ... I am the more solicitous respecting forming this settlement from the probability having in contemplation to make a settlement ...

While this missive was making its way to England, further rumours forced King to take precautionary action to ascertain the intentions of the French in the area. He sent a schooner, the *Cumberland*, whose crew included the NSW Surveyor-General, Charles Grimes, to follow the French and plant the Union Jack wherever they might happen to land. When the two parties met on King Island, to the north-west of Van Diemen's Land, the commander of the French expedition, Captain Nicholas Baudin, was eager to reassure the British authorities that his mission was for scientific rather than colonial reasons. Armed with this message for Governor King, the schooner headed for the mainland with instructions to further explore the land in the vicinity of Port Phillip.

The *Cumberland* entered Port Phillip Bay on 20 January 1803 and travelled for a fortnight up the eastern side of the bay until coming to the mouth of what Grimes called the Freshwater River (now known as the Yarra River). This, he concluded, was 'the most eligible place for a settlement that I have seen'. The rest of Port Phillip Bay, from its difficult entry to its sandy soil and sparse supplies of fresh water, failed to impress Grimes, however. Yet his report wouldn't reach London until after the Duke of Portland had sent an expedition in response to King's dispatch.

While the *Cumberland* was exploring, King's earlier letter had received a positive reception in London. Somewhat fortuitously, it had arrived just as preparations were being made to send a convict ship to Australia. Changing the destination would not be that difficult. King's second-hand enthusiasm for Port Phillip Bay was paraphrased without attribution in the *London Times* newspaper, which helped to generate favourable publicity for the proposed colony.

The person chosen to lead the settlement was Lieutenant David Collins, who had sailed to New South Wales with the First Fleet in 1788 and became its judge advocate. Collins hated the ocean and didn't much like being

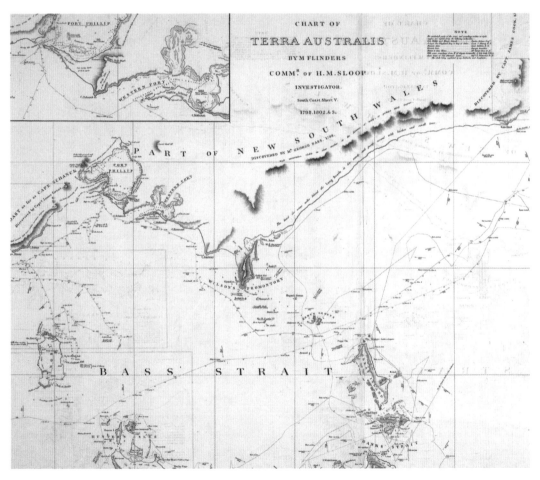

Matthew Flinders' chart of Bass Strait, with an inset of Port Phillip Bay

in Australia. In many ways he was the classic English enlightened amateur gentleman, who lacked sufficient family money to live independently and had thus been forced to choose between the military and the clergy in order to earn his keep. Collins had opted for the Royal Marines, a decision he would later regret, but as a young man it at least offered the prospect of adventure. He fought in the American War of Independence and met his wife, Maria, while garrisoned in Nova Scotia, Canada. Impoverished by half pay when he returned to England, he was encouraged by his father to join the New South Wales venture, where he enjoyed an excellent relationship with Governor Phillip and gained a sense of purpose in the colony. He was sufficiently good at his job that, when Phillip returned to England and Collins wanted to follow, he was pressed to stay because he was deemed indispensable. Collins lacked the connections and requisite skills to plot his own career trajectory, and stayed.

When he returned to England in 1797, several years after he'd originally hoped, Collins found himself in financial difficulty only partially alleviated by sales of his *An Account of the English Colony in New South Wales*. Promotion was difficult to find since Collins, who believed his character was better cut for the cloth than the military, was something of a fish out of water when it came to the Marines. The only area where Collins had unique knowledge was the Antipodean colonies, and when the decision was made to found a settlement at Port Phillip Bay

he was offered the job, with the new title of lieutenant-governor of the proposed new colony. Although he was loath to leave his wife again, there were no other offers on the table. Given that their only child had died soon after birth, he also perhaps felt the desire to see two illegitimate children born to his convict mistress in Sydney. While Collins hated the sea and believed himself better suited to the clergy, he nonetheless seemed to have a girl in every port.

The reluctant governor

In April 1803, HMS *Calcutta* set sail from Portsmouth in the south of England for Port Phillip Bay. On board were 150 civilian men and over 300 male convicts, as well as a number of officials and a detachment of Marines; wives and children accompanied the men. A second ship, the *Ocean*, a former coal freighter, had been hired to carry supplies, settlers and the remainder of the civilian officials and their families. All up, over 600 people embarked on the voyage.

Of the convicts, over 260 had a trade at the time of their trial: there were sawyers, carpenters, blacksmiths, gardeners, bakers, brickmakers and bricklayers, in addition to less obviously necessary tradesmen, including a button-maker and a carpet-weaver. The majority were sourced from the prison hulks at Woolwich on the River Thames, meaning that most of them had been convicted for crimes committed in London. As a result, while Collins was content with the trade credentials of his complement, he was concerned about the relative lack of agricultural experience.

The *Calcutta* sailed via Tenerife, Rio de Janeiro and Simon's Town (Cape Town), while the *Ocean* sailed directly to Port Phillip Bay from Rio de Janeiro. During the trip Collins decided to take Hannah Power, wife of convict Matthew Power, for his mistress, apparently with her husband's consent. The last leg of the voyage was particularly rough. Humane captaincy with an eye to hygiene limited the casualties, however.

The ships arrived at Port Phillip at the beginning of October. Collins was almost immediately disenchanted by the difficult entry to the bay with the strong currents caused by the long, narrow tip of Mornington Peninsula. The risk of running aground was amplified by the powerful winds common to the area. From the start therefore, the Lieutenant remained sceptical about the value of Port Phillip Bay as a place to establish a settlement, particularly as trade with the whaling and sealing industries was anticipated as a major economic component. He thought it unlikely that captains would be willing to risk their ships to enter the bay.

Because Collins had left before Grimes's report reached England, he did not have access to the information identifying the mouth of the Yarra as perhaps the only really suitable place to locate a settlement. Nor had Collins had any contact with Governor King, whose initial enthusiasm for Port Phillip Bay had considerably receded. Faced with a cargo

of convicts and settlers who had endured a torrid trip through the Roaring Forties, and no doubt eager to establish his land-based authority and get on with the job of establishing the settlement, he sent out a boat to make some cursory explorations. When they found nothing ideal, Collins chose a bay (close to today's seaside village of Sorrento) about 6 kilometres (4 miles) east of the heads that was partly sheltered from the fierce winds blowing from Antarctica. He named it Sullivan Bay, after the Undersecretary of State at the War and Colonial Office.

Any vestige of optimism that Collins possessed for the settlement site soon diminished. To begin with, the bay was so shallow that the two ships had to be anchored more than half a kilometre (500 yards) offshore. Much of the supplies, and those livestock and fowls that had survived the journey, had to be lugged ashore by convicts stripped to their waists and wading through the shoals. Once the goods were landed on the shore, and the tents were erected, the most pressing problem became the lack of a suitable supply of fresh water. Water was accessed by sinking eight water casks into the ground. Two tonnes of fresh water was obtained this way, but when they attempted the same thing several days later, the water proved to be brackish.

In contrast, the Arcadian vista that confronted this motley lot of colonists was encouraging. Like the explorers before them, the Sullivan Bay settlers were quick to comment on the beauty of a setting that appeared to be regulated nature rather than pure wilderness. Lieutenant James Tuckey, for instance, gave the following description:

> *The face of the country bordering on the port is beautifully picturesque, swelling into gentle elevations of the brightest verdure, and dotted with trees, as if planted by the hand of taste, while the ground is covered with a profusion of flowers of every colour.*

Tuckey was certainly prone to waxing lyrical. Elsewhere he wrote:

> *I beheld a second Rome, rising from a coalition of banditti. I beheld it giving laws to the world and, superlative in arms and in arts, looking down with proud superiority upon the barbarous nations of the northern hemisphere.*

His expansive prose was usually in synchrony with his alcohol consumption. Yet Tuckey was not alone in his praise of the landscape. The reason for the glorious scenery which inspired such Wordsworthian fancies was probably that the local Boonwurrung tribe of Aborigines were in the habit of burning the forest so it wouldn't get too thick, in order to make it easier for them to hunt game.

Meeting the locals

Despite its appearance, the land soon revealed itself to be something of a disappointment in utilitarian terms. The soil was sandy, and although Collins was quick to think that his settlers were a mob of whingers and more useless in general than the convicts, their failure at cultivation was partly justified by the poor quality of the soil. Just as disappointing were the supplies of timber, harvesting of lumber being one of the colony's main tasks.

With Sullivan Bay having proved unremarkable, Lieutenant-Governor Collins, sent a boat with six men under Lieutenant Tuckey on a reconnaissance mission of Port Phillip. They traced the eastern shore of the bay and then the northern shore, where they found signs of increased population density, which they quite rightly concluded pointed to superior supplies of fresh water. While Grimes had indicated the mouth of the Yarra as his preferred location for a settlement, Tuckey favoured a snug bay he found on the western shore of Port Phillip, an area with sufficiently deep water for the ships to anchor. Today it is the site of Victoria's second-largest city, Geelong, and the bay is known as Corio Bay. There was copious fresh water there in a series of ponds, while the soil also seemed richer than in most places. The area now known as Limeburners Point contained materials such as clay, limestone and shell deposits crucial for the making of bricks.

Although the settlement at Sullivan Bay had occurred without much interaction with the local Aborigines, Tuckey and his men found themselves visited by members of the local Wathaurong tribe while camping at Limeburners Point. Initially the tribespeople seemed friendly and curious; they were happy to receive some gifts. However, when Tuckey returned to one of the dinghies while his colleagues were preparing dinner, the situation rapidly changed. Perhaps the lieutenant had committed a breach of etiquette by leaving, or perhaps the Wathaurong perceived that his absence made the men vulnerable to attack.

All of a sudden, 200 Wathaurong warriors appeared, singing war songs and brandishing their spears. Their chiefs, carried aloft, were resplendently dressed in cloaks made of possum fur, wore necklaces made from reeds and human hair, and sported headpieces created from the wing feathers of swans. The faces of the warriors were painted with patterns of red, white and yellow clay; their noses were pierced with bones up to 61 cm (2 feet) long, and their skins were ritually scarified. From one of the small boats, they seized a tomahawk, an axe and a saw.

As Tuckey hurried back to the camp, a man named Gammon was grabbed by the warriors, who also took possession of one of the tents. At this point, the Wathaurong retreated—only to soon return in greater numbers.

In keeping with his romantic demeanour, Tuckey chose to play the Noble Savage gambit. He put his gun on the ground and approached the warriors with peace offerings in his arms. This failed to sufficiently pacify them, however, and as they continued to advance, Tuckey ordered his men to fire at the most aggressive member of the tribe. Boatswain Innis and two other men levelled their muskets at one of the gesticulating warriors and fired from a range of 45 metres

(50 yards). The man dropped dead on the spot. The other attackers immediately fled, leaving his body behind.

Relations with the Wathaurong remained fraught, although this was as close to all-out conflict as things got. In general, Collins took a more humane approach to the Aboriginal people than did many of his colleagues in Australia. In January 1804, eager to maintain peace with a people who vastly outnumbered his isolated contingent, he issued orders stipulating that the taking of any articles belonging to native tribespeople, whether from their huts, from the beach or from the people themselves, would be treated as theft, and punishable as such; while anyone 'wantonly or inconsiderably' killing or wounding a member of the tribe or offering violence on an Aboriginal woman would be tried for their life.

Running away

No one would be convicted of a capital offence during the short life of Sullivan Bay. Infractions of the regulations, followed by floggings, however, were an all too frequent occurrence—as also was the escape of convicts from the camp. There were twenty-seven absconders in all, and the ease of escape was another reason for Collins to prefer Van Diemen's Land, with its ocean boundaries.

One of the persistent rumours motivating convict escapes was that there was an overland route to China. Others believed that they might be able to join up with the sealing

THE AMAZING MR BUCKLEY

The son of a smallholder near Cheshire, William Buckley had served a bricklaying apprenticeship before joining the British Army. In 1799 he was wounded in battle while fighting against Napoleon's armies in the Netherlands. Three years later, in August 1802, he was convicted of knowingly receiving stolen goods—two lengths of cloth, no less—and sentenced to transportation for life. When he arrived in Sullivan Bay, Buckley was just twenty-three years old, but his physical size belied his young age.

A giant of a man, Buckley stood at 2 metres (6 foot 6 inches), when the average height at the time was less than 170 centimetres (5 foot 7 inches). It was this physical characteristic that appears to have saved his life in the early weeks of 1804, while his fellow escaped convicts perished. Having parted company with the small party at Corio Bay, in the west of Port Phillip Bay, Buckley then encountered the Wathaurong people, whose chief had just died and been buried nearby. It should have been the end of him, but in fact it was a new beginning.

Seeing this large white man in the vicinity of their chief's grave, the tribespeople assumed he was a reincarnation of their former leader. Buckley befriended the Wathaurong, who showed him how to survive; he took a Wathaurong wife and had a number of children. Revered as a sacred spirit, he was forbidden to fight in their frequent tribal wars.

Buckley's popularity among his new companions was undeniable. Many years later, when he made contact with a party led by Victorian entrepreneur John Batman, he led them to his home where, the visitors noticed with some awe, 'three men, five women and about twelve children' rushed to greet him. 'Buckley had dismounted and they were all clinging around him and tears of joy and delight running down their cheeks,' recorded J.T. Gellibrand, the first attorney-general of Van Diemen's Land. 'It was truly an affecting sight and proved the affection which these people entertained for Buckley.'

This was in July 1835, when the former convict hadn't been seen or heard from in over thirty years. By this time, so legend has it, Buckley had forgotten how to speak English. On another occasion, having heard his fellow Wathaurong planning an ambush on the colonists, he apparently wandered into the Englishmen's camp shouting one of the few words he could still remember: 'Bread!' The ambush was averted.

His English eventually returned to him, and Buckley became valuable to the second generation of Port Phillip settlers as an interpreter between them and the local tribes. For this service, he received a pardon and an annual salary of £50. But before long, he grew dissatisfied of his go-between status. Trapped between worlds, he enjoyed the full confidence of neither the Aborigines nor the whites and chose to move to Van Diemen's Land at the end of 1837. In 1840 he married a widow, with whom he had two daughters. Buckley worked as a gatekeeper at the female prison in South Hobart, among other things, before his death in January 1856.

William Buckley

William Buckley returns to civilisation after thirty years living with the Wathaurong

and whaling boats then plying Australia's southern coast. Many of these vessels were American, and their masters therefore were no great fans of English law, so it was not an outrageous hope that an absconder might find himself picked up and from there work his way to a free life in America, even if this scenario appears never to have eventuated.

Of the escapees from Sullivan Bay, twenty had returned to the camp by the time the *Ocean* took away the final settlers in May 1804. Of the other seven, six perished. The only successful escape was carried out by young William Buckley, who flew the coop as part of a mass breakout on Christmas Day in 1803.

Having correctly guessed that the Marines might not have their minds on the job on Christmas Day, Buckley and his fellow escapees stole a number of items, including a gun. One man was shot in the gut by a sentry, while several others gave themselves up soon afterwards. By New Year's Eve, seven of the fugitives were still at large. Buckley and his party traced the eastern and northern shores of the bay, dispersing a potentially hostile gathering of Wathaurong locals by firing a gun in the air before they crossed the Yarra. Their anticlockwise circuit continued down the west of Port Phillip until they'd made their way to Corio Bay, the place that had so impressed James Tuckey. The men were hungry and exhausted, and were relieved to find fresh water there and shellfish to eat.

Most of the escaped convicts had already returned to the colony by this point, and Buckley and his companions were down to three. While at Corio Bay, they too decided that a flogging and an extended sentence in a civilisation they knew was better than an unknown death in an unknown place. Each night they built a bonfire, in the hope that their countrymen over in Sullivan Bay would come and take them back to civilisation. The fires were noticed, but no action was taken. Knowing that the colony was soon to be abandoned, the trio decided to return, but two of them never made it. Whether they were killed by Aborigines, died of exposure or starved to death, or perished through something more exotic, such as snakebite, remains unknown. William Buckley was more fortunate, although it was a long time before he returned to civilisation. He would be discovered some thirty years later by a party of Victorian pioneers, a free man, living in peace among the Wathaurong people.

Abandon colony

The escaped convicts weren't the only ones who were keen to flee their environment. From almost the moment he arrived there, Lieutenant-Governor Collins had wanted to be elsewhere, and as the few remnants today attest, Sullivan Bay resembled more of a tent city than other abandoned antipodean colonies, such as Port Essington in the north (see page 220).

Having anchored in October, by November, Collins had sent a cutter (a small single-masted yacht) crewed by six men to Sydney, seeking leave from Governor King to relocate the colony to either King Island, in Bass Strait, or Van Diemen's Land. The cutter had a rough trip and was eventually picked up 95 kilometres (60 miles) short of its destination and towed into Sydney by the *Ocean*, which was also Sydney-bound. On 24 November, they arrived at Port Jackson. King assented to a move to Van Diemen's Land, and even gave Collins a choice of north or south of the island: either Port Dalrymple, in the vicinity of present-day Launceston, or the Derwent River, where King had already sent a contingent of men to deflect any attempt by the French to settle there.

The news reached Collins on 12 December with the return of the *Ocean*, and despite two of the runaway convicts reporting that they'd found excellent fresh water and pasture in the vicinity of the Yarra River, the lieutenant-governor was determined to move. He immediately set about organising the transition. His plans were slowed somewhat by the departure on 18 December of the *Calcutta*, the other ship that had brought the settlers and convicts over from England in April. Its captain had become edgy when hearing that England and France were at war.

Collins had hoped that the captain and his crew would be staying until the move was finished, since he considered his own manpower to be insufficient to quell a rebellion should the convicts became organised enough to start one. But his humane treatment probably stood him in good stead, and other than the Christmas runaways—during which time he armed and deputised some of the most trustworthy convicts—there were few inklings of a possible mass rebellion. Collins put the convicts to work building a 380-foot pier out into the bay in order to facilitate the loading of the *Ocean* while he waited for another ship to arrive.

After the first replacement ship, the *Francis*, proved unseaworthy, it was substituted with the *Lady Nelson*, the same vessel that Grant and Murray had used to explore the coastline to the east of Port Phillip Bay. The free settlers and civilian officers boarded this ship, while on 24 January, 120 convicts with twenty Marines to guard them boarded the *Ocean*, which was otherwise packed with supplies. The remaining 170-odd convicts would remain at Sullivan Bay with Lieutenant Sladden's guard detail until the *Ocean* was able to return.

Two days later, Collins joined the ship. On 30 January, after waiting at the heads for a gale to blow over, the *Ocean* sailed and reached the Derwent on 15 February. Once the cargo, both human and material, had been successfully unloaded, the ship returned to pick up Sladden and his contingent. They sailed on 18 May, at which point William Buckley became the only European in Port Phillip Bay.

Second chances

By the time David Collins died of a heart attack in March 1810, at the age of fifty-six, without ever having returned to England, he must have felt vindicated in his decision to abandon Port Phillip. Instead he founded what is now the city of Hobart. It might be added that at some point he abandoned his Port Phillip mistress for sixteen-year-old Margaret Eddington, who bore him two further children.

A second attempt to settle contemporary Victoria, at Western Port in 1826, also failed and it wasn't until John Pascoe Fawkner and John Batman returned to the area in the 1830s that the optimum site for settlement, on the Yarra River, became the first permanent Victorian settlement and the nucleus for the metropolis of Melbourne. While Sullivan Bay proved unfruitful for Collins and his convict colonists, the same cannot be said of the area today, in its modern guise of Sorrento. In April 2008, a 1.2-hectare (3-acre) beachfront site, which includes some of the very few remnants of the Collins settlement, sold for $18.4 million, the most expensive residential property deal ever in the state.

FIRST-GENERATION HIGH ACHIEVER

The life of Sullivan Bay settler John Pascoe Fawkner was one of the many chains-to-riches stories of colonial Australia. The son of a metal refiner, also called John, young Fawkner must have got the shock of his life in 1801 when his father was convicted of receiving stolen goods and sentenced to fourteen years' transportation. For two years, Fawkner senior was imprisoned on one of the convict hulks on the Thames—the decommissioned ships that had been used as a temporary solution to England's burgeoning gaol population ever since the American War of Independence caused a hiatus in the transportation of convicts. In 1803 Fawkner senior was chosen as part of the Calcutta contingent to settle Port Phillip Bay. His wife, Hannah, must have loved him, since she chose to go with him and take their children, ten-year-old John and his little sister Elizabeth. (Young John would be eleven by the time he arrived at Sullivan Bay, his birthday having fallen late in the journey.)

Following the abandonment of Sullivan Bay in early 1804, the Fawkners relocated to Sullivan Cove (now in Hobart), where the family lived in a primitive hut and in great poverty while Fawkner senior continued to serve his term. Severe food shortages in the early years of the settlement meant that the family, like many others in the fledgling colony, suffered from scurvy. Although the relationship between scurvy and fresh food had been shown more than fifty years before, the wisdom was bizarrely slow in filtering through to everyday medical and dietary practice.

It wasn't long before the family's fortunes took a turn for the better. By 1806, Fawkner senior had received his ticket of leave, along with a 20-hectare (50-acre) land grant 11 kilometres (7 miles) out of Hobart. Young John was given the job of shepherd and lived in a turf hut on the property. He was granted an adjacent 20 hectares (50 acres) by Governor Macquarie in 1811. Combined with an inheritance that his mother went to England to claim, the family was becoming well off—better off than they had been. In addition, the now twenty-year-old John Fawkner became a baker, which brought them further income.

In 1814, Fawkner showed he had inherited his father's capacity to get into trouble, when he tried to help some of his convict associates escape to South America in a boat. They hardly got anywhere, and Fawkner was sentenced to 500 lashes and three years' hard labour, which he served in the penal settlement at Newcastle, New South Wales. When he was freed in 1816, he returned to his trade as a baker and also entered the lucrative illegal liquor trade. In 1822, he married Eliza Cobb, who had been transported as a seventeen-year-old for stealing somebody else's baby. He moved to Launceston, where he reinvented himself as a builder, opened a pub, worked as a bush lawyer and started the Launceston Advertiser newspaper, which advocated the rights of emancipees in the face of snobbery and discrimination from the government and free settlers.

Fawkner was clearly a restless soul, and merely becoming a successful businessman was not enough for him. In 1835, he charted a boat to return to his first Antipodean 'home', Port Phillip Bay. While he was forced by the courts to remain in Van Diemen's Land to settle a dispute, the ship he hired, the Enterprise, captained by John Lancey, sailed into Port Phillip Bay and set up camp near the mouth of the Yarra River, where they encountered another former Sullivan Bay inhabitant: William Buckley. Fawkner followed soon afterwards and began to establish a fortune built on newspapers, bookselling, pubs and landholdings.

By 1851, his respectability was complete when he joined the state of Victoria's first Legislative Council as the member for Talbot, where he battled the greed of the squattocracy and fretted over the social upheaval caused by the Gold Rush. He remained on the council until his death in 1869, and was famous for his unchanging parliamentary uniform of an old-fashioned cloak paired with a velvet smoking cap. By the time he died, Fawkner's colonial life had taken him from being the eleven-year-old son of a convict and subsequently a convict himself, to becoming the grand old man of Victorian politics and one of the first politicians to represent the Aussie battler.

CHAPTER 19

The British outpost of Victoria, Port Essington, North Australia, New South Wales (1838–49)

Located on Cobourg Peninsula in what is now the Northern Territory, the outpost of Victoria was the third attempt by the British to establish a settlement on the northern coast of Australia. In October 1838, Sir Gordon Bremer arrived on board the Alligator and founded a naval base that initially showed great promise, despite a catastrophic cyclone necessitating a rebuild in its first year. Later on, it was the turn of malaria-carrying mosquitoes to wreak their own form of devastation among the colonists. Crucial decisions made in London also jeopardised its success, and Victoria never did graduate from its military beginnings to become a trading or farming settlement. Even Britain's urgent need for a new transportation colony couldn't throw Victoria a lifeline.

When Napoleon Bonaparte annexed the Netherlands in 1810, thus gaining control over the Dutch East Indies, the British became anxious about possible French encroachment into Australia—or the north of New South Wales, as the eastern half of the mainland continued to be called. To prevent this, they invaded Java and took possession of most of the Dutch East Indies. For five years, under the governorship of Sir Stamford Raffles, British trade in the region flourished.

The Netherlands regained independence from France in 1813, a year after which a treaty restored to it the Dutch East Indies, much to the chagrin of the British traders who had found the region lucrative. By way of compensation, Britain established a trading centre on the island of Singapore in 1819 and maintained a presence at Malacca on the Malay Peninsula, which now forms Malaysia. The Dutch resented this intrusion into their former monopoly markets and tried to defuse the newfound popularity of machined cotton products from England's mills by imposing large tariffs on English products imported into their territories. They also agitated against the British settlements at Singapore and Malacca. This state of affairs forced the negotiation of another treaty, in 1824, whereby Britain agreed to withdraw its outposts on Sumatra, while the Netherlands agreed to recognise British sovereignty over Singapore and withdraw from the Malay Peninsula.

Having established territories and markets in the north of the region, Britain's attention turned to the formation of a trading outpost in the south, which, it was hoped, would rival the success of Singapore. Because Australia nominally belonged to Britain already, it was envisaged that goods traded from there would escape the onerous duties exacted by the Dutch. Just as importantly, the north coast of Australia was where the Bugis people (originally from the current-day Indonesian island of Sulawesi) sailed down from the Malay archipelago on the north-western monsoon to trade with the local Aborigines while they caught and dried sea cucumbers, known as trepang. The latter were highly valued in Chinese markets as a delicacy, not the least because of their supposed aphrodisiacal properties; and given the balance-of-trade difficulties between Britain and China that eventually led to the Opium Wars (as a result of Britain forcing China to accept Indian opium), it's possible that the British were attracted to trepang as a possible export.

In January 1824, the warship *Tamar*, under the command of Captain J.J. Gordon Bremer, was sent from England to northern Australia, with a brief to find suitable sites for settlement between the western coast of Bathurst Island and the eastern side of the Cobourg Peninsula. Two sites had been given preference in an earlier survey carried out by Captain Phillip Parker King (who was the son of the third governor of New South Wales, Philip Gidley King), namely Port Essington and Melville Island, although Bremer decided he had only sufficient manpower to settle one.

In September, he arrived at Port Essington, some 350 kilometres (215 miles) to the north-east of present-day Darwin in an inlet of the Arafura Sea. Set in the northern shore of the peninsula and measuring some 31 kilometres by 11 kilometres (19 miles by 7 miles), the inlet had first been explored by the Dutch around 1636 and more recently by Matthew Flinders, in 1803, fifteen years before Captain King's visit on behalf of the Royal Navy. But Port Essington wouldn't be settled on this occasion: an unsuccessful three-day search for water convinced Bremer that Melville Island would have to be the superior destination.

Bremer's settlement site at Fort Dundas, on the north-western side of the island, soon proved less than ideal, however, for the 100-plus Marines, soldiers and convicts who landed. To begin with, the site was ill chosen: mangroves and dense foliage surrounded it, cutting it off from cooling sea breezes. The mangroves were excellent incubators for mosquito-borne diseases, though. Two ships sailed towards the islands of the Malay archipelago with the intention of initiating trade, only to be captured by pirates, plundered and their crews put to the sword. Even worse for the long-term prospects of the colony was that, when choosing the site, the British had failed to research the route the Bugis took in their *prahus*, and the anticipated arrival of the trepang fishermen from the north failed to occur.

As the heat took its effect and provisions dwindled, morale at Fort Dundas plummeted. To add to their troubles, they'd failed to reach a peaceable agreement with the local Aborigines, the Tiwi, who had fatally speared sufficient members of the garrison that no one was prepared to leave the fort unless they had an armed guard. When the second commandant, Major John Campbell, arrived, he found the settlement in a parlous state. The East India Company, unwilling to give up on the idea of settling northern Australia, argued that another settlement to the east of Melville Island might prove more amenable in terms of natives, sea breezes and trade. The British government acquiesced, and in June 1827, a settlement called Fort Wellington was established at Raffles Bay, on the eastern coast of the Cobourg Peninsula.

This proved a far better site. Unlike Fort Dundas, Fort Wellington caught the sea breeze and was perfectly located to catch the passing trade offered by the Bugis trepang fishermen on their way east. The settlement experienced widespread illness during its first year, however, a situation that provoked the commandant, Captain Smyth, to write adverse reports on the place, in the hope that he might be removed from his post. Smyth eventually obtained his wish and was invalided home, to be replaced by Captain Collet Barker, who arrived in September 1828.

Barker's presence soon revealed the truth of the incompetence and cowardice of his predecessor. The health of the settlers improved, relations with the local Aborigines were largely good, and gardens were grown successfully, creating the promise of self-sufficiency. In addition, the increasing number of Bugis traders suggested that a permanent base at Fort Wellington was feasible.

It seemed that Britain now had its southern trading capital in the region, its second Singapore. Barker wrote effusive reports to his superiors in London about Fort Wellington and its potential. Yet, as was often the case with top-down colonial management from afar, by the time his reports arrived, the fate of the settlement had been sealed. No doubt motivated by the desire to protect his own reputation, Smyth had painted an exceedingly bleak picture of Fort Wellington and had received support from the governor of New South Wales, Ralph Darling.

In August 1829, an order arrived from the Colonial Secretary spelling out the end for the settlement. Captain Barker apparently considered ignoring the instruction to leave, in the correct belief that his reports had not been read in time. Discretion got the better part of valour, however, and to the disappointment of those who had invested their effort in making it work, Fort Wellington was abandoned at the end of the month.

Use it or lose it

In 1836, British interest in settling the north coast of the colony of New South Wales was renewed when the well-connected trader and traveller George Windsor Earl began making enquiries to the Colonial Office in London as to whether there were any plans to establish a permanent settlement there. Earl argued that the abandonment of Fort Wellington had been based on the poor information provided in Smyth's reports and that trepang could become a staple commodity for trade in the region. The case for the establishment of a new colony was eventually taken up with the Colonial Secretary himself, Lord Glenelg.

Rather than trade though, the decision was sealed by strategic considerations. If the north coast remained unoccupied, then there was a risk that another power, most likely the Dutch or possibly the French, could establish a settlement there.

The history of European colonisation showed that just sticking a flag in the ground was not always sufficient to maintain sovereignty of territory, especially when other nations also had interests in the region. The Dutch could well argue that they had discovered northern Australia first and that the abandonment of Fort Wellington was tantamount to the relinquishing of sovereignty. To an extent, the reality of colonisation was use it or lose it.

With two failed attempts weighing on its conscience, the British government, while agreeing to the settlement, was quite cautious in planning the new venture. The site selected was Port Essington, an excellent natural harbour, larger than Port Jackson in Sydney, where Captain Bremer had stopped briefly in 1824. The colony there was to be restricted to a naval base, and only once the viability of that seemed likely would the settlement be expanded to become a permanent trading port. This cautiousness would be a contributing factor in the colony's eventual failure.

Gordon Bremer, who had been knighted since returning from the earlier expedition, was again chosen to lead. The colony's population would consist primarily of a garrison of Royal Marines. A man-of-war would be stationed in the inlet for defence purposes, while the settlement would facilitate the rescue of stricken sailors from the frequent shipwrecks in the region, as well as serve as a supply point for ships making their way from the Indian Ocean to Britain's assets in the Pacific. The commander of these Marines would be Captain John McArthur, nephew of the fractious soldier, entrepreneur and governor John Macarthur who, despite being an unpleasant character, introduced the merino sheep to Australia and was thus responsible for much of the early prosperity of the colonies.

George Earl, the trader who had advocated so strongly for a trading presence in the north, was included in the expedition as a translator. Another non-military addition was John Armstrong, an English horticulturist from the Royal Botanical Gardens at Kew, in London.

Australia's first Victoria

On 19 February 1838, HMS *Alligator* and HMS *Britomart* set out from the Devonshire port of Plymouth. There were delays for heavy weather and stops at Tenerife, Rio, the Cape of Good Hope, the newly proclaimed state of South Australia, and Sydney. In Sydney, they took on most of the provisions needed to begin the settlement: enough food to supply 318 people for just over a year, seeds for growing tropically suited fruits and vegetables, and a number of prefabricated timber buildings, as the fees demanded by tradesmen to travel to the settlement and build on-site were deemed too expensive. There were also cows, sheep, pigs, poultry and a pack of greyhounds specially trained for use in the hunting of kangaroos.

The fleet left Sydney on 17 September 1838. With the winds against them, it was a slow trip and they didn't arrive at Port Essington until the morning of 27 October. Having weighed anchor in deep water some 400 metres (435 yards) offshore, the officers immediately ordered an exploration of the inner harbour to find a source of fresh water, the lack thereof having prevented Bremer from choosing it as a site of settlement some fourteen years before. This time Bremer's men had better luck. A spring was discovered about 800 metres (half a mile) from where the ships were moored. A schooner was then dispatched to the island of Kissa, 480 kilometres (300 miles) to the west, for fresh supplies and to advertise the fact that the settlement was open for trade.

Bores were sunk to augment the supply of fresh water and an area of long grass, where Bremer had chosen to put the buildings, was cleared by burning off. A pier was constructed to make it easier to transfer goods between ship and shore, while various sectors were designated for the livestock and the establishment of the settlement's garden. The buildings acquired in Sydney were erected: a two-room weatherboard house for the commandant; officers' quarters, and two barracks blocks for the men; kitchen, storehouse and hospital buildings; and a church provided by the Lord Bishop of New South Wales, with a 200-person capacity. By December, most of the essential work had been done. Bremer named the settlement Victoria, in honour of the new Queen.

The first months of settlement were highly promising. There were very few deaths and a visit by Bremer to the Portuguese settlement at Dili in Timor had been a diplomatic and trade success. The Bugis trepang traders were also pleased by the presence of the British, since it would lessen the local Iwaidja's attacks against them during their annual visits from the north. And to a certain extent, the Iwaidja saw the colonists as protection against the Bugis, whose trading was often combined with raiding. With the exception of the odd light-fingered moment, relations between the English and the Aborigines were fairly good. Some of the local tribespeople remembered the efforts taken to establish harmonious relations at Fort Wellington. During Victoria's early months, in fact, the only significant aberration in this most satisfactory state of affairs was the sinking of one of the ships after it hit a hidden reef.

On 27 March 1839, two French ships were spotted near the previous settlement at Raffles Bay and the rumour quickly spread that they too had been sent to establish a colony on the coast. An emissary from Victoria was sent to meet the ships, who were under the command of Captain Jules Dumont d'Urville. It turned out that they had been engaged in a peaceful scientific mission since 1837, and had taken refuge in Raffles Bay after being buffeted by a storm. Despite the French flag flying from their tent on the beach, they had no intention of forming a settlement, and the two groups of officers exchanged hospitality before the French sailed off for their next destination.

Produce flourished in the tropical climate. Cabbages and pumpkins were the most successful vegetables. Bananas, oranges, lemons and tamarinds also grew well, while of the crops, sugar cane and cotton showed some promise. Bremer noted, though, that the private gardens of McArthur's Marines were producing greater quantities of food than the public garden under the control of John Armstrong. As was commonplace in these colonies, the problem was one of snobbery. Armstrong believed that his social status should excuse him from growing such lowly vegetables as the cabbage and much preferred to spend his time collecting botanical specimens, even if it did come at the price of risking the health and viability of Victoria.

The initial success of the colony created interest in a variety of people eager to settle there, some wanting to establish trading posts, others interested in the agricultural potential.

FOLLOWING PAGES: A view of the harbour at Port Essington

One man wrote to Bremer proposing to establish a sugar cane plantation. Getting people to invest their time and energy in establishing farms demanded the granting of freehold land, however, something the British government, in restricting the initial settlement to a naval base, was unprepared to do. Given the marked superiority of the private gardens over the horticulturist's public garden—remarkable considering that the private ones were the work of off-duty Marines—Bremer became convinced that the future of Victoria lay in fast-tracking its development to a normal colony.

He visited Sydney, where he asked the governor of New South Wales, now Sir George Gipps, for the right to grant land and received an ambivalent response. The colonial government was insistent on hedging its bets and gave Bremer the authority only to grant seven-year leases of land up to 2 hectares (5 acres). As a consequence, rumour spread throughout Sydney that the northern colony was destined to be abandoned, and with freehold land cheap in settlements in less isolated parts of the Australian colonies, no one took up the offer. A major opportunity to inspire confidence in Victoria had been lost.

Bremer sailed for Victoria, but the prevailing winds in November meant that it was too difficult to pass through the Torres Strait from east to west. The alternative route, via the Great Australian Bight, became something of a long-cut. Bremer's ship sailed first to Panang, then Madras and finally to Trincomalee in Ceylon. It was there in the

north-east of modern-day Sri Lanka that he decided to stay, having been promoted to commander-in-chief of the Indian station. The powers of commandant of Victoria were vested in his deputy, Captain John McArthur, who would prove to be a consistent enthusiast for the settlement.

The winds of change

While Sir Gordon Bremer was sailing towards his new job, the wet season arrived, and on 25 November 1839, Victoria was visited by its first cyclone. It's hard to imagine the terror of the wind howling, of the sea roaring, of trees being ripped out of the ground, of sheltering in a small hut before it too was lifted by the wind and smashed, of running into the jungle in the middle of the night, dodging invisible flying objects, with no idea of whether there was shelter to be found. Out in the deep-water harbour, the stationed ship, HMS *Pelorus*, was driven onto the beach and embedded in 2.7 metres (9 feet) of mud. Eight of its crew were killed.

On land the damage was horrific. The church was blown down and most of the little cottages were demolished. At 2 am, with the barometer having dropped to 960 millibars, the wind got under the colony's administrative building and blew it off its stone piers, 3.5 metres (12 feet) into the air. Worse still, the sea rose up and flooded the entire settlement, penetrating the badly damaged storehouses and destroying much of the supplies. In the morning, the survivors discovered a swathe of land up to 13 kilometres (8 miles) wide where the cyclone had caused hundreds of trees to topple over. The gardens were devastated, and their fresh water supplies had been compromised by sea water and detritus entering and blocking the wells.

Victoria seemed to have had the bad luck to be at the epicentre of the cyclone's fury. The *Beagle* was some 435 kilometres (270 miles) away on a surveying mission and experienced only strong winds, while the French ship *Astrolabe*, under Admiral d'Urville, had been prevented from entering the Torres Strait. Neither crew could have guessed at the carnage wrought at Port Essington. Even the Aborigines were shocked, suggesting that such a destructive cyclone was by far the worst in living memory; a blessing to an extent, since it meant the colonists needn't expect another one in a hurry. Given the ferocity at its epicentre, it was surprising that more of the colonists weren't killed.

It was a serious setback for the colony. The rains had set in, making repair work difficult. And with many of the supplies destroyed and the gardens in no shape to compensate, food rationing was introduced, with staples such as bread being reduced by a third.

By the end of the wet season, things were starting to improve. The Bugis arrived to fish for trepang, with the advent of the north-western monsoon winds, while several European ships came to trade. The gardens were resuscitated and the livestock replenished. The next problem faced by the colonists, minor in comparison to the cyclone, was one that was entirely of their own making.

The skipper of HMS *Pelorus* was replaced by Captain William Chambers, formerly of the *Alligator*. In naval terms, he was the superior of McArthur, yet the latter was commandant by virtue of deputising for Bremer. Throughout 1840, the settlement became divided by one of those asinine disputes over status that frequent the records of colonial endeavour. A squabble regarding a team of oxen crossing the front lawn of Chambers' temporary residence escalated and soon led to petty-minded spats between him and McArthur regarding matters as trivial as cedar logs, twine and stone. Most crucially, their subordinates were forced to mediate between the two senior officers, the pinnacle of absurdity being reached when Chambers

> ✳ *The wreck which the forest trees still present—the effect produced on the animals and animal nature in general, bear silent and solemn testimony to the desolation and terror accompanying this destructive visitation.*
>
> Captain John McArthur, writing of matters cyclonic, more than three months after Port Essington had been devastated by a tropical hurricane

Aboriginal tribespeople at Port Essington

decided that all communication between them should be made in writing. The situation was only alleviated when the *Pelorus*, now restored to seaworthiness, sailed under Chambers on 17 March 1841, ostensibly for supplies. But the captain's true intention was to abandon the colony, and he did, leaving Victoria without a ship of its own.

Fortunately for Victoria, this silly imbroglio occurred at a time that was relatively crisis-free. The rebuilding of the settlement had largely been successful, while the public gardens were improved by the resignation of their haughty horticulturist, John Armstrong. Although rats destroyed most of a rich pumpkin crop, by the middle of 1841 the banana, pineapple and lemon plantations had started to bear fruit again, and some success was being achieved with the sugar cane and sweet potatoes. While the livestock weren't faring quite so well, the protein intake of the colonists was helped by trading clothes, bread and rice with the Iwaidja in return for oysters, crabs and fish.

Fever

In March 1843, HMS *Alligator* and HMS *North Star* arrived in the colony with supplies rendered surplus by the end of the First Opium War. The commander of the *North Star*, Captain Sir Everard Home, had been ordered to visit Victoria and compile a report on its progress.

After spending more than a month there, Home's report was extremely positive. He argued that Chinese and Malays should be allowed to settle permanently in the area, and that trade with the neighbouring islands would increase, since the islanders hankered after the British goods that were only available from Singapore. He also noted that since the establishment of Victoria, there had been no cases of piracy from the islands north of the Torres Strait, where a number of ships had been plundered in the past and their crews murdered, including the first two trading vessels dispatched from Fort Dundas,

in 1824. At the very least, Home insisted, Victoria functioned as an excellent deterrent against attacks on British shipping.

With the damage from the cyclone mostly repaired and a positive report on its way to the Admiralty, it seemed as if the future of Victoria was looking good. But no one had reckoned on an outbreak of malaria that would decimate the garrison, especially since the first four and a half years of the settlement had generally been free of serious illness.

Soon after the arrival at Port Essington of the 1000-tonne merchant vessel *Manlius*, with a metre (3 feet) of water in its hold and a third of its crew stricken with scurvy, one of the fittest and strongest Marines went down with malaria and died a few days after. By the time Captain Home departed, in April, men were falling sick in droves. From this point on, the history of Victoria, like that of so many European ventures into the tropics, would inextricably be entwined with malaria and its capacity for multiple relapses, which weakened its victims further and prevented their full recovery.

During May that year, more than a third of the Marines were on the sick list. By August, that number had grown to half, and included McArthur himself. And by the time the commandant's son, yet another John, became seriously ill, every man in the settlement bar one had caught the fever. While malaria had been associated with swamps and marshes since ancient Roman times, its cause (minuscule *Plasmodium* parasites being transmitted to the bloodstream by mosquito bite) wouldn't begin to be unravelled until the 1880s. Supplies of quinine helped alleviate some of the symptoms, but no more than that.

Within the space of a few months, Victoria went from a place of promise to one of desperation. Of the non-commissioned Marines, around half were off duty at any given time due to illness. McArthur built a convalescent post on a bluff overlooking the ocean, where his idea of giving the men fresh sea air happened to also keep them away from the source of further infection, mosquitoes being no great fans of the wind.

The consequences for the settlement were disastrous: building work stopped, the livestock went untended and the gardens were overrun by weeds. If land had been granted to private citizens earlier, notably to Malays and Chinese, who likely had developed greater immunity to malaria than the British, perhaps things wouldn't have been so bad. In addition, with Chambers' abandonment on the *Pelorus*, the colonists were forced to rely on visiting ships, the crews of which viewed this outpost of illness with some trepidation. Orders were issued in Sydney to relieve the sick Marines, but the requisite ship was slow to arrive, while others carrying vital medical supplies were delayed due to damage sustained while navigating to Port Essington.

Somewhat paradoxically, Governor Gipps had only recently received a letter from the Colonial Office awarding him the discretionary power to grant freehold land in Victoria. As encouraging as this might

have been, now was hardly the time to be marketing the settlement's prospects. Any slight hope was further dampened by the British government's decision that, despite Home's positive report, it didn't consider Victoria worthy of further development as a trading centre on the Singapore model. Although the status quo was to be maintained, this announcement was tantamount to an expression of a lack of confidence in the settlement. It certainly served as a major disincentive for Europeans, Malays and Chinese alike to gamble their wealth and wellbeing on a place that, like its predecessors, could one day just vanish into thin air.

Fresh hands and short-stay guests

The long-suffering garrison of Royal Marines was finally relieved in December 1844, with the arrival of HMS *Cadet*. Of all the original settlers, only Captain McArthur remained. For a while, things began to look up again. Fresh hands refurbished the buildings that they were to live in, and the lassitude caused by the illness and the long sojourn of the previous cohort was rectified. Only temporarily, however.

Before long, some of the new Marines began to fall ill also. As for the healthy ones, McArthur observed them going about their work with a definite sullenness. When questioned about this, the men replied that they'd been led to believe they were going to a penal colony, and had arrived at Port

Essington with the expectation that convicts would be doing the heavy manual labour. Finding that such dirty work, amid the heat and humidity, was down to them, with not even Chinese or Malays available to be hired as labourers, the Marines felt they'd been conned. And they most likely had been.

Not everyone was disgruntled to be at Victoria, however. On 17 December 1845, explorer Ludwig Leichhardt emerged from the scrub after travelling for more than eighteen months and over 4800 kilometres (3000 miles) overland from Moreton Bay, near Brisbane. Having been given up for dead, Leichhardt and his men were arguably the happiest people ever to see Port Essington. Their presence certainly added extra cheer to the Christmas celebrations that year.

Another visitor was a Catholic priest, who started a mission with a view to converting the local Iwaidja. These arrivals were the exception more than the rule, however. The tentative status afforded Victoria by the government, and the attendant rumours, continued to dissuade either European or Asian civilians from making it their home. Every year, McArthur hoped that some of the Bugis traders would settle there, tempted by the lease of cheap land on whose produce they didn't have to pay taxes as they did under the Dutch. Every year, they promised to settle, but when they blew down on the annual north-west monsoon winds, they stayed for the trepang and turtles and then went home. One of the reasons for this was that the Dutch, having got wind of the

British invitation, had lessened the duties they charged.

Another reversal of governmental opinion occurred on 17 February 1846, when it was announced that a new colony called North Australia had been excised from the vast territory under the control of New South Wales. The primary reason was the British government's desperate need to find a new place to which it could transport convicts. Transportation to the colony of New South Wales had been abolished in 1840, while South Australia had refused to be a penal colony on its founding in 1836. Only Van

Portrait of the German explorer Frederick Wilhelm Ludwig Leichhardt

Diemen's Land (modern-day Tasmania) and Norfolk Island were accepting convicts, and both were becoming overburdened.

William Gladstone, then Secretary of State for War and the Colonies, advocated that a party of convicts be sent to Port Essington

> ✳ On the Vollir [river], we came on a cart road which wound round the foot of a high hill, and having passed the garden, with its fine Coca-nut palms, the white houses, and a row of snug thatched cottages burst suddenly upon us; the house of the Commandant being to the right and separate from the rest. We were most kindly received by Captain Macarthur, the Commandant of Port Essington and by the other officers, who, with the greatest kindness and attention, supplied us with everything we wanted. I was deeply affected in finding myself again in civilised society, and could scarcely speak, the words growing big with tears and emotion; and, even now when considering with what small means the Almighty had enabled me to perform such a long journey, my heart fills in grateful knowledge of his infinite kindness.
>
> Ludwig Leichhardt, on his arrival at Port Essington after an amazing odyssey through northern Australia

in order to ascertain if it was a suitable destination for transportees. At the same time, however, the First Lord of the Admiralty was requesting that the Marines at Victoria be withdrawn, as it was not standard procedure to place corpsmen in permanent garrisons in either Asia or Australia. Once again the shilly-shallying of the government prevented the colony from being given a sense of its future. McArthur himself was unsure whether a colony situated in the vicinity of Cape York, on the far side of the Gulf of Carpentaria, might not be more useful, both as a trading centre and as a point from which to send out rescue teams to the frequent shipwrecks on the Great Barrier Reef.

Catch-22

The dry season of 1847 was particularly cold for the region, and while the British breathed a sigh of relief, the Iwaidja, with whom the settlers remained on fairly good terms, were afflicted by influenza and died in droves. As usual, the Bugis came and failed to settle. It was a catch-22 situation: without growth in the settlement, there wasn't enough trading potential for the fishermen to maintain a permanent base, yet without some of them settling, there was little chance of the colony escaping its temporary character as a military camp. In December 1847, as if reading this stalemate from afar, the proclamation of North Australia as a colony was rescinded.

When Earl Grey replaced Gladstone as Colonial Secretary, the writing was on the wall for Victoria. Grey managed to convince Van Diemen's Land to continue accepting convicts, while plans were afoot to begin transportation to Swan River, in what would become Western Australia. Port Essington, however, was deemed unsuitable, due to its climate and the fact that it presented too many opportunities for escape.

The settlement itself, with the prevalence of malaria, had become a listless and tawdry place. The naturalist Thomas Huxley visited Victoria in 1849 and famously described it as 'the most wretched, the climate the most unhealthy, the human beings the most uncomfortable and houses in a condition most decayed and rotten'. By that time, the decision had finally been made to close the settlement down.

When the India and Australia Steam Packet Company informed the government that Port Essington was a long way from the route it proposed to take to Australia, so ruling out the possibility of any settlement there continuing as a coaling station, that was it. On 13 November, HMS *Meander* was sighted approaching the colony. The warship carried the orders for Victoria to be abandoned, and seventeen days later it was.

Port Essington was never settled again, although northern Australia finally received its first permanent settlement with the establishment of Palmerston (now Darwin) in 1869 to the south-west. The ruins of Victoria now reside in Garig Gunak Barlu National Park and are visible to those visitors who manage to overcome its inaccessibility.

CHAPTER 20

 # The post-Civil War Confederate colonies, Mexico (1865–67)

In early 1865, with the war for the American South almost lost, many
of the Confederate top brass were considering where they could take
their tattered way of life. While a large number of them decided
to capitulate and hold on to their plantations, or head west, where
there was land without the law, for some the answer lay further south.
A number of Confederate colonies were established in Brazil. Others
chose to build their new lives somewhat nearer to the old, in Mexico.
They were supported by Emperor Maximilian I, a liberal who had
been offered the throne by Mexican monarchists, with the support
of Louis Napoleon's French army. Around half-a-dozen colonies
were founded, but homesickness, high land prices and the ordeal
of agriculture without slaves disheartened many. The Confederate
settlers were eventually undone by Mexico's shifting political
circumstances, the downfall of Maximilian and the ruthlessness
of the Juaristas.

236

When the leaders of the Confederate Army began to think the unthinkable in early 1865, a number of them hoped to be able to continue their military careers by offering to join Mexican Emperor Maximilian, who had been installed on the throne in April 1864 by an alliance of European investors and Mexican monarchists. Maximilian was dependent on the French army to defend his regime against the Juaristas, as the forces of ousted Republican leader, Benito Juarez, were known. General E. Kirby Smith, commander of the Confederate Trans-Mississippi Department, for one, offered to provide 10,000 men to Maximilian, particularly to defend himself against any incursion from Union forces, who supported the Juaristas.

On 13 May, a month after General Robert E. Lee's surrender at Appomattox, Virginia, a group of Confederate leaders met at the house of former Texan senator Louis T. Wigfall and resolved to marshal their troops in the direction of Mexico. They approached General Smith to lead the expedition, but he wasn't going to leave the battle until Jefferson Davis, the President of the Confederate States, gave the final order to disband the troops. Their second choice, General Simon Buckner, also declined, because Smith was yet to release him from his duties. While these generals waited for the official end to the war, most of the rank and file decided with their feet, and left the Confederate encampments before being formally discharged. As a consequence, the forces that marched to Mexico would never remotely match Smith's promise.

On 1 June 1865, Missourian general Joseph O. Shelby assembled a troop of 300 men at Pittsburg in north-eastern Texas and set a course for the Rio Grande, the river marking the border with Mexico. Shelby, also known as Fighting Joe Shelby, was the leader of the famous Iron Brigade, which had enjoyed a daring and successful 2500 kilometre (1500 mile) cavalry raid that inflicted more than 1000 casualties on the Union forces in the trans-Mississippi theatre. Born in Kentucky, Shelby had moved to Missouri as a young man, where he had been a steamboat captain and hemp plantation owner before the war.

The Confederate force travelled through Corsicana to Austin, in central Texas, where they picked up further troops and Southern luminaries such as the governor of Texas, the tubercular Pendleton Murrah. Arriving in San Antonio after a two-week march, Shelby's troop was further augmented with governors Henry Allen and Thomas Reynolds, from Louisiana and Missouri, respectively, as well two former governors, Thomas Moore and Edward Clark. The star-studded cast was rounded out by a number of other Confederate generals. In violation of the surrender agreement, they took with them all the arms, ammunition and rations they could carry. Most of the force then crossed the Rio Grande at Eagle Pass and Piedras Negras, points strategically chosen to avoid being engaged by Federal patrols.

Reaching Mexico fully armed, Shelby and his troops, now numbering around 1000, encountered 5000 Imperialist Mexican and French soldiers in the vicinity of Monterrey, just south of Piedras Negras. Their commander, General Jeanningros, refused to let them join the Mexican Army there and then, but he did allow them to continue their march towards Mexico City.

The further south the Confederates travelled, the smaller their force became. Men such as Pendleton Murrah died of their ailments. It had been a long, hard war and the casualty rates were phenomenally high for a conflict of the time. Faced with a long march through hot and dusty northern Mexico, often without food or adequate water, many of Shelby's former soldiers decided to cut their losses, thinking they would be better off taking their chances in familiar territory, in what was now the United States of America. After all, they had fought bravely and it was likely that only their leaders would be held to account for decisions made before and during the war. Others were killed by bandits or the Juaristas, or peeled off towards the coast to try their luck in other climes.

When Shelby's group reached the mining town of San Luis Potosí, in the centre of the country, around mid August, they encountered General Felix Douay, the commander of the French army in Mexico. When questioned as to their reason for being in Mexico, Shelby answered that he and his men had come to join the Imperialist forces, and that if his offer was accepted, he could supply up to 50,000 men. Faced with passionate opposition from the Juaristas as well as the threat of an invasion by the United States Army, Douay was elated and forwarded the offer to his superior, Marshall Bazaine in Mexico City. Shelby was soon invited to the capital to discuss the issue.

The talks in Mexico City played out somewhat differently from how the Missourian general had expected. It must have been clear to the Imperialist hierarchy that Shelby's claims were something of an exaggeration, and besides, Emperor Maximilian was loath to incorporate his men directly into his army, because it would jeopardise the chances of reaching an early peace with the United States. General Philip Sheridan, for instance, whose job it was to enforce the peace in Texas, was wary of the Confederate rump heading into Mexico and its potential for a rearguard action. So instead of a chance for military redemption, the Confederates under Shelby were offered the chance to colonise tracts of Mexico.

A man with a plan

The main mover behind this scheme was Matthew Maury, an agent for the Confederate Navy, who had been en route from England to Virginia when he heard of the loss of the war. Maury had decided that Virginia was no longer safe for him. In his pre-war career as an internationally famous oceanographer (he is considered by many as the father of modern oceanography and naval meteorology) Maury had made the acquaintance of King Leopold of Belgium, whose daughter Charlotte was

Maximilian's wife. When the Civil War appeared lost to the Confederacy, he headed to Mexico, where he was received generously and appointed Imperial Commissioner of Colonisation, just as Shelby and his entourage arrived in Mexico City.

While the Confederate brass were not incorporated into the Mexican army as active officers, some of them were given ranks and salaries. Henry Allen, the Louisianan governor, was given a grant by Maximilian to start an English-language newspaper, the *Mexican Times*, whose purpose was in part to encourage American immigrants. The first issue was published in September.

With the support of the Mexican government, Commissioner Maury employed immigration agents in Virginia, Texas, the Carolinas, California, Louisiana, Alabama and Missouri. These initial appointments were soon followed by a number in Union strongholds, such as New York City, Boston, Philadelphia and Chicago. Meanwhile, the former Confederate officers were employed in Mexico to reconnoitre for the best places to establish the colonies. Parties set out for Durango, Mazatlán and Guadalajara, in the west of the country; Monterrey, up north; and the eastern towns of Orizaba, Córdoba and Vera Cruz.

On their return, Maury determined to form a number of agricultural colonies with a secondary military purpose along the planned railroad line from Mexico City out to the east coast at Vera Cruz. This was a model that strongly resembled the United States, where property development was closely entwined with the growth of the railroad, so much so that railways were often built for the purpose of realising a profit from the subsequent rise in property prices.

Maury's grand dreams for the colony could not be realised, however, without considerable emigration of the Confederates who remained in the United States. He embarked on an American publicity campaign that rather exaggerated the virtues of the new terrain. 'In some places', he wrote, 'it crowns the labor of the husbandman regularly with two, and in others with three harvests annually; and in each, one gathers one hundred, two hundred, sometimes three hundred and occasionally four hundred fold'.

Like all great salesmen, Maury had already sold the dream to himself, even if his wife remained in the United States, apparently sceptical. In November 1865, he wrote to her, insisting that colonisation was 'a fact, not a chimera'. He continued: 'By the time these lands are paid for [in five years] they will be worth, even if no more settlers come to the Empire, $20, $30, or even $100 the acre, because they produce everything under the sun, and yield perpetual harvests'. With the assistance of the glowing reports in the *Mexican Times* the propaganda machine to attract Confederate exiles was in full swing.

Sweet home Mexicana

The first and most substantial of the Confederate colonies was Carlota, named after the Empress of Mexico, and located some 115 kilometres (70 miles) west of Vera Cruz and 15 kilometres (9 miles) east. Around 200,000 hectares (500,000 acres) of land in the vicinity had been appropriated from the church during the previous incumbency of Juárez, land which, on his becoming emperor, Maximilian had then annexed for himself. At the centre of this holding was a former village, with a square shaded by a grove of mangoes and, crucially, a well offering good-quality water.

Under the scheme concocted by Maury and agreed to by the Emperor, land from this parcel was offered to ex-Confederate soldiers at $1 per acre on five years' credit, as many of the men under Shelby's command had blown most of their capital on gambling, drink and women during their enforced hiatus in Mexico City. Married men were permitted to purchase a plot of 260 hectares (640 acres), while single men were allotted half this area.

Each person who bought a tract of land was also given a block in the town of Carlota. Other colonies in the vicinity, such as Omealco, followed a similar pattern. In acknowledgment of his service, Maximilian granted General Shelby a fully kitted-out hacienda with whitewashed walls and terracotta tiled roof, which had been expropriated from exiled politician Antonio López de Santa Anna. It was 3.2 kilometres (2 miles) out of Córdoba, whose hotel became a major meeting point for the American expats.

According to Maury's publicity material, Mexico's climate made 'existence itself an enjoyment'; it was a place where 'the vegetable kingdom displays its wealth and its powers most gorgeously, and with the utmost vigor and concentration'. He went on to list cotton, corn, olives, grapes, tobacco, coffee, sugar cane, cocoa, rice, indigo, cochineal, rubber and henequen (a tequila agave-related plant whose leaves were used for making rope and twine) as crops that could be fruitfully grown in the Córdoba region. If the material was to be believed, the settlers at Carlota could expect a paradise.

To help exploit the agricultural potential of Mexico, Maury had proposed the importation of African slaves. But this did not happen, and when the settlers took up their allotments, they either did the work themselves, or hired Mexican labour to do it for them. Unsurprisingly, they found the work more arduous than they might have expected. The Carlota district, a good way inland from the Caribbean Sea and at 600 metres (2000 feet) above sea level, was on the wet side of the Sierra Madre Oriental. The climate was hot and wet, although not unusually hot for those from the Deep South.

And while the land was fertile, much of it was effectively jungle. In order to make the land arable for the staple crops they were used to, the Americans had to clear tracts of jungle that included dense thickets of bamboo, bananas and hibiscus. When it rained, the red earth turned to a thick and difficult mud.

Portrait of Confederate officers in Mexico, including Sterling Price

The plant that seemed to best respond to the environment was coffee. However, coffee takes three years of growing before it can be commercially harvested and the colonists needed to survive in the interim. Perhaps unsurprisingly, given the circumstances under which they had been formed, the colonies tended to look like army camps rather than actual towns. Most of the dwellings consisted of tents, and while a number of houses were constructed and a number of haciendas taken over, the accommodation was a long way short of the grand plantation houses of the ante-bellum south. Although Carlota was the main settlement, the main meeting place for the colonists was the hotel in nearby Córdoba, where men and women went to conduct business and mimic the society they had left behind.

The previous inhabitants of the haciendas whose ruins the Southerners inhabited had planted crops of mangoes, pineapples and papayas, as well as oranges, figs and bananas. The colonists also grew foodstuffs such as corn, beans and sweet potato, while sugar cane was grown to produce a rum that substituted for the bourbon whisky they had left behind.

Two worlds colliding

The occupation by the ex-Confederates of expropriated land wasn't particularly popular with the locals. Although Maximilian was trying to improve the lot of the Mexican poor and thus win their support as their leader, it was largely a futile quest, given the popularity of Juárez, Mexico's first non-European, non-military leader. While Maximilian wanted to win over the population by being an enlightened despot, he was increasingly forced to rely on his imported French army to keep himself on the throne. Although he had resisted admitting the Americans into his army directly, one of his key reasons for supporting Commissioner Maury's colonisation scheme was that the fortified Confederate villages would provide a means for Maximilian to subdue both the Juaristas and the bandits on the crucial route between Mexico City and the port of Vera Cruz. When the railway was completed, Maximilian imagined that the ex-Confederates would defend it, since it would raise the value of their investment and provide the means for them to ship their goods to market. An added advantage was that Maximilian could subdue antagonistic forces in a key part of the country without being directly responsible, and without having to rely on the largesse of Louis Napoleon.

While the Confederates got good land at reasonable prices, they also earned the enmity of both the Mexicans and the Juaristas. By being so closely identified with Maximilian, their fate was effectively contingent upon the continuation of his tenure. Given that the former owners of the Confederate farms often still resided in close proximity, the relationship between the Americans and the locals was tense. In one instance, Shelby planted 5 hectares (12 acres) of coffee; but after a trip away to visit friends, he returned to find that the crop had been pillaged by bandits. In order to safeguard the remaining crops, he started to pay the leader of the bandits protection money, a practice that spread throughout the colonies.

Relations between the Mexicans and the Confederates were also not helped by the employment of locals on the Americans' farms. While Mexico was a hierarchical society with a peasant class, the Southerners were used to slave labour. The attitude they tended to take towards their workers, combined with the inevitable language difficulties and nationalistic resentment of the interlopers, meant that employer–employee relations were less than ideal. On one occasion, a Confederate farmer rounded up his Mexican workforce at gunpoint and forced them to pick a crop after they'd earlier walked off the job.

Shelby supplemented his agricultural income by running a transportation business between Vera Cruz and Mexico City, and earned most of his money through contracts with the French Army. He was strongly identified with Maximilian's forces, and his men often had to fight off bandits who attacked his wagon convoys for political reasons as well as theft.

The dream unravelling

When Maury envisaged the Confederate colonies, he imagined an idyllic plantation life that was apparently lost to the South. This never eventuated. The main farm in Carlota was owned by former Missouri politician and general Sterling Price, who had also fought in the Mexican–American War of 1846–48. Far from a grand Southern house, Price's abode was comprised of a bamboo and adobe cottage, protected from bandits by a high adobe wall with jagged glass implanted on the top. Many of the settlements around him were sadder still, and a visiting New York *Herald* correspondent in 1866 described Carlota as 'a few tents scattered here and there, and at about five hundred yards a cluster of about a dozen unfinished houses'.

The fertility of the land was not in question, and under different circumstances it's very likely that Carlota and the other Confederate colonies could have been a success. But by the time the political situation turned against them, the colonies weren't sufficiently developed to overcome local animosity.

One of the problems was that the land rapidly became too expensive, largely due to property speculation. While the rate set by Maximilian was fair, once the land had been traded several times over, it became more expensive than comparable land in America. This was compounded by the difficulty in getting to Mexico. The United States Army was actively patrolling the border between Mexico and Texas, which made it difficult for former soldiers (especially armed ones) to make it through. Most of the colonists who arrived after Shelby and his men did so by ship: travelling from the United States to Havana and then to Vera Cruz. But it was

A newly constructed railway station in the Mexican countryside, late 1860s

an expensive exercise, particularly after four years of war and when travelling with all of one's worldly possessions.

Shifting sands

Hostility from the locals, the unsuitability of the land, delays on the Mexico City–Vera Cruz railway—only 215 of the 425 kilometres/134 of the 264 miles—were built by the time Maximilian was overthrown), the lack of African slave labour, and difficulties in attracting further Confederate exiles from the US—all these factors worked to stop Matthew Maury's grand plan from ever coming to fruition. But the real reason for the decline of Carlota and the other colonies was the shifting political situation.

President Lincoln and his government had long supported the Mexican Republic under Benito Juárez, but had been unable to continue support during the Civil War. Since mid 1865, however, they had been supplying arms to the Juaristas, who then won a number of battles against Maximilian's forces. On 12 February 1866, the United States upped the ante by posting 50,000 troops along the Rio Grande under General Sheridan, who threatened hostile engagement with the Imperial forces. He also demanded the withdrawal of the French troops from Mexico and established a naval blockade to prevent reinforcements from landing.

MAXIMILIAN OF MEXICO

As a liberal-minded emperor fighting against the liberal Republicans in Mexico, Maximilian von Habsburg found himself in an awkward position. Born into the noble House of Habsburg, his official father was Archduke Franz Karl of Austria, and he was the younger brother of Franz Joseph, Emperor of Austria and King of Hungary. However, there were strong rumours that he was the bastard son of an illicit union between the Princess of Bavaria, Franz Karl's wife, and Napoleon II (son of Napoleon Bonaparte).

As a youngster, Maximilian was interested in the arts and botany, yet he chose the navy as a career. Distinguished service in the first Italian War of Independence saw his brother reward him by appointing him Viceroy of Lombardy–Venetia in February 1857. Soon after this, he married Princess Charlotte, daughter of King Leopold of Belgium. Charlotte would become Carlota, Empress of Mexico, and an active supporter of the Confederate colonists, who named their most promising colony in her honour.

Maximilian was a creature of the European Enlightenment and not unsympathetic to the socialist currents of the time. As ruler of Lombardy–Venetia, he was able and rather liberal—so much so that his conservative brother sacked him after less than two years in the job. Soon after this sacking, Austria lost most of its Italian possessions.

When President Benito Juárez, a Zapotec Indian of great talent, suspended the repayment of foreign debt in 1861, Spain, Britain and France collectively seized the Customs House in Vera Cruz. The former two countries soon withdrew their troops, but Louis Napoleon determined on a full invasion of Mexico while the United States was too busy fighting its Civil War to react. Part of French Emperor Louis Napoleon's plan was to install an amenable government to replace that of Juárez. Maximilian was approached by members of the Mexican aristocracy, keen to sound him out about becoming the country's first emperor. He refused the offer, in favour of a botanical expedition to the Brazilian jungle. In 1863, however, he was presented with the result of a plebiscite indicating that the Mexicans would happily accept the installation of an emperor, and he accepted the re-offered job on this basis.

Maximilian seems to have been a decent if somewhat naïve man. He was shocked to discover when he arrived in Mexico that the plebiscite had been dodgy, and that the forces of Benito Juárez and much of the country actively opposed his reign. Emperor Maximilian set about trying to win over the hearts of the people by building infrastructure, expanding the voting franchise, reforming land ownership and improving the lot of the poor. In doing so, he offended many of his original backers, but it wasn't enough to gain the support of the people. Without the military sanction of the French Army, he wouldn't be able to hold on to his throne.

Emperor Maximilian

When Louis Napoleon withdrew his troops in 1866, the writing was on the wall for the Emperor. Maximilian was advised to abandon Mexico, but the place had gotten under his skin and aroused his sense of noblesse oblige. As the Juaristas, supported by the United States and most of the population, gained control of the country, Maximilian withdrew to Santiago de Querétaro, where he was captured following a three-week siege on 15 May 1867. He was court-martialled and sentenced to death by Juárez. Many influential Europeans, monarchs as well as liberals such as Italy's great freedom fighter Giuseppe Garibaldi, pleaded with Juárez for clemency on Maximilian's behalf. But Juárez was sick of Europeans meddling in the affairs of his country and was determined to set an example. On 19 June, Maximilian and his two closest generals were executed by a seven-man firing squad, an act that also sealed the demise of the Confederate colonies of Mexico.

At home, Louis Napoleon had problems of his own, in the form of the rising power of Germany under Chancellor Otto von Bismarck, which would lead to the French Emperor's disastrous defeat in the Franco–Prussian War of 1870–71. Suddenly, Mexico was a faraway problem he couldn't afford. As of 31 May 1866, he ordered the withdrawal of French troops. With this act, both Maximilian and the Confederate colonies were doomed.

Between May that year and the following February, the Juaristas regained control of Mexico. On 15 May 1866, the Confederate colony of Omealco, 50 kilometres (30 miles) from Córdoba, was attacked by Juaristas and destroyed. Its captured inhabitants were forced to walk for miles, until they were eventually released in Vera Cruz. Smaller attacks on the other colonies began to increase. With the French gone, there was no one left to defend them. Maximilian himself fled to Querétaro, in central Mexico, where he was captured after a siege in May 1867.

As it became clear that they had picked the wrong side in the battle for Mexico, and were unwelcome by the new government, the settlers of Carlota and the surrounding colonies began to drift back to the United States. In cases such as Tuxpan (another Shelby venture, in the north-east of Mexico), the dissolution was aided by local hostility, with the colonists being forced to flee after a series of skirmishes with Toluca Indians had culminated in a fully fledged assault. By the time that Maximilian was executed, in June 1867, only two families of former Confederates remained in the Córdoba region, along with a number of men whose fortunes prevented them from leaving.

General Sterling Price returned to Missouri a bitter man and died of cholera soon after. Shelby returned to Missouri, too, where he resumed farming. In 1893, he became a US Marshall, a post that he held until his death in February 1897, long after the dream of a Mexican Dixie was dead. Maury returned to Virginia and became Physics Professor at the Virginia Military Institute. He helped launch the American Association for the Advancement of Science, and travelled widely promoting the new science of meteorology. He died in Lexington, Kentucky, in 1873. Benito Juárez, meanwhile, is remembered today as Mexico's greatest national hero.

CHAPTER 21

The racially pure colony of Nueva Germania, Paraguay (1886–93)

Inspired by racist beliefs and the romantic notion of the German *Volk*, anti-Semite schoolteacher Bernhard Förster set off to South America with his wife, Elisabeth, and a small group of fellow travellers to establish an Aryan paradise. Unfortunately for this motley crew, the wild animals, insects and microbes of the Paraguayan jungle weren't aware of the new arrivals' racial superiority and it didn't take long for the colony to founder. Faced with the rising disgruntlement of his ill-adapted settlers, Förster retreated into booze and self-pity, leaving his Elisabeth to run the show. After her husband died from a self-administered overdose in a San Bernardino hotel room, Elisabeth returned to Germany to look after her mad brother, the philosopher Friedrich Nietzsche, while some of her poorer colonists were stuck in Nueva Germania, condemned to generations of subsistence farming in a place they didn't want to be.

Compared to England, Germany came relatively late to industrialisation. The process by which the countryside was abandoned en masse for the factories of the cities didn't fully kick off there until the middle years of the nineteenth century. Its arrival was connected with the 1871 unification of Germany under Otto von Bismarck, whereby twenty-six member states, from the kingdoms of Bavaria, Prussia, Saxony and Württemberg to various duchies and minor principalities, were joined to form a nation that was largely controlled by imperially minded Prussia.

The upheaval and exploitation of this era gave rise to a number of German thinkers with alternative philosophies. On one hand, Karl Marx and Friedrich Engels, the founders of communism, imagined a workers' paradise driven by industrialisation, set in the future, at the end of an economic tale they projected onto their particular interpretation of history.

> ✳ *Enthusiasm for the fight—since every German is a fighter, he only feels great in the heat of the battle— enthusiasm for thinking and meditation and finally enthusiasm for singing.*
> *The true German is a fighter, a thinker and a poet.*
>
> Bernhard Förster on the essence of the German character

Others held that industrialisation itself and the increasingly metropolitan nature of society was a corruption of humanity. The cure, this latter group believed, lay in a geographical removal from the scene of the degradation, and the re-establishment of society with an emphasis on the organic community of *Volk* (whose meaning is roughly synonymous with the English word 'folk'), thus reversing the shift from an agrarian, village-based society to an industrial one. One man who adhered to the latter philosophy was Bernhard Förster, an anti-modernist academic from Saxony, a German state in the east of the newly unified nation.

Part of the reason for Förster's and others' nostalgic vision was related to the disappointment that many nationalists felt regarding the German nation's failure to live up to expectations. It hadn't taken long for the euphoria of unification to wear off, and many soon came to believe that it hadn't served the German people well. Scapegoats were looked for, and as is often the case in European history, people began to blame the Jews.

Förster, who was born in 1843 and had fought in the Austro–Prussian War while still a student, was teaching in a Berlin high school when he launched his career as a political reactionary. His rise to prominence at the ratbag end of the political spectrum was swift. He founded the Deutscher Volksverein (German People's League) in 1881, one of a series of political parties that were the forebears of Adolf Hitler's National Socialists and shared their anti-Semitic platform. As the leader of the Deutscher Volksverein, Förster organised anti-Semitic rallies and congresses. The pinnacle of his dubious achievements came with the submission to Chancellor Bismarck in 1881 of an anti-Semitic petition signed by more than 250,000 people. Its requests included the limitation of Jewish immigration to Germany and the exclusion of Jews from holding senior positions in government employment. Bismarck was not interested in pandering to anti-Semitism, however. Having lost its galvanising moment, the movement soon disintegrated under the weight of infighting and personal conflict, a fact that didn't bode well for their leader's future plans.

The germ of an idea

By the end of 1881, plans were already in train for the settlement of what would become Nueva Germania. Förster's inspiration came from the publication that year of Richard Wagner's *Regenerationschriften*, in which the famously anti-Semitic composer argued that the true German *Volk* could be regained by selective emigration to the underdeveloped but fertile regions of South America. A keen acolyte of Wagner's, Förster was soon mixing in circles that included the Nietzsche family.

In 1885, Förster married Elisabeth, the sister of philosopher Friedrich Nietzsche. If anything, his wife's politics were more right-wing than his own. Elisabeth's brother and mother disapproved of her relationship with

A portrait of Elisabeth Förster-Nietzsche, 1882, just before she met Bernhard

Förster, on account of both his personality and his anti-Semitic politics. Although Friedrich Nietzsche's notion of the *Übermensch* (Superman) would later be manipulated to fit the Nazi advocacy of Aryan supremacy, his ultra-elitism was actually racially indifferent. Nietzsche's terms of superiority were artistic and philosophical, and he considered himself an anti-anti-Semite. A strong and influential friendship with Richard and Cosima Wagner had fallen apart partly because of Nietzsche's refusal to buy into their politics. He considered his sister's marriage to Förster as a schism between them and described her at one point as a 'vengeful anti-Semitic goose'.

The failure of his petition to Bismarck had increased Förster's disillusionment with the prospects for achieving his ideals in Germany. He took up Wagner's idea with gusto, and from 1882 he undertook out a series of lecture tours to publicise and raise funding for the endeavour. In 1883, he travelled to South America on a reconnaissance mission, during which he visited Paraguay, a former Spanish territory in the centre of the continent, landlocked by Bolivia, Brazil and Argentina. There he met with President Bernardino Caballero to discuss the details of his upcoming venture. In 1885 he returned home and set about trying to attract other settlers, publishing reams of propaganda about the potential of Paraguay and how a new Germany could be built from scratch.

The settlement he proposed was unlikely to appeal to most people. Essentially it was a small-scale prototype of a fascist society that also owed a debt to ancient Greece. Förster envisaged a strictly hierarchical community organised on military lines, similar to Sparta, and in many ways a precursor to Nazi Germany, but with elements of European feudal society, such as the guild system, included. Within it, sexual relations were to be strictly patriarchal; decadent behaviour was to be frowned on, and individual freedoms subordinated to the perceived needs of the group. In order to purify the new race of Germans, there would be compulsory calisthenics and vegetarianism, in an alcohol-free environment. Unsurprisingly, Förster had trouble raising money and finding subscribers for his venture.

Another new Germany

When he and Elisabeth set sail in February 1886 from Hamburg, only five families accompanied them. And despite Förster's four-year campaign to publicise the venture, only fourteen families ever showed up. When they arrived in Paraguay, they were granted around 20,000 hectares (50,000 acres) some 350 kilometres (200 miles) to the north-east of Asunción, in what is now the San Pedro administrative area. In contrast to the land granted to William Lane and the colonists at New Australia and Cosme (see page 271), which had a natural combination of pasture and forest, Nueva Germania was almost entirely forested. To get there, the settlers had to make a 24-hour canoe trip up the Aguaray River, the alternative being a long horse ride through thick jungle.

Soon enough, the folly of the endeavour became apparent. To begin with, Förster had drastically overestimated the fertility of the land. Just because jungle is thick, it does not necessarily follow that the land, once cleared, will be suitable for growing crops or grazing animals. Often, it is the density of the forest and the constant cycle of decay and regeneration of plant life under the canopy that makes for such lush environs. Once the trees were chopped down at Nueva Germania, the land, its ecosystem unbalanced, quickly lost its fertility. And given their vegetarianism, the would-be settlers were technically unable to supplement their diets through hunting and fishing.

While the Germans attempted to purify themselves on their vegetable diets, this wasn't reciprocated by the local animal population. Situated beside the Aguaray River, Nueva Germania was a haven for mosquitoes, flies and gnats, the latter of which had a particularly painful bite. The place was also rife with ants, snakes and spiders.

Before too long, the colonists abandoned vegetarianism out of necessity and began to supplement their diets with wild boar, venison, birds, monkeys and agoutis, a relative of the guinea pig. Some of the settlers found this quite distasteful. One wrote that he did not like shooting monkeys because 'the animal with the bullet in its fur looks at one so painfully pleading. After it has been skinned it resembles a small child'. Eating meat also eroded the utopian conviction that had motivated them to move there in the first place.

The main crops they planted were manioc, corn, beans and oranges. In his desperation to establish the colony, however, Förster had taken pretty much anyone who wanted to come. Many of his fellow nostalgics for the old agrarian ways were city dwellers, particularly from the industrial region of Saxony—a hotbed of radicals both left and right, no doubt because the brown coal mines and the heavily polluting industry powered by them created an environment of modernity easy to dislike. Förster's minions included cobblers, schoolteachers and a variety of other trades, but unfortunately for the colony's future very few farmers.

In the early years, the colonists were far from self-sufficient and had to trade with the local Paraguayans (whom they detested as inferior) in order to survive. The nearest market to the settlement was a difficult day's ride away. More importantly, the hierarchy of Nueva Germania was disturbed by the fact that those colonists who had means were able to enjoy a better standard of living than those who didn't. This eroded the primacy of the group.

Some of the better-off colonists were not only able to buy extra food at market, but they were also able to hire Paraguayans, and even some of their fellow settlers, to help farm the plots of land that Förster had sold to them. And on this last point, their leader contributed to the problem, since the land wouldn't legally be granted by the Paraguyan government until 140 families had settled there—Förster's property deals with his compatriots were fraudulent. While he and Elisabeth used the money from the sale of the land to build themselves a nice house, many of the Germans went into debt, often to their fellow colonists, merely in order to live.

With this lapse into financial inequity, Nueva Germania quickly abandoned its utopian ideals. The practical problem of survival put the settlers under pressure— and above all Nueva Germania was not in a good spot. In addition to the issues of clearing the jungle and access to markets, there were difficulties establishing a reliable water supply, and many of the colonists got sick from drinking bad water. Others died from tetanus, while tropical ulcers were also a problem.

The colony was perpetually in danger of falling apart, a consequence not only of its ill-suitedness but also of the wacky spatial organisation Förster had put in place. Based on descriptions of the ancient German village by the Roman historian Tacitus, Förster had spaced out the houses so that each family lived in effective isolation, only occasionally alleviated by social events. The isolation placed great mental strain on the colonists. When there were festivals to celebrate German holidays and the like, the no-alcohol clause was ignored and the men behaved like sailors stuck for a long time at sea—furiously consuming *cana*, the local rum, with the day more often than not ending in a fight.

The burden of leadership

As the inequity between the colonists increased in an environment of collective scarcity, pressure naturally came to bear on its leadership. Förster, who could quote reams of the classics, but who knew nothing about farming, simply wasn't up to the task. When faced with dissension in the ranks, the former schoolteacher retreated into a sulk. He was also prone to abandoning the colony for large chunks of time. Despite the avowed patriarchal structure proposed for Nueva Germania, for most of its existence the effective ruler of the colony was Elisabeth. She knew as little about farming as her husband, but was at least made of sterner stuff and became known, with Teutonic sentimentality, as 'the Mother of the Colony'.

By mid April 1889, with next to no new colonists and an increasing awareness among those stuck in Nueva Germania of how their Führer had built the colony on flimsy, if not deliberately fraudulent, financial foundations, Bernhard Förster decamped to a hotel in San Bernardino, the lakeside town originally named New Bavaria which had been founded by another group of German utopians in 1881. He stayed there for six weeks, drinking his way through a nervous breakdown brought on by the clear fact of his abysmal failure. On 1 June he wrote to a German supporter:

> My physical and mental condition is such that I can see my departure from these harsh obligations in the near future. My last request to you: keep placing your wonderful talent, astonishing energy and youthful enthusiasm into this good cause I have begun. Perhaps it will grow better without me than with me.

Two days later, in a funk exacerbated by a bad hangover, he took a lethal dose of strychnine and died in agony.

Twisted legacies

The colony did little better without him. Elisabeth Förster remained in charge of Nueva Germania until 1893, when she returned to Germany to look after her brother, who had gone mad. Most of the settlers who were able to afford it returned to Germany around the same time, and even though some did stay, the utopian vision behind the colony effectively died with the disappearance of the Försters. The prevailing attitude towards Förster from the remnants of Nueva Germania was one of bitterness. Those settlers condemned to stay eked out a subsistence as farmers in a location with poor access to markets. Things improved for a while during the 1890s when they planted yerba mate, a caffeine-containing plant that was used to make beverages. But this window of prosperity came to an end in 1907 when the market for yerba mate collapsed.

Elisabeth Förster-Nietzsche with Hitler in her later years

GERMANS IN PARAGUAY

There have been thirty-seven different attempts by idealistic Germans to establish agricultural communities in Paraguay, since New Bavaria (later San Bernardino) was founded in 1881. Their founders ranged from Berlin utopian socialists to Aryan supremacists and persecuted Christian sects. Not all of the colonies were as stark a failure as Nueva Germania, though.

In the 1920s, German Mennonites, a Protestant sect that shares its heritage with the Amish, began to settle the inhospitable region of western Paraguay known as the Chaco. While originally German, many of the Mennonites arrived in Paraguay via Canada from Russia, where colonies organised according to similar principles had been disbanded because of the Bolshevik Revolution. The first Mennonite settlers arrived in 1926, and while many of them died of typhoid, they were hard-working, experienced and competent farmers. Consequently, they were able to make a go of much poorer land than that granted to Bernhard Förster and his misguided companions. More Mennonites arrived, and today there are twenty colonies still in existence. More than 30,000 Mennonites live in Paraguay and many of their original communities remain functional. Some native Paraguayans have also converted to the religion, including the wife of former president Nicanor Duarte Frutos.

A less savoury form of German emigration to Paraguay was the arrival of escaped Nazi war criminals at the end of World War II. Helped by organisations such as the Catholic Church and, according to some sources, the CIA, Nazi war criminals came to South America in their droves, and were welcomed by the right-wing dictatorships in control of countries such as Argentina, Chile, Paraguay and Uruguay. From 1954 until 1989, Paraguay was ruled by Alfredo Stroessner, whose father was Bavarian, while his mother was the daughter of a wealthy Paraguayan family. Although Förster would never have approved of such miscegenated origins, under Stroessner's long dictatorship Paraguay became a haven for former Nazis, to whom President Stroessner sold new identities, a process made easier by the country's pre-existing German population.

Perhaps the most famous Nazi war criminal to settle in Paraguay was the Angel of Death himself, Josef Mengele, whose medical experiments on the prisoners at Auschwitz were cruel and barbaric. Spooked by the Mossad kidnapping of Adolf Eichmann in Buenos Aires early in 1960, Mengele fled to Paraguay, where a connection close to Stroessner helped him acquire citizenship. For a few months Mengele lived on a farm in Hohenau, a successful German colony on the Paraná River, founded in 1900. Some people have claimed that he also lived in Nueva Germania for a period. Mengele stayed in Paraguay until moving to Brazil late in 1960, where he died in February 1979. Most of the Nazis sheltered by Stroessner have long since died of natural causes.

Portrait of a Mennonite family of fourteen from Colonia Mexico, Paraguay, 1994

After Nietzsche's death in August 1900, Elisabeth Förster invested her considerable ambition into twisting her brother's philosophy to fit into her own anti-Semitic beliefs. She was close to the Nazi Party, and when she died in November 1935, Adolf Hitler was one of the mourners at her funeral. Elisabeth's long-deceased husband was not forgotten by the Nazis either. In 1934, Hitler ordered a memorial service for this prototype Nazi, and German soil was scattered over his Paraguayan grave.

Today Nueva Germania is a small town of 500 families, a seven-hour bus ride from Asunción. The atmosphere could easily be described as anti-modern, but it is far from paradise. In fact, its inhabitants are among some of the poorest inhabitants of one of the poorest countries in South America. When *New York Times* reporter James Brooke visited the colony in the 1990s, the closest paved road was 25 kilometres (15 miles) away. Only sixteen houses had electricity and eleven had telephones, while the televisions connecting them to the outside world were run off a car battery. Just seventy of the 500 families claimed any German heritage. Most of those that did couldn't speak any German, and while there were more than 100,000 people of German descent in Paraguay, Nueva Germania was considered by the German government to be the least important German settlement of all.

CHAPTER 22

The Cossack colony of New Moscow (Sagallo), Northeast Africa (1889)

Renegade Cossacks, the kingdom of Prester John, the Suez Canal, arms dealing, the Russian Orthodox Church and the geopolitics of European imperialism were the motley factors behind this short-lived Russian colony at Sagallo, on the Red Sea coast of Africa. Founded by Cossack wheeler-dealer Nikolai Ashinov, it lasted a few chaotic weeks before his rowdy mob exhausted France's patience and invited a shelling from one of its gunboats. Despite having given the enterprise tacit support, after the colonists' surrender Tsar Alexander III described the fiasco as 'a sad and stupid comedy'. He was right.

Unlike most European powers, pre-revolutionary Russia's imperial ambitions were traditionally landlocked. Its empire stretched as far west as Poland, and to the Grand Duchy of Finland in the north, while its sphere of influence extended south into the Slavic cultures of the Balkans. Most of the empire, however, had come about through a huge expansion out to the east, to Siberia and (until 1867) Alaska. It also extended into the 'stans' of Central Asia, reaching as far as Afghanistan, where geopolitics and espionage reached new heights of intrigue in the so-called Great Game, played out between Russia and Britain over the spoils of Persia's declining empire. The gradual disintegration of the Ottoman Empire saw Russia expand into the Balkans, with the concomitant dream of achieving a warm-water port through control of the Dardanelles Strait, leading from the Black Sea to the Mediterranean and beyond.

It was this last point that continued to be a stumbling block for the fortunes of the Romanov tsars. For while Russia's Baltic Sea ports and those on the Pacific were prone to freezing over during winter, the warm-water ones that it did possess, on the Black Sea, were compromised by the country's inability to gain free access to the Dardanelles. Movements south into Central Asia had also failed to give Russia an all-year-round harbour facility.

By the end of the nineteenth century, most of the New World had been divided up among the major colonial powers. The remnant most contested was Africa, which had become a

frenzy of colonial expansion that also involved imperial minnows such as Belgium, Germany and Italy. For a short time too, the Russians had a stake in the Dark Continent. Yet it is more a tale of tolerated chicanery and populist buffoonery than anything else.

Russian interest in northern Africa began with the assertion of parallels between the Russian Orthodox Church and the Ethiopian Orthodox Tewahedo Church, the only pre-colonial Christian denomination in Africa. One of the tenets of the ultra-nationalism prevalent in Russia throughout the nineteenth century was the sentimental belief that the Russian Orthodox Church was the great protector of Orthodox Christianity. Some Russians believed that the Ethiopian Church was the remnant of the kingdom of Prester John, the mythical Christian king whose potential whereabouts were a common motivation for the Asian and African sorties of the early European explorers. With the French and the British controlling Egypt and the Italians moving in on Abyssinia (the former name for Ethiopia), the Russians were keen to protect the Ethiopian Church from the depredations of Western Christianity. In 1861, Russian priest Porfiry Ouspensky advocated turning Ethiopia into an ecclesiastical colony of Russia, as part of a plan to assert religious control over the entire Near East. The plan lay fallow for a while, but interest was revived in the scramble for Africa in the 1880s.

Not all of the Russian interest in the area had to do with the maintenance of spiritual

A satiric cartoon presents the 'grab-bag' approach of Russian, German and British imperialism in the 1880s

traditions, however. With the opening of the Suez Canal in November 1869, connecting the eastern Mediterranean with the Red Sea and through to the Indian Ocean, the Red Sea area had become even more crucial to world geopolitics and trade than before. To some, therefore, the idea of a Russian colony on the sea's western shore held a definite strategic attraction, especially given the scramble to exploit Africa was the main colonial fashion at the time.

Also, lingering grievances over the terms of peace following the Crimean War of 1853–56, particularly in regard to the regulation of the Dardanelles, meant that some Russians were eager to forestall Britain's control of Suez. Influence over the Canal, they reckoned, might be a useful bargaining chip for Russia in its constant battle to secure unconditional access through the straits of the Dardanelles.

Cossack by name, Cossack by nature

It was this web of motives that Nikolai Ashinov was able to cultivate and manipulate in his scheme to begin a colony at Sagallo, on the Red Sea coast in present-day Djibouti, a tiny country on the Horn of Africa. Ashinov was a Terek Cossack, a group of Cossacks who had settled in the Black Sea kingdom of Georgia in the sixteenth century. The Cossacks were a proud and hard-to-govern people. Famous for their military and nautical prowess, and unscrupulous in their

allegiances, they had often carried out the dirty work for the tsars during the early expansion of the Russian Empire. Yet they were just as renowned for being self-serving brigands and pirates.

Ashinov himself was no stranger to colonial impulses. In 1883 he led his self-titled 'Brotherhood of Free Cossacks' to found a colony on the Black Sea coast near Batumi, in territory newly ceded by the Ottomans (in contemporary Georgia). Although he'd attracted a number of investors for the venture, including railway speculators and influential pan-Slavic enthusiasts with high-level access to Tsar Alexander III, Ashinov clashed with the local authorities and found it difficult to get land grants for his men. Due to their criminality and unruliness, the governor-general of the region, Prince Dondukov-Korsakov, eventually ordered the Cossacks' expulsion as he considered them a threat to security. Worse still, he put out a warrant for Ashinov's arrest on the charge of misappropriating public funds. Ashinov fled to Constantinople, where a second plan, to start a Russian colony in Africa, began to take shape.

In 1885, the exiled Ashinov met four Circassians who seduced him with tales of Ethiopia as a cornucopia populated by ancient Christians. He began to think that Abyssinia might be an excellent destination for his band, whose dreams of land on the Black Sea had been shattered. The problem of funding was solved by stealing money from the British. Hearing of his disaffection with Russia, British agents had contacted Ashinov and asked him if he would like to smuggle weapons into Afghanistan on their behalf, to be used against the Russians. Having accepted an advance of thousands of roubles, Ashinov had a moment of patriotism and informed the Russian government of the scheme. Before the British discovered his perfidy, the Cossack hopped on a steamer for Cairo, from where he used the British money to fund a reconnaissance expedition to north-eastern Africa.

Ashinov arrived in Abyssinia in early 1886. He formed a good relationship with the powerful Ethiopian chief Ras Alula, who was on the northern front line of resistance against the incursions of Italy and the Sudanese Muslims known as the Mahdists. The two men's friendship was cemented over Ashinov's promise to source Alula modern European weapons to help him in his battles.

The Ethiopian emperor, Johannes IV, was less welcoming, however. Nine years earlier, he had tried to form an alliance with the Tsar's father and predecessor, Alexander II, but had been rejected. His regal pride was wounded, and as a consequence he refused to receive Ashinov, especially when he discovered he was not even an official emissary from the tsar. Emperor Johannes ordered Alula to prevent the Cossack from travelling any further than the Ethiopian citadel of Asmara. By the time Ashinov reached the coast, however, he was carrying 'gifts' from Johannes to the tsar, as well as a fraudulent commission to buy weapons on

the emperor's behalf. Most probably, the gifts and written orders were supplied by Alula, whose situation on the front line had led him to ignore the protocols demanded by his monarch.

Ashinov was convinced he'd pulled off a major coup, one that would be feted by Tsar Alexander III on his return to Russia. But that would have to wait. Because his Black Sea shenanigans had resulted in the issuing of a warrant for his arrest, he had to cool his heels for several months in north-eastern Africa until his pan-Orthodox supporters were able to get it rescinded.

Wheeling and dealing

When Ashinov finally arrived at St Petersburg, the pre-revolutionary capital of Russia, he tried to see the Foreign Minister, Nikolay Karlovich Giers. But Giers was a cautious man, who saw political risk in Ashinov's meddling in the complex imperial politics of Africa, particularly in terms of the burgeoning alliance between Russia and France. Giers was also a Protestant of Teutonic descent and thus immune to the passionate excesses of Russian pan-nationalism, with its emphasis on the divine mission of the Russian Orthodox Church. He refused to see Ashinov and advised that the tsar do the same.

But Ashinov had associates with access to Alexander, one of whom was Konstantin Pobedonostsev, the Procurator of the Holy Synod of the Russian Orthodox Church and arguably the tsar's most influential advisor as well as the most prominent pan-Slavist of the time. Ever the schemer, Ashinov gained the interest of Pobedonostsev by gross exaggeration, claiming that the Ethiopians were the community of lost Christians prophesied since the times of Prester John and that they were desirous of reunion with the true keeper of the Christian faith, otherwise known as the Russian Orthodox Church. The church hierarchy became interested, and while Ashinov busied himself in fundraising and arms dealing, a Cossack monk by the name of Vasily Paisy, whom Ashinov knew from Constantinople, entered a monastery in Russia to be trained to go to Ethiopia as an emissary of the church.

Members of the Russian court

Christianity and patriotism were only ever strategies of convenience for Nikolai Ashinov, whose morals were little higher than the gangster capitalists of contemporary Russia. But his amorality, scheming and lust for the filthy lucre, combined with his impatience and inconsistency, meant that he was eminently capable of shooting himself in the foot. He antagonised the entire merchant community of Moscow, for instance, when he tried to sell goods intended as gifts for the Ethiopians from Russia's wealthiest industrialist, T.S. Morozov, on the open market in Odessa. In true Houdini fashion, the wily Cossack successfully capitalised on this sale by investing the profits in France, where he bought 20,000 rifles to take back with him to Abyssinia.

Before Ashinov left for Africa again, he wrote a note advising Johannes of his success in procuring the guns. He also suggested that the emperor might like to send some religious ambassadors to Russia for the celebrations marking the 900th anniversary of its conversion to Christianity.

He landed at the Red Sea port of Tadjoura, a sultanate under French protection, in April 1888, with the arms and eight fellow Cossacks. They were met by a delegation from Johannes. Ashinov left his comrades behind to guard the guns and returned to Russia with the emperor's emissaries. In St Petersburg, with his eyes as always on European diplomacy, Giers attempted to block Ashinov from meeting the tsar, but his efforts were undermined by lobbying from the church. For a while, Giers succeeded in preventing Tsar Alexander from receiving the Ethiopian monks, but eventually he lost that battle too. The church expedited Paisy's monastic training and elevated him from monk to deacon to priest to archimandrite (one rung below the rank of bishop) in less than a week.

Russian nationalist sentiment soon decreed Ashinov's African experiment to be a worthy one. Money for the adventure was raised by subscription through the Palestine Society, headed by the tsar's brother, Grand Duke Sergei Alexandrovich, a noted ultra-nationalist. One of Ashinov's allies petitioned the tsar for a licence to establish a Russian trading company in Africa, to be based at the Gulf of Tadjoura settlement of Sagallo, which Ashinov planned to rename New Moscow. In the latter part of 1888, men and goods gathered in Odessa, on the northern coast of the Black Sea, the designated point of departure.

Meanwhile, Ashinov was busy, as usual, buying guns. From a Russophile French viscount named Jean-Robert de Constantin, an occasional special agent for the French government with high-powered connections, he obtained an agreement to supply Johannes with 100,000 rifles, superseded technology in European terms, but capable of changing the political balance of north-east Africa.

This apparent alliance between France and Russia particularly alarmed the British and the Italians, both of whom also had designs on Abyssinia and were extremely wary as to who controlled the shipping lanes leading to the Suez Canal. Russian foreign minister Giers was concerned that the small party of Cossacks, with their reputation for mayhem and unpredictability, could easily cause a disproportionate reaction in the delicate balance of European diplomacy. Alexander III may even have listened to his foreign minister, for although he hadn't shut down Ashinov's activities, he was reluctant to give them his royal imprimatur.

To a certain extent, Ashinov and his Free Cossacks gave the tsar some insurance against the antipathy of other European powers. If they succeeded, Russia would benefit, and the tsar, who had offered them informal assistance, would be well reflected in the glow of their achievement. Yet if they failed, he could cut them loose, dismissing them as a bunch of untrustworthy miscreants who had acted without his authority. Alexander was definitely attuned to the kind of rogue Ashinov was, at one point commenting to Pobedonostsev, his religious advisor: 'I think this sly old fox Ashinov will dupe everyone, rob everyone, and throw them out'. Quite rightly, he concluded that the Cossack leader could not be sufficiently trusted to be blessed with overt support.

Steaming to New Moscow

By the end of 1888, all that remained was confirmation from Ashinov's ally Jean-Robert de Constantin that the French government was still willing to supply the arms as agreed. Here, Ashinov ran into problems. News of the agreement had leaked. Not only had the British, Italian and also the German ambassadors to France protested, but Giers himself had summoned the French ambassador to his ministry and expressed his displeasure. Consequently, the arms deal was cancelled, although with the caveat that it might be revisited once the furore had died down. France continued to grant permission for the Russian 'religious' mission to pass through territory under its control.

On 10 December, 20,000 patriotic Russians were gathered at the Odessa docks to cheer on the 175 Cossacks and forty religious emissaries as their goods-laden steamer, the *Amphitrite*, set off for Africa. The trip was initially uneventful. But once the ship reached the African coast, the unruliness of the Cossacks and their inability to behave inconspicuously became an issue. At the Suez terminus of Port Said, they went on a drunken debauch that reached the newspapers of Europe, with Ashinov being accused in one Italian publication of raping two women.

Of all the powers competing for turf in Africa's north-east, the Italians were the most worried about the Russian expedition—so much so that they sent a gunboat to shadow the *Amphitrite* through the Canal and into the Red Sea. With no clear sense of the line between bravery and stupidity, many of the Cossacks wanted Ashinov to usurp control of their unarmed steamer, turn it around and ram the Italian ship. When he refused, there was almost a mutiny. The two ships were parted by a storm before the situation reached a climax.

Ashinov and his fellow colonists landed at Tadjoura on 18 January 1889; a week later, they occupied a dilapidated former Egyptian fort at nearby Sagallo and began to rebuild it. France already had a fort of its own at Obok, further east along the Gulf of Tadjoura's northern coast. Initially, it seemed that the French were unconcerned about the Russian presence, as long as the Cossacks accepted their primary sovereignty in the region. But when Ashinov refused to fly the tricoleur above New Moscow, the French became less accommodating, claiming that while they had granted the Cossacks permission to cross their territory en route to Abyssinia, which was inland, they had not sanctioned the occupation of the fort. Once again, Ashinov had deceived an ally in the pursuit of his goals.

The French protested to Ashinov, but to no avail. He claimed that the Sultan of Tadjoura had sold him the land. (The sultan had conveniently ignored the fact that the previous sultan had already sold it to the French.) If not for its strategic location—set in a protected gulf hugging the western shore of the gateway to the Indian Ocean—the colony wouldn't have incited such controversy. The land around Sagallo was pretty much a stony desert,

where agriculture could never thrive. But the French were under pressure from the Italians and the British, who argued that France's tacit support of the Cossacks was in violation of a treaty against the proliferation of weapons in Africa. As the French became increasingly exasperated with the behaviour of Ashinov and his cohorts, Ashinov insisted that he would recognise no authority other than that of the tsar.

By this time, Alexander had decided that the colony was bound to fail. Having stood on the fence for so long, he now cut the Cossacks loose. He instructed Giers to inform the French ambassador that Ashinov's mission was an enterprise undertaken at the Cossack's own initiative and peril. If Sagallo belonged to the French Protectorate, then, in Tsar Alexander's opinion, Ashinov was bound to observe the French rule of law or suffer the consequences.

Even while this diplomatic to-ing and fro-ing was taking place in the embassies and foreign ministries of Europe, New Moscow had already started to implode. By February, two groups had defected to the French settlement at Obok, where they accused Ashinov of brutality and murder. The Danakil tribal chiefs, who had originally seen the Cossacks as potential allies against the French, also began to find the Russians troublesome, on account of their violence and vulgarity. Given the only prospects for the colony were to be found in trade, it was an invidious position.

THE RUSSIAN EMPIRE

Although the colony at Sagallo was an utter fiasco, of all the European empires in the nineteenth century, Russia's would prove the most enduring. Perhaps this was because, in contrast to the other powers, the Russian Empire had territorial integrity.

Most of Russia's empire was a result of its extension to the east. This began in the sixteenth century with the conquest of Siberia by Cossack mercenary Timofeyevich Yermak. Russia gradually expanded across the forests, taiga and tundra of Siberia until it reached the Pacific coast. In 1742, following the expedition of Vitus Bering, Russia claimed Alaska as part of its empire. The colony there failed to be extremely profitable, however, and in 1867, Russia sold the territory to the United States for $7.2 million—a move it must have regretted during the Klondike gold rush thirty years later, not to mention the immense mineral deposits yet to be exploited in those icy climes. However, it's hard not to wonder whether the Cold War might've been hotter had Alaska remained in Russian hands during the Soviet era.

By the end of the nineteenth century, a formidable one-sixth of the world's landmass belonged to the Russian Empire. In addition to the current borders of Russia, this

Portrait of Yermak Timofeyevich, the Cossack leader who first claimed territory for the Russian Empire

included: Ukraine, Belarus; Moldova, Finland, Armenia, Azerbaijan and Georgia; the Central Asian states of Kazakhstan, Kyrgyzstan, Tajikistan, Turkmenistan and Uzbekistan; the greater part of Lithuania, Estonia and Latvia; and large chunks of Poland, as well as the Turkish provinces of Ardahan, Artvin, Idır and Kars. Only Britain's empire was larger.

Yet while the British Empire was in recession for most of the twentieth century, Russia's actually expanded in its Soviet incarnation, from 1917 onwards. Parts of Turkey were lost, but the USSR's western reach into Europe was increased dramatically through its post-1945 control over the countries situated behind the Iron Curtain. These included East Germany, Poland, Czechoslovakia, Hungary, Bulgaria and Romania, all of which had Soviet-installed governments until the fall of the Berlin Wall in November 1989. Ten years before that, Russia made the strategically poor decision to invade Afghanistan, in many ways an disaster equivalent to America's involvement in the Vietnam War.

The fall of the Berlin Wall marked the end of the Soviet regime and its empire, although today Russia remains the largest country in the world, at 1.8 times the size of the United States. The last two decades have seen something of a surge in Russian imperialism, as evidenced by the harsh response to independence movements in Chechnya and, as of August 2008, in Ossetia, where there have been skirmishes between Russia and Georgia over territory.

By the middle of February, the Russian colony at Sagallo was left without an ally in the world. Under continuing pressure from Britain and Italy, the French sent a light cruiser and three gunboats to Sagallo with instructions to force the Cossacks' surrender. The ultimatum was delivered to Ashinov on 17 February by a junior officer from the *Seignelay*, and promptly rejected. The officer returned to his ship and the French guns opened fire. As much as Ashinov and his remaining allies wanted to fire back, they were vastly outgunned. Only six shells had been fired and already five people, including a pregnant woman, had been killed and twenty more wounded. The survival instincts of the majority prevailed and the Russian flag was lowered in favour of a white piece of cloth. The colony was finished.

Out of Africa

This was the first and only time that Russia tried to stake a territorial claim in Africa. It wasn't until the post-World War II era, in its incarnation as the USSR, that Russia would become a major player in African affairs, albeit through aid rather than colonisation. The French shipped the Cossacks back to Russia, where most of them vanished into obscurity. Nikolai Ashinov was banished to Chernigov in the Ukraine, while Father Paisy, who was as vulgar a man as Ashinov, only dressed in the garb of a priest, disappeared into a monastery.

The French expanded their foothold at Obok until it became the territory known as French Somaliland, which gained independence in 1977 to become Djibouti.

CHAPTER 23

The utopian colonies of New Australia and Cosme, Paraguay (1893–94 and 1894–99)

Watching the brutal repression of the Shearers' Strike of 1891 and Australia sliding into drought and depression, socialist William Lane decided that his dream of a just society could only be realised if he established a whole new one. He turned to South America, where the Paraguayan government, its population decimated by war, was happy to provide assistance. More than 200 utopian Australians decamped there to build their perfect world, but human relations soon began to deteriorate. Lost in the rigidity of his own ideals, Lane was a poor leader. Schisms developed, and Lane left New Australia with a number of loyal supporters to found Cosme. Despite a number of recruitment drives, both colonies continually lost members, while those who remained became increasingly factionalised. In 1899, William Lane left Cosme for New Zealand and resumed his career in journalism. The two settlements eventually abandoned all pretences to utopianism and were absorbed into Paraguayan society.

Australians are fond of telling themselves that they live in the lucky country and for many this has proven to be true. However, things were not looking quite so lucky for the rural working classes in the early 1890s, and in 1891 the social agitator, journalist and pipe-dreamer William Lane was determined to do something about it.

Born in 1861 in the English city of Bristol, Lane was no stranger to hardship himself. His father was an alcoholic Irish Protestant landscape gardener, whose boozing had kept the family poor. Although he did well at school, young William left home at sixteen and crewed on a ship to pay for his passage to Canada, where he worked in Montreal at a time when industrial relations were frequently violent. He then moved to Detroit, Michigan, where he discovered the work of utopian socialist thinkers such as William Morris, Edward Bellamy and Henry George. He married a Scottish girl, Ann, in Michigan before deciding to join two of his brothers out in Australia.

The Lanes arrived in Brisbane sometime in 1885 and before long he was working as a radical journalist, pitching his articles to the rural working classes: shearers, drovers, farm labourers, harvesters and the like, a large audience since Australia was still living off the sheep's back. It was an era, too, when the idea of journalistic objectivity had yet to become entrenched, and Lane's journalism was always more about political activism than balanced reportage. Like many of the working-class nationalists in the period leading up to Australian federation in 1901, Lane was an appalling racist. This was notably on show in his paranoid 'yellow peril' fantasy, *White or Yellow? A Story of the Race-War of A.D. 1908*. Lane was one of the key founders of the Australian Labor Federation in 1889, and he launched his radical magazine *The Worker*, that year also, funded through union subscription.

The genesis of New Australia probably came about through the poor result the Australian Labor Federation achieved during the Queensland Shearers' Strike of 1891. On 5 January that year, shearers had decided to down tools until four key demands were met: the maintenance of existing pay rates; protection of workers' rights and privileges; the establishment of just and equitable agreements; and the exclusion of low-cost Chinese labour. They were opposed by the Pastoralists' Federal Council, a group of squatters that had the Queensland government on its side. Lane covered the strike as a journalist, although many claimed he was also one of its central organisers. It was a bitterly fought episode, with armed camps of up to 1000 shearers ranged against the police. Sheds that employed non-union labour were torched, while key members of the union were arrested on trumped-up charges. For a while it seemed that the shearers might even prevail, but by August the strike was officially over. After a wet summer and a consequent delayed start to the shearing season, many of the workers had simply become too hungry, exhausted and poor to continue their fight.

It was a seminal moment in Australian history. The utopian strand of socialism favoured by William Lane was now abandoned in favour of a Fabian socialist model focused on achieving legislative reform in Parliament. This led to the founding of the Australian Labor Party, and also to the sidelining of Lane. He wrote the satirical novel, *A Working Man's Paradise*, the proceeds of which he donated to cover the legal fees of the shearers who'd been arrested. But, deeply disillusioned with the direction of socialism in Australia even before the strike was over, his thoughts had turned to the idea of founding a utopian colony elsewhere.

The spruiker

Lane had been in correspondence with the Mexican utopian colony at Topolobampo and he was also cognisant of the Icarian colonies, those utopian communities based on the vision of Robert Owen, which had briefly flowered in the United States. In May 1891, *The Worker* advertised that the New Australia Co-operative Settlement Association was seeking land in South America on which to establish a colony on socialist and racially exclusive principles.

That same year, Lane appointed several men to scout around the continent for suitable land. They initially looked in Argentina, but in neighbouring Paraguay they found an opportunity that was too good to refuse. Once one of the most powerful nations in South America, Paraguay had been greatly

diminished by the War of the Triple Alliance, which lasted from 1865 to 1870. Fighting against Brazil, Uruguay and Argentina, the landlocked nation had lost not only more than a quarter of its territory, but also two-thirds of its population. From 800,000 people at the beginning of the bitterly fought and particularly nasty conflict, the Paraguayan population now comprised 150,000 women, 81,000 children and just 14,000 men.

Paraguay was facing one of the greatest man droughts experienced by any society in history. There weren't enough men either to farm the land or defend the shrunken territory should its neighbours decided to wage war again. And there weren't enough men to keep the women of Paraguay happy either. One emergency response the Paraguayan government took to resolve this demographic crisis was to encourage the establishment of colonies by people from other parts of the world, particularly those Germans disillusioned with their recently unified nation. In 1881, utopian socialists from Berlin founded a colony at San Bernardino, on the shore of Lake Ypacarai, and in 1887, Nueva Germania was established in the north-east of the country by the rabid anti-Semite Bernhard Förster (see page 249). In both cases the utopian impulse soon wore off even if many of the settlers begrudgingly stayed on.

On 19 January 1893, Alf Walker, one of the New Australia Association's four representatives in Paraguay, came to an agreement with President Juan Gualberto

González's government and cabled a message to Lane. They had been granted 75,000 hectares (185,000 acres) of land in the south of the country, a lush combination of pasture and woodland 25 kilometres (15 miles) from the railway track between Asunción, the capital, and the city of Villarrica. In addition to the land, the Paraguayan government offered the colony a ten-year tax exemption. In return, the New Australia Association promised to settle 1200 families in the space of six years; half the land would be available immediately, with the remainder to be granted once the first 600 families had arrived.

Back in old Australia, Lane had been busy spruiking for colonists, both in person and in print, particularly through the November 1892 launch of *New Australia* magazine. Although a short man with a clubfoot and a moustache that resembled a fat caterpillar lodged on his face, he was a gifted orator, whose romanticising of the Australian bushworker fed his audience's sense of its own natural nobility. On hearing the good news from Alf Walker, Lane and his associates went into full gear organising the exodus from Australia.

Not nearly so impressed by their progress was the *Bulletin* magazine, an Australian nationalist publication that had competed with Lane's various newspapers for the hearts, minds and wallets of the bush worker, and as such bore a historical enmity towards him. While reporting on the departure of Lane's colonists the following July, the magazine's editorial cattily observed:

On the assumption that life among wild oranges and yerba mate scrub has capabilities which it does not offer in Australia, one of the most feather-headed expeditions ever conceived since Ponce de Leon started out to find the Fountain of Eternal Youth, or Sir Galahad pursued the Holy Grail, is about to set forth.

But the *Bulletin* was being overly harsh. Compared to many colonial ventures, Lane's was a relatively sensible one. The land was known and had been freely granted; it was fertile and there was access to plentiful water. It was unlikely anyone was going to starve. The part of Paraguay they had chosen to settle was also free of the debilitating mosquito-borne tropical diseases whose attritional effect had destroyed colonies such as Port Essington, in northern Australia (see page 220). Moreover, in contrast to many of the early settlements in the Americas, where soldiers had to perform the labour of farmers, the colonists heading to New Australia included a high proportion of agricultural workers. And rather than the lowly status usually accorded to such employment, the value system of Lane's utopian socialism (to which all the colonists at least superficially aspired) glorified the agricultural worker as the bedrock of civilisation. In comparison to many colonies, in other words, New Australia had a lot going for it.

Starting out

On 16 July 1893, the sturdy barque-rigged sailing ship *Royal Tar* sailed from Sydney, en route to the Uruguayan capital of Montevideo and thence on to Asunción by river. On board were 220 emigrants, William and Ann Lane among them, as well as other members of his family, including his brother John.

With the Australian colonial states deep in the grip of an economic depression, hundreds of people lined the foreshore or crammed into boats to wave farewell to what many considered to be a brave contingent of men and women. Echoing the *Bulletin*'s scorn for the venture, however, was a dinghy full of sceptics who had dressed themselves up in straitjackets and were waving a banner that read: 'Lunatics farewell their brothers and sisters'.

The Royal Tar *in port in Australia*

✴ SELLING THE UTOPIAN DREAM IN THE PAGES OF NEW AUSTRALIA

DID YOU KNOW

That all our modern social ills—poverty, unemployed, prostitution, ignorance and all the evils attending these wrongful conditions— arise wholly and solely because selfish greed more than counter-balances all the advantages of civilisation?

That the wealth production of the world is vastly in excess of all ordinary requirements, but that the greater part is carelessly wasted by the rich who do not work while only a comparatively small portion goes to give a scanty subsistence to the poor who, roughly speaking, produce it all?

That in what are called barbaric times, among our own race, every man had a home and a wife and every woman a home and a husband, every man was sure of opportunity to live free and of seeing his children grow up free and equal; and that civilisation takes from us this freedom which must be the basis of all happiness and gives us wage slavery and degradation in return, only because we have not realised true co-operative conditions suited to modem civilisation, as the common ownership of land and cattle was suited to the barbarism of our forefathers?

That all the energies of earnest and determined men and women are necessary, not only to convince the world that things are wrong, which is very easy, but to show the world by practical means what is the best way out,
which is very hard; and that the best way is certainly to build up a community enjoying plenty and happiness and individual liberty, which will be an object lesson and an example to all who seek a better order of things, proving to all nations that better things are possible?

That such a community can only be built up by those who give their lives to the work which will live after they are dead and gone and forgotten, and who for the sake of that work, and in the faith of winning humanity, are strong enough to take every precaution towards success no matter what such precautions may cost—are ready to 'go out into the desert' to live in their own way?

DO YOU BELIEVE

That though some men are unreliable and selfish and brutal, having been made so by the unnatural conditions under which we are forced to live, that many men are square and straight and honest, particularly if they have any thing like a chance to be?

That there is pluck enough and honesty enough in the straight men to enable them to trust one another through difficulties and discouragements and pull them through to a state of industrial organization in which every man will be a mate and in which no man would dream of taking advantage of another?

That there is intelligence enough and power of organisation enough among the workers to enable them of their free will to organise the present conditions of industry and to give the world an example of a peaceful and self-sustaining industrial community in which there are none but workers and in which all are equal?

DO YOU FEEL

That the weakness of the social movement is in men themselves, in their lack of faith, in their hesitation of thought, in their doubts as to what is best to be done?

That year by year, generation after generation, demoralising conditions are having an effect upon men equally with the degenerating influence of modern ideas?

That the greatest gift which men could bring to their fellow men would be faith, absolute unalterable faith in a tried and proved form of industrial organisation and in the divine truth that happiness is only possible so far as we care for one another?

That you can make one of an association whose members are pledged to give up everything and to join one another in earnest effort to help one another live a life worth living as an example to the world?

IF YOU DO, JOIN THE 'NEW AUSTRALIA' MOVEMENT.

This movement has been two years in preparation. Its principles and articles of association have been discussed and rediscussed a score of times by its original members. It is almost unanimously agreed, by all who have considered the movement, that Australia does not offer for the purpose the advantages offered by other continents and that those who love Australia most love the movement more. The names of the Provisional Board of Trustees show the genuineness of the movement, and that it is worth every honest man's consideration.

WILLIAM LANE,
19 NOVEMBER 1892

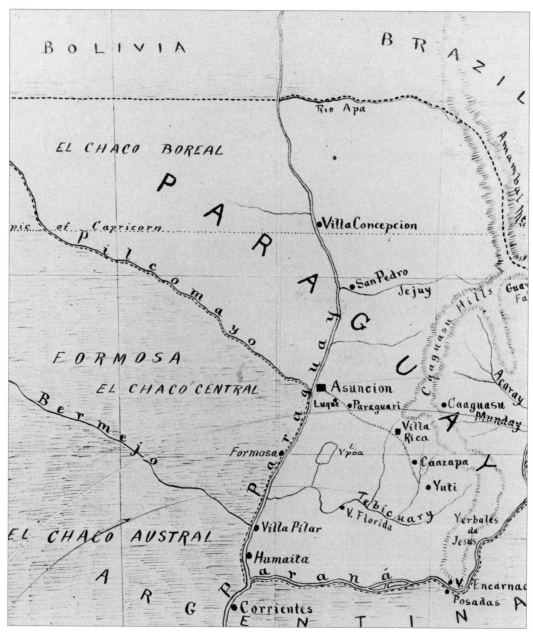

Map by John Lane. Cosme was located south-east of Asunción, close to the town of Villarrica (Villa Rica)

When the *Royal Tar* passed New Zealand's North Island, it was the last land they would see before the Chilean coastline, on the far side of the Pacific. The ship sailed south of Cape Horn, where the colonists were treated to the sight of floating icebergs, before heading north through the Atlantic Ocean towards Montevideo. Even before they'd arrived, cracks were appearing in the firmament of utopia.

The first example of this occurred as a result of a flirtation between one of the single women, Nurse Clara Jones, and a single man, Dave Stevenson. This wasn't a problem in itself. The single women were essential to Lane's vision of a racially homogenous colony. However, Lane's wife had promised to keep an eye on Stevenson on behalf of her friend and future colonist, Mary Cameron, who later became famous as an author under the name of Mary Gilmore. In response to this Lane issued an executive order that single women weren't allowed to appear on decks after 6 pm unless they were accompanied by their parents. Nurse Jones, being the only single woman on board without accompanying relatives was the obvious target of the order, yet many of the colonists considered Lane's order compromised the rights of the individual as enshrined in the colony's 'Basis for Communal Organisation'. Lane's response was both pedantic and petulant. He told the others that the Basis for Communal Organisation was not yet in force—a ridiculous argument, given that the colony was supposed to be about ideals

rather than regulations. Lane then retired to his cabin and sulked; he even had a table installed there so he wouldn't have to eat with his fellow utopians. Understandably, his brothers and sisters in idealism began to wonder about the judgment of the man who had inspired them to join this adventure.

When the *Royal Tar* arrived in Montevideo, Lane had a similar moment of petty autocracy that further eroded his authority. With everyone excited to set foot on dry land for the first time in months, Lane went ashore leaving the order that no-one was to leave the ship until he returned. This behaviour might have been expected from the captain of a ship, but from the founder of a socialist colony, it was idiotic. Unsurprisingly, some of the colonists took umbrage. A group of them went ashore and broke the Association's temperance rules by behaving like true sailors and going on a bender. When they returned, other colonists who were unswervingly loyal to Lane called the merrymakers 'scabs', slang for non-union labour used to break up a strike, and one of the worst things you could call a socialist. Consequently a brawl broke out on the ship. With more than 1000 kilometres (600 miles) to go before they even reached New Australia, the bonds of common purpose the colonists depended on were beginning to wear thin. One of the illicit shore-leavers, Tom Westwood, wrote in his diary: 'I can't help feeling that the movement cannot result in success if that incompetent man Lane continues to mismanage so utterly as he has done up to the present'. Although Lane had his supporters, Westwood was far from alone in holding this opinion.

It had been hoped that the *Royal Tar* could take the settlers up the Paraguay River as far as Asunción. However, there was insufficient draft and the colonists had to transfer their belongings onto a smaller boat, a process that was repeated at the confluence of the Paraguay and Tebicuary rivers, where the waterway became even shallower. They arrived in Paraguay's capital to be greeted by official dignitaries including the British Consul, the Paraguayan Minister for Colonisation and President González himself. As flattering as the welcome party was, Lane's settlers were less thrilled to hear that the site of the land grant had been changed to a new location, even further away than what they'd been told in the prospectus.

From Asunción, the 220 Australians travelled south-east by steam train to Villarrica, before transferring to twenty massive carts, or *carretas*, each pulled by a team of eight bullocks over the rough tracks that constituted the last leg of the journey. They finally arrived at New Australia on 28 September and began to build their new society within an abandoned orange grove, in the centre of 185,000 hectares (463,000 acres) of grassland surrounded by forest—more than double the area originally negotiated by Alf Walker.

For a while it seemed as though the troubles on the way over might be put behind them. The colonists were too busy to squabble. A temporary wattle-and-daub structure was built, while timber was cut for more permanent dwellings and fences. Expeditions into the forests discovered fruit trees including peaches, limes, figs, lemons and guavas. The colonists took cuttings to plant next to the oranges. Crops planted included sweet potato, mandioca (cassava), french beans, melons and potatoes. The initial signs were good, as only the potatoes failed. By the end of 1893, 15 hectares (40 acres) of land had been cleared, half of them planted with crops, and stockyards had been built to hold 2500 head of cattle. From wattle-and-daub beginnings, New Australia came to resemble a genuine village, with a blacksmith, butcher's shop, school and twenty thatched cottages. Quarter-acre blocks—the standard parcel of land for an Australian suburban block—were pegged out in anticipation of the colonists to come.

Splitting up

After several months, a visitor to New Australia might have assumed the colony was well on its way to success. In fact, it was already imploding. By mid November, New Australia had split into two factions: 'the royals', who remained loyal to Lane, and 'the rebels', who did not. Complicating things further was the fact that the rebels were themselves divided, between a mob of malcontents who broke the rules on a regular basis, and others who kept to the rules but were becoming increasingly mistrustful of Lane's autocratic tendencies.

Much of this dissension came about because wives who had been persuaded against their better judgment to follow idealistic husbands to the ends of the Earth, had found the reality considerably less ideal that what had been promised. Among the drinking crew, there were also issues regarding the bartering of communal property for drink and possibly assignations with Guarani women—both of which were anathema to Lane. On several occasions, these disputes led to punch-ups. As with many co-operative ventures that hit strife, people soon became very calculating about the effort they were putting into the community in comparison to others.

Rumour and paranoia exacerbated the tension between the factions. One of Lane's allies, John Sibbald, had been appointed postmaster and at one point was accused of steaming open the rebels' mail. Given the deteriorating situation, Lane again showed poor leadership. Instead of attempting to defuse the problems between the colonists, he insulated himself via an inflexible sense of his own moral rectitude. For someone with the reputation as an inspiring talker, his constant failure to adequately communicate his intentions to his fellow colonists exacerbated the situation even more.

While much of this was going on, Lane was often in Asunción sorting out the legal status of the colony with the Paraguayan government. As a legal convenience, Lane had the society registered as a limited liability company. However, he forgot to ask his fellow colonists for permission to do this, despite the fact that many of them had invested their life savings in the venture.

While Lane's decision wasn't made for his own advantage, he should have known that an autocratic rendering of a utopian socialist community into a capitalist entity might incite disapprobation in an atmosphere already poisoned by the eroding trust in his leadership.

The damage gradually became irreparable. On 5 December, twenty-four of the colonists wrote a letter to the Paraguayan government, complaining of Lane's mismanagement and asking for individual grants of land closer to the Asunción–Villarrica railway line. On 15 December, in what seems strangely like a real-life rehearsal for reality TV shows such as *Survivor* or *Big Brother* a century later, Lane issued a public notice of expulsion to three of these men—the ringleader, Fred White, together with Tom Westwood and Louis Simon—for breaching the temperance rule. They were given until 7 o'clock the following morning to leave, otherwise the police would be asked to intervene. White was in Asunción but Simon and Westwood, who was recovering from a bout of dysentery and had a blind son, were in the colony and refused to leave. In an unfortunate inversion of the role he had played during the Shearers' Strike, Lane called in the Paraguayan police, who arrived that morning brandishing swords and bayonets and evicted the men and their families.

That same day, nineteen of the colonists, including the three evictees, signed a petition for separation and presented it to Lane. The document must have made for very difficult reading:

> In our opinion we have been unjustly treated, and our individual liberties have been unduly interfered with. Hard words have been said and deeds have been done, which in our opinion, render reconciliation upon our existing basis absolutely impossible. There remains but one remedy—separation. If collectively we fail to ensure that harmony which we all seek let us divide the camp, and let each party try and achieve its objects without hindrance. We have all worked hard in improving the land and doing necessary work, and we deem it right that the Association shall give us a substantial dividend in order that we and those whom we brought with us, and those whose wishes in the matter were not consulted, may be placed beyond the reach of starvation while we are struggling to make a new home.

Lane refused to divide up the colony, however, and instead offered a paltry dividend to those who wished to leave. Despite the inequity, by the end of the month close to one-third of the original New Australians had left; some moved to Asunción and other parts of South America while others returned to Australia

Meanwhile, the second batch of colonists was preparing to depart from Adelaide on the *Royal Tar*. A telegram was sent to the intending settlers, partly explaining what had happened, but curiously, the figure for

those who had quit the colony was fudged. Instead of eighty-one, the telegram sent to Adelaide mentioned the loss of only eight New Australians.

Travelling in the southern hemisphere summer, the second wave of settlers had an easier passage than the first and arrived at the colony in February 1894. By March, the split between royals and rebels had replicated itself, however, with the exception that this time the rebels outnumbered Lane's loyalists. The new leader of the rebels, a short pugnacious character by the name of Gilbert Casey, tried to convince Lane to take advice from an elected board, to which Lane responded grandiosely that he was tired of pandering to the majority.

A meeting soon afterwards voted yes to establishing a board of management by 104 votes to four. Knowing the numbers were against them, Lane's supporters had abstained from voting in order to undermine the legitimacy of the ballot. Rather than conform to the dictates of democracy, William Lane decided to withdraw from the New Australia Association.

Reborn in Cosme

On 12 May, amid scenes of considerable acrimony, Lane and his sixty-odd supporters removed themselves from New Australia to other land granted to them by the Paraguyan government. On 7 July they re-established their utopia at Cosme, 75 kilometres (45 miles) to the south, on 9000 hectates

(23,000 acres) of land in two separate allotments, nestled between twin tributaries of the Tebicuary River. In order to fund the new colony, Lane pulled a tricky financial manoeuvre over the sale of the *Royal Tar*. But this time, things were going to work. All the crooked elements, as Lane described them—the shirkers, slackers and drinkers who had corrupted his ideal—had been expunged.

Cosme was not immediately as prosperous as New Australia had been. In the first few years, the colonists were forced to resort to eating eels and monkeys. But then the crops began to prosper: maize, sweet potatoes, melons, mandioca, sugar cane and tobacco were all successfully grown.

While there were piranhas in the river, there were also several varieties of local catfish. One of them, the manguruyú, was capable of growing to 200 kilograms (440 pounds) in weight. Aside from these supplements, the colonists still had insufficient red meat in their diets, which was somewhat surprising in a culture as famous for its barbecues as the one they had come from. During those early years, the bullocks were needed for clearing land and planting crops, and the Cosme settlers lacked the money to buy a herd. This would change as the colony developed.

The small imported society was able to enjoy a social life that included square dances, variety nights, public lectures and poetry readings, in an atmosphere free of alcohol. While the material circumstances of the colony continued to improve, however, there were serious problems in terms of its demographics. Firstly, there weren't enough people. While Cosme grew in its first two years from sixty-three people to ninety-five, to fulfil the terms of the land grant by the Paraguayan government, they were supposed to have settled seventy-two families by 1898. In 1896 they had only sixteen. Secondly, the ratio of single men to women was unbalanced. At the first dances, there were thirty-eight available men to ten available women. By the second anniversary, in July 1896, the ration had worsened to thirty-three single men to only three single women—something that was bound to cause a degree of friction in any non-monastic community. While no one had explicitly prohibited romance with the locals (whose gender balance was the opposite), the racial prejudice of the colonists continued to permeate their sense of social hierarchy, and 'going native', to adopt a phrase from British imperialism, was considered poor form.

Despite almost dying from an obstruction of the bowel, William Lane appeared to have drawn closer to his idea of utopia second time around. If Cosme were to survive, however, it needed more people, and in 1896 he set off on a recruitment mission. Instead of going to Australia, where the story of New Australia might have sullied his reputation, Lane chose Britain. Perhaps this was a marker of the emerging Anglo-Saxon imperialism that

FOLLOWING PAGES: A group of colonists, including Mary Gilmore, at Cosme

would dominate his politics in later years. Lane travelled around the old country giving talks, and while there were a few takers, they only ever came in dribs and drabs. This lack of success meant that Lane stayed away from the colony until February 1898, so that the British recruits began arriving in his absence.

The newcomers inevitably clashed with the Australians who had long adapted to harshness of frontier life. One of Lane's original arguments was that Australians were better suited to this kind of endeavour than the English, precisely because they had learned how to operate in a radically different environment, and it seems there was some truth to this.

To the veterans of Cosme, the new arrivals were materially far better off and complained too much, while the English settlers resented the barriers of entry the originals had created in order to establish a sense of ownership in the colony. At the same time, though, the clannish veterans were being riven by their own internal ructions.

When William Lane returned, matters were coming to a head. With his typical insensitivity, he managed to turn an episode involving the non-communal eating of a pig by a colonist and some of his friends into a major fracas. Two of the pig-eaters were expelled from Cosme by a vote of a two-thirds majority. Six dissenters and their families then decided to leave the colony of their own free will.

By April 1898, Cosme had lost thirty-eight people—more than 30 per cent of the colony. Lane's recruitment drive to England, which had occurred at the colony's expense, was undone and more in less than two months after his return. One of the colonists who left in sympathy with the evictees, Larry Petrie, wrote the following regarding his former leader:

> He is a madman, a knave seized with the madness of ambition, overpowered with a sense of the divinity of himself and his mission, and for that he will barter truth justice and the whole of the world plus the handful of bigots he terms the faithful. I believe everybody can perceive how shamefully he betrays his friends, cheerfully leaving them to bear a burden of reproach which he at least should share.

While undoubtedly written in anger, such a judgment was not a wholly inaccurate assessment of Lane's approach to leadership and his delusional perception of his own role in the scheme of things. In May 1899, embittered by the failure of others to inhabit his vision, Lane resigned as chairman of Cosme. His brother John, a less dogmatic and more practical character, was elected in his stead.

No longer the leader, Lane was soon no longer in Cosme either. In August that year, just before his thirty-eighth birthday, Lane, his wife Ann and their children left for Auckland via London. He worked for the *New Zealand Herald*, but before long he had accepted a post in Sydney, as editor of *The Worker*. He soon discovered he'd become too conservative for the labour movement, however, and resigned after three months to return to Auckland and the *Herald*. There, the same imperialist outlook that had once seen him hoping that Paraguay might become part of the British Empire became increasingly reactionary and anti-labour. This seemed to suit both his employers and the newspaper's readers. He was promoted to editor in 1913, a position that he held until his death in August 1917 at the age of fifty-five.

Fading to Paraguay

Unlike many failed colonies, neither New Australia nor Cosme was abandoned. However, with Lane's departure, their mode and organisation shifted towards private ownership and greater integration with the rest of Paraguyan society. By 1908, the population of New Australia was 161. This figure was considerably less than it had started with in September 1893, but more than double that of 1897, when an agreement was reached with the Paraguayan government to grant each colonist 45 hectares (110 acres) of personal land while retaining 11,000 hectares (28,000 acres) for common use. The restrictions on drinking and temporary membership were removed, and the people who arrived there came from as far afield as Sweden, Britain and the United States, as well as Australia; in addition, there was increasing miscegenation with the Paraguayan locals.

Although the colony was hampered by the difficulty of access to markets, being

> ✳ *To me turning with aching heart from wrangling and groping, Truth has whispered. To me, sinking in self-knowing agony on the dungeon-floor of life, Freedom has shown what might be. To me, faltering often because Wrong triumphs, the knowledge of how justice is ever done has come. For God has given a task to me who am unworthy, and has not deserted me altogether, though for years I have tried to do his work without declaring Him openly, relying on my own intellect rather than on the Supreme will, and shrinking from the scoffs and jeers of men. It is reaping of my own sowing that the Settlement we have tried to build has been uncemented by the sense of God, without which there can be no trust among men.*

William Lane displaying his wounded messianic streak, as well as his emerging conservatism, in the face of his failure to lead New Australia

relatively far from either the railway or a navigable river, the prosperity of New Australia grew. From 1900 to 1926, the colony's administrator was James Kennedy, who gave it the stability that the utopians had been unable to provide. By 1924, when Australian genealogist George Reeve raised the question of repatriation for the New Australians, there were only around two dozen Australian-born residents remaining. Most of the next generation had married Paraguayans, and in most cases the third generation didn't speak English.

A number of Australian Paraguayans fought in the Australian armed forces during World War I, but almost all of the survivors returned to Paraguay rather than Australia at the cessation of hostilities. Some of the colonists and their children left New Australia to work in other parts of Paraguay or in Argentina. The dwindling Britishness of the colonists would have appalled William Lane, as would the number of distilleries built in the colony for the making of *cana*, the local rum-like spirit.

In Cosme, a similar thing happened, albeit more slowly. In 1961, Mary Davey, the last of the original colonists, died. By that time, none of the ideals on which Cosme had been founded remained, although by most accounts it was a pleasant, slow-paced, if primitive, backwater to live in.

Some of the descendants of the Australians have prospered in their country. They include Robin Wood, a bestselling author of comic books throughout Latin America. There have been famous anthropologists, wealthy businessmen and cattle ranchers, while some still eke out a largely subsistence living at Cosme. It could easily be argued that both New Australia and Cosme should be considered a success. There was no great period of starvation, and most of the people who stayed enjoyed relatively comfortable lives. But the true ghosts of these two colonies are the ideals of establishing a perfect society, especially when filtered through the cranky persona of their instigator, William Lane.

CHAPTER 24

The Finnish socialist colony of Sointula, British Columbia (1901–04)

In 1901, after a failed attempt to establish a colony at Chillagoe in tropical northern Queensland, Finnish utopian socialist Matti Kurikka set his sights on Malcolm Island, wedged between the northern shore of Vancouver Island and mainland British Columbia. Named after the Finnish for 'place of harmony', Sointula experienced difficult beginnings caused by the settlers' lack of experience in the two staple industries of lumberjacking and fishing, not to mention a lack of capital. Conflict arose from Kurikka's radical ideas on sexual mores and child rearing, and the whole sorry situation was compounded by a tragic fire in 1903. Amid accusations of fraud and financial incompetence, Kurikka and half the members left in October 1904, seven months after which the colonisation company was liquidated. It seems that Sointula was anything but a place of harmony for its first European inhabitants.

Born in north-west Russia to bourgeois Finnish parents in 1862, Matti Kurikka was arguably Finland's premier socialist during the mid 1890s. In terms of historical context, his career trajectory bore some similarity to New Australia's William Lane (see page 271), and indeed he shared his Australian counterpart's facility for charismatic speech, as well as his pig-headedness and impracticality. Kurikka was editor of *Työmies* (meaning 'the worker'), Finland's main labour newspaper, for two years from 1897. His form of socialism was

Portrait of Matti Kurikka from his time at the Harmony Island colony

highly nationalistic and earned him the ire of the Russian government, which was pursuing a course of Russifying Finland at the time. Ironically, it also earned him the contempt of Finland's Marxist socialists, whose emphasis was international and who scorned Kurikka's utopian impulses from the sureties of their historical determinism. When the production of his radical play *Tower of Babel* managed to offend his supporters among Finland's nationalistic upper classes, Kurikka decided it was prudent to leave the country with the idea of organising a utopian society based on a mix of Tolstoy's Christian socialism and theosophy, which were the foundations of his political beliefs.

The place he chose was Queensland, in soon to be federalised Australia, where William Lane's utopian dream of a shearers' paradise had come to nothing some years before. The Queensland government initially approved of the Finnish colony and offered Kurikka's eighty-odd settlers free railway travel to their intended base at Chillagoe, in the far north of the state, where they established a tent city. When their utopian socialist principles became evident, however, government support dried up. The colonists were forced to resort to manual labour, such as cutting railway sleepers, to put together enough money to buy some beachfront land in the vicinity of Cooktown, further north, but the money they earned wasn't sufficient and the men became disenchanted.

The women and children had been left behind in Cooktown, and when the sleeper-cutting got too much, the men returned there. They soon became so broke that Kurikka had to resort to busking in the local pubs to get enough money for food. Nonetheless, he remained undeterred.

From Cooktown, Kurikka led his band of colonists on a trip further north into the wilds of the Gulf of Carpentaria, with the intention of founding a settlement there. As before, it was a debacle. The Finns were forced to eat wild honey and other bush tucker to escape starvation while their socialist messiah led them into the wilderness. Like most messiahs, Kurikka was immune to seeing himself at fault.

It was at this time that he received a request from some Finnish coal miners in the western Canadian province of British Columbia, who were hoping to establish a socialist paradise where the profits of their labour would be more evenly distributed than was currently the case. They were looking for a life that took them out of the bowels of the earth and into a place where they could live in harmony with each other and nature. Rescued by the offer, and no doubt deeply flattered, Kurikka left Queensland with the claim that:

> The labourers in Australia ... are too drunk, too vulgar and too hateful against all foreigners that are as sober, friendly and honest as the Finns ... My friendly hope is only that the people of Queensland will rise to the same level of civilisation as the other cultured peoples of the world.

Perhaps the patrons of Cooktown's pubs weren't too fond of Finnish folk music.

New harmony

Kurikka arrived in the coastal town of Nanaimo in British Colombia in August 1900 and he and his new colonists immediately began to look for suitable territory around the Vancouver region. The government of British Columbia was somewhat more generous than that of Queensland towards the Finns, who had incorporated themselves as the Kalevan Kansan Colonization Company.

They were granted conditional title of Malcolm Island, in a strait below Queen Charlotte Sound—some 30,000 hectares (80,000 acres) of land wedged between Vancouver Island and the mainland, and about 290 kilometres (180 miles) north-west of the city of Vancouver. Full title would not be granted for seven years, by which time the company was to import one settler for every 32 hectares (80 acres) of land, making the minimum population 250. The Finns had to become British subjects and have their children educated in schools where English was the primary language of instruction; they also had to improve the land to the value of $2.50 per acre and provide the colony's infrastructure, such as buildings and bridges.

On 15 December 1901, the first five settlers arrived on Malcolm Island and named the site they chose for settlement Sointula, meaning 'place of harmony'. People trickled in and by the summer of 1902 the population had reached 127.

The most immediate problems they faced were financial. While Kurikka was capable of building inviting fantasies of utopian socialism, the practicalities of getting a colony off the ground eluded him. Each new settler was supposed to stump up $200 seed capital to help get the settlement running, but despite Kurikka's exhortations most of the colonists were reluctant, preferring to work the amount off instead, or wait until the future of the colony seemed secure before departing with their life savings. The irony of this was that Sointula fell into debt before it had the means to pay it off. By withholding this crucial money, the settlers seriously compromised the colony's chances of survival.

At the same time, their caution was probably prudent. Money alone was not going to solve the economic problems that the Finnish expats faced. While natural resources on Malcolm Island were abundant, little of the land was immediately available for agriculture, and most foodstuffs had to be imported. It was decided that the best chance of earning money to pay for food before agriculture could be established was to harvest the lumber from the forest that covered most of the island, and to fish for the salmon that inhabited the turbulent waters of Queen Charlotte Strait in droves. While the ideas were solid, the execution was lacking. Most of the colonists were coal miners, urban émigrés and utopian thinkers, and

had little experience in either lumberjacking or fishing. This put them at a competitive disadvantage to the established businesses in the region. Their inefficiency at cutting timber was compounded by the distance between Malcolm Island and the markets in Vancouver. Besides, timber was plentiful in British Columbia, prices were low and the market was glutted; between Sointula and Vancouver were many places with better quality lumber, cut cheaper.

The hope of achieving economic self-sufficiency through fishing also proved elusive. Once again, few of the Finnish utopians had the necessary expertise. Even if the settlers had been able to catch large amounts of salmon, there was still a considerable distance to the markets, and as for raw timber, prices were very low due to supply outweighing local demand. Perhaps the only way to make fishing work would have been to build a cannery. But this conflicted somewhat with the aesthetic of getting back to nature—and it was impossible anyway, because the colonists lacked the capital to construct one.

The timber felling at least had the benefit of clearing the land for agriculture, as well as providing the colony with fuel and building materials. While they weren't competitive in terms of raw lumber, the colonists decided that finished lumber might actually be the way to go.

In December 1902, as Sointula entered its second year, a sawmill assembled from spare parts was brought to the island and began to turn out finished-lumber products, and a small tugboat was acquired to tow the goods to market in Vancouver.

With a great deal of the forest now cleared, agricultural endeavour proved discouraging. The only crop successfully grown was potatoes, although at least the tending of livestock became easier. While the colonists were able to supplement their diets through deer hunting and fishing, they still had to import much of their food.

Harmonic bickering

Matti Kurikka had been invited by the coal miners to lead them, but he failed to be a harmonious influence on Sointula. Like Bernhard Förster and William Lane before him, Kurikka was deeply egocentric and only ever really measured the success of things in terms of himself. Another man of words rather than action, before the colony was even established he'd threatened to quit the

Felling timber in the dense British Columbia forests during the late nineteenth century

THE MANY FACES OF FINNISH UTOPIA

Finns have been searching for utopia since two brothers, Jaakko and Erik Eriksson, and the mystic-separatist sect they led were banished by the conservative Lutheran church. In 1734, the Erikssons' sixty men, women and children left Finland on a ship and spent the next eleven years travelling between Denmark, Holland and Germany before moving to Sweden. There, the group dissolved after the death of Erik, and in conjunction with a more liberal religious climate back in Finland.

In 1792, another group of Finns combined with Swedes and some English in a plan to establish a Swedenborgian (another Christian mystical sect) utopian colony in Sierra Leone. Given that one proposal was to transport the colonists from England in a flotilla of hot-air balloons, a new invention at the time, it is perhaps no surprise that this particular project never really got off the ground.

An attempt in 1868 to set up a Finnish colony near the Amur River on the Pacific coast of Siberia was slightly more successful. Comprised predominantly of fishermen and their families, it lasted several years before its dissolution: the inhabitants either returned to Finland or melted into nearby Russian communities. In 1899, a group of Finnish nationalists, seeking to escape the new tsarist policy to Russify Finland drew up plans to establish a colony in Alberta, Canada.

The grand dreamer of Finland's utopian exodus was Matti Kurikka, although none of the four colonies he attempted to establish were successful. Yet his failures did not deter other Finns from trying. Two nationalist colonies with socialist inclinations were founded in Cuba in 1904 and 1906, but neither lasted long. More successful was Colonia Finlandesa, founded in 1906 by an eccentric aristocrat named Arthur Thesleff. Set in the subtropical Misiones region of Argentina, near the border with Brazil and Paraguay, Colonia Finlandesa's population peaked at over 500 in the 1930s. Like many émigré colonies in South America, it gradually lost most of its cultural distinctiveness, and when the settlement celebrated its 100th anniversary, almost no one there could speak Finnish.

In the late 1920s, three Finnish colonies were founded in South America on vegetarian principles. One group settled in Paraguay, in the pre-established colony of Colonia Villa Alborada. A more substantial effort was the colony of Penedo, in Brazil, located on a former coffee plantation; founded by Toivo Uuskallio, the intention was to live in harmony with nature, which involved adhering to a strict vegan diet. Utopia was forestalled at Penedo since the coffee had leached most of the nutrients from the soil. Many of the settlers returned to Finland, and most of the others were forced to abandon their strict ideals. Dairy and poultry farming entered the community, and other than the Finnish architecture, Penedo merged into Brazilian society. A third colony, Viljavakka, in the Dominican Republic was established a year after Penedo.

During the 1920s, several Finnish communes were founded in the Soviet Union. In 1971, some Christian Finns even established a kibbutz in Israel. Despite consistent attempts to found colonies, however, only 10,000 Finns ever emigrated in this way out of a total of more than one million who have left the land of snow and reindeer for warmer, greener pastures.

venture until his compatriots agreed to divert scarce funds to the creation of his Finnish newspaper, *Aika*, so that Kurikka would have a vehicle to expound his views.

Consternation was also caused by their leader's attitude towards domestic arrangements. Kurikka's marriage had ended in divorce, and his behaviour no doubt brought other marriages to the brink of the same. He had a reputation as a ladies' man, and given his egocentricity it's easy to imagine that his attempts to undermine the institution of marriage—arguing that women should not live with the men who fathered their offspring, for instance, and that children should be raised separately from their families—were partly intended to facilitate his own nocturnal liaisons.

Fishing at Kanaka Creek, near Sammon Takojat, in the early 1900s

There were always twice as many men in Sointula as women, and while this imbalance caused problems of sexual competition, some of the men believed that women should not be part of the colony at all. One grumpy settler, clearly a dedicated bachelor, complained:

I came to Harmony Island to seek refuge in the arms of nature. I hoped to be freed of the world's meaningless bustle and fuss, to live in a tent, or under a tree, eat potatotoes, clams and berries. I thought that women would remain far away. But what happened? I had scarcely arrived here, when a lady came from New York, another from Pori [a city on the west coast of Finland], a third from St Petersburg. And now there are many dozens of them. Of course they must have knives and forks, sheets and linens. Oh, the banefulness of this world! Is this the way to get back to nature?

On the basis of his theories of sexual relations and child raising, Kurikka insisted that most of the colonists abandon the idea of separate cabins and instead live together in a three-storey log construction which his adversaries disparaged as 'the Barn'. The first two floors were partitioned into rooms for sleeping, while the top floor became a meeting hall. On 29 January 1903, while a meeting was being held upstairs, tragedy struck when the building caught fire. Chaos ensued as people tried to flee down the one narrow stairway or threw themselves out of the windows and into the cold. The untreated timber building quickly became an inferno. Eleven people died, eight of them children, which amounted to almost one-tenth of the population. Many more were badly burned.

False dawn

Following the fire at the Barn, a number of the colonists argued that if it wasn't for Kurikka's weird ideas, the casualties would have been far less. The sniping and dissatisfaction already prevalent intensified. Many of the Finns left Sointula, so beginning a slow exodus that never really reversed itself. Reconstruction tended towards log cabins designed for single-family occupation, a sign of more conventional arrangements in the colony's second incarnation.

Despite the internal dissension at this time, the colony's economic circumstances did seem to be improving. Finished lumber yielded a profit in Vancouver and so a new sawmill was planned. A brickworks was established and a new meeting house constructed, and there were further plans to build a hospital and a school. However, the colony remained in debt, and became more so due to its inability to make itself self-sufficient in terms of food.

Again, Kurikka thought he had the solution, and again it was a terrible failure. In early 1904, on the colony's behalf, he bid on a public tender to build bridges in northern Vancouver; for $3000, the Finns undertook to erect two 55-metre (180-foot) long timber bridges over the Seymour and Capilano rivers.

They were awarded the contract, simply because their bid was so absurdly low. Although many of the Sointulans were in favour of reneging on the deal that had been agreed, Kurikka insisted, arguing that otherwise the colony would lose the $150 deposit paid when submitting the tender. He also reasoned that if the settlers completed this project, they would be able to earn further income through other public works contracts for the British Columbian government.

Kurikka's arguments prevailed. For more than four months, almost the entire productive energy of the colony was devoted to felling trees, sawing logs into timber and transporting it to the sites on the mainland, where they then had to build the bridges. And all for nothing, as it turned out. Kurikka had underestimated the cost of construction so badly that the $3000 fee hadn't even covered the cost of buying the necessary tools. At the end of the project Sointula was in a worse financial position than it had been before winning the contract.

The blame was fairly levelled at their disaster-prone leader. Kurikka blustered for a bit, then took a leaf out of William Lane's book of colonial management under fire. In October 1904, Kurikka resigned from the company and left Malcolm Island, taking with him the utopian socialist dream that had failed to be realised in the colony of Sointula, just as it had in either of his Queensland efforts.

Soldiering on

After the departure of Kurikka and thirty or so others, Sointula struggled on under a new leader, but the financial situation was grim. In May 1905, a group of Vancouver creditors took hold of a load of lumber intended for market and sold it for less than its value. In response, the remaining thirty-six members of Sointula dissolved the Kalevan Kansan Colonisation Company. Most of them then left the island.

Meanwhile, Matti Kurikka had been working his magic elsewhere in British Columbia. With a few loyal believers from Malcolm Island, he'd gone on to found a new colony, Sammon Takojat, some 50 kilometres (30 miles) east of Vancouver in the Fraser Valley. This attempt to create utopia also dissolved, with any colonists who remained becoming part of the general community.

In 1906, a disenchanted Kurikka returned to Finland, where he found the times had usurped him. He eventually returned to North America and worked for a Finnish newspaper in New York, before buying a farm on Rhode Island, which is where he died in October 1915, at the age of fifty-two.

Sointula eventually became a viable community, albeit in a far more conventional way than had originally been the plan. Today, around 800 people live on Malcolm Island and some of its early utopian ethos remains. The co-op store founded by the Finns is still in existence and is heralded by locals as the oldest in British Columbia. During the Vietnam War, the island also became a haven for draft dodgers from the United States.

The Peoples' Temple, Jonestown, Guyana (1974–78)

On 18 November 1978, 909 members of the People's Temple Agricultural Commune, Guyana, committed collective suicide soon after visiting US Congressman Leo Ryan and his entourage were murdered by gunmen on the orders of Temple leader Jim Jones. It is perhaps the strangest, most extreme end to any of the colonies in this book. Even more so if you consider that compared to many, the colony was a relative success, despite the fact its population was largely drawn from the dregs of American society and peppered with middle-class idealists. No one was starving and there were no hostile barbarians at the gates eager to destroy them. While the discipline and blackmailing were unpleasant, by the standards of this book, the conditions in Jonestown were mild. Yet the megalomania of Jim Jones, a man corrupted by his own immense charisma, had created circumstances by which the colonists were convinced collectively to make the most extreme decision of all.

When the Reverend Jim Jones began his anti-racist Christian socialist activism in Indiana in the 1950s, the tragedy that would befall his congregationalists two decades later would have been impossible to imagine. Nevertheless, the signs were there in his upbringing that the charismatic leader might not necessarily use his gifts for the benefit of those around him.

Born in the small town of Crete, Indiana, in May 1931, Jones was the son of James Thurman Jones, who'd fought in World War I and come back shell-shocked. In the 1920s, Jones senior had spent five years in a psychiatric hospital. He was lucky to marry Lynetta Putnam, fifteen years his junior, since he never really worked again and was notable for being an alcoholic member of the Ku Klux Klan. Jim was their only child. Something of an outcast, Jim preferred to play with younger children, because he could control them. He also liked acting as a preacher, and was fond

Jim and Marceline Jones with their adopted children and other family members in California

of conducting funerals for animals, some of which he'd killed himself.

As a kid, Jim Jones worked hard to transcend his dysfunctional childhood through academic achievement. In addition to school texts, he studied works on Stalin, Hitler, Marx and Gandhi. By the time he moved to Bloomington, Indiana, to attend university, in 1949, he was a confirmed Marxist and had married a nurse named Marceline Baldwin. In 1951, the young couple moved to Indianapolis, where he acquired a degree in secondary education. However, it was through religion rather than school teaching that Jones decided to find an audience for himself and his brand of philosophy.

He initially became a student pastor in the Methodist Church, but left because he was forbidden from presiding over a racially integrated congregation. At any rate, the Methodist mode of worship was too conservative for Jones, while the church hierarchy quite rightly judged him to be 'too free a spirit' for the constraints required of his post. After witnessing a faith-healing service at a Baptist church, Jones decided that this was more his style. Faith healing created an aura of excitement, which was ideal for a man wanting to live on the power of his charisma. It also brought in the money necessary to fund the social programs he'd planned for the local community.

In 1955 Jones started up his first People's Temple church, in Indianapolis, which he helped finance by selling pet monkeys door to door. The religious services soon became known for their theatrical intensity. Blacks and whites sang together and grooved in the aisles to rich gospel music, while Reverend Jones 'healed' people and delivered sermons on the importance of equality and the radical message of Jesus Christ. Away from the services, the People's Temple provided a soup kitchen for the indigent and nursing homes for the elderly. The congregation boomed just as its preacher began to be seduced by the power of his role in the spotlight. According to sources at the time, after taking a busload of churchgoers to visit the wealthy Philadelphian revivalist preacher Father Brown in 1957, Jones returned to Indianapolis convinced that he was God. This corrupting sense of omnipotence was reflected in his behaviour as he began sleeping with his parishioners, boozing and taking drugs.

That Jim Jones was a powerful campaigner for the cause of racial integration cannot be denied. In 1961, he and Marcey became the first white couple in Indiana to adopt an African-American child, before which they had already adopted several Korean children as well as having a natural son of their own. The Joneses became referred to as a 'rainbow family'.

When the mayor of Indianapolis, Charles Boswell, appointed him a director of the Human Rights Commission in 1960, Jones ignored the request to keep a low profile and embarked on a series of anti-racist public gestures. One was making the beds and emptying the bedpans of African-American hospital patients after he was accidentally put in a black ward instead of one designated for whites. Subsequent political pressure from Jones forced the authorities to desegregate the wards. As Indianapolis was a stronghold of the Ku Klux Klan at that time, these gestures were not universally popular. The People's Temple church was graffitied with swastikas, while a stick of dynamite was deposited in its coal pile.

California dreaming

Perhaps it was understandable that Jones started to grow paranoid in the racially charged, Cold War-obsessed environment of the 1960s. But paranoia can be a very dangerous thing when you think that you are God. In 1962, Jones's belief that Indianapolis would be demolished by nuclear weapons led him to take his family off to live in Belo Horizonte in south-eastern Brazil, one of nine places that had been named in an *Esquire* magazine article earlier in the year as being likely to avoid the fallout from a nuclear war. Jones failed to prosper there or later when he moved Marcey and the clan on to Rio de Janeiro. While there was plenty of work for him in trying to address problems associated with the country's harsh poverty, Brazil was already racially integrated, while the language barrier made it hard for him to work his charisma.

After three years away, Jones returned to America in 1965 to find that the church in Indianapolis had far from prospered in his absence. Having prophesied that a nuclear war was to take place in July 1967, he led about 140 people from Indiana to establish a new People's Temple in California. The site he chose was near Ukiah, in the Redwood Valley north of San Francisco, a place that *Esquire* had also deemed capable of escaping the effects of nuclear attack.

Once settled in Redwood Valley, the People's Temple grew enormously, as did its wealth. Yet it came to resemble a Christian church less and less as Jones embraced the concept of apostolic socialism, which denied the existence of God. In his sermons, he frequently threw the Bible on the ground, arguing that it was a tool of oppression. In the words of his wife, Marcey, he 'used religion to get people away from the opiate of religion'.

When the nuclear holocaust failed to eventuate, Jones began to think about expanding his influence into the urban areas of California. In 1971 he set up a church in Geary Street, San Francisco, and in 1972 another one in Los Angeles, both at the sites of disused synagogues. Through a series of recruitment drives, the People's Temple expanded from a few hundred members to more than 3000, each paying at least 25 per cent of their income to the church as a tithe. Many handed over their entire salaries and assets in return for a guarantee of care. One such new recruit was Timothy Stoen, an idealistic and highly capable assistant district attorney with the local Mendocino County's civil division, and a man who would play a central role in the Temple's fortunes through to the end.

The increased membership base and expansion into new Californian locations allowed Jones to pursue his programs on a greater scale and cultivate allies among the state's political leaders. One of the ways he did this was by offering them the services of his Temple disciples to help bolster the numbers at political rallies and campaign events. They were the perfect rent-a-crowd for liberal causes: racially integrated, of all ages and classes, and well behaved. While the actual membership of the People's Temple never got above 5000, those who were affiliated with it numbered up to 20,000. In closely contested elections, the bloc vote of Jim Jones's People's Temple could make the difference between winning office or not. Most notably this occurred in the San Francisco mayoral campaign of 1975 undertaken by Democrat politician George Moscone. He won the election by a mere 4000 votes, and it was widely recognised that the campaigning and voting of the People's Temple had made the difference.

Moscone was certainly grateful. In recognition of Jones's support, the new mayor appointed him chairman of the San Francisco Housing Authority Commission, at the same time giving the influential preacher access to the upper echelons of the Democratic Party, such as Walter Mondale and Californian governor Jerry Brown. Aside from providing the numbers, politicians liked Jones because he took the pressure off their social-welfare bottom lines: under 'Reverend Jim', soup kitchens, nursing homes, drug rehabilitation

Jim Jones raises his fist in a black power salute while preaching in the United States

and welfare accommodation were all provided without causing a strain on the public purse. For while Jones courted the country's politicians and high-flyers like Tim Stoen, the People's Temple encouraged anyone, no matter how abject, to enter its fold.

False confesssions and conditional love

Once someone became a fully subscribed member of the People's Temple, the pressure to conform was intense. In many cases, these people were entirely dependent on Jones, having been coerced into giving up all their assets to his church. During some services, Jones initiated the practice of catharsis by which devotees were ritually humiliated. Sometimes they were spanked for minor indiscretions, at other times beaten with a paddle. As a student of Joseph Stalin, Jones had learned the value of divide and rule. Temple members were encouraged to report each other for infractions, which would then be publicly punished. Many were forced to sign false confessions saying that they had sexually abused their children, so that Jones and the Temple hierarchy would have leverage over them if they ever decided to leave.

While a good deal of the achievements of the People's Temple were admirable as examples of living rather than theoretical socialism, the means of patrolling collectivity were suspect. Like many utopian socialists and megalomaniacs, such as Finnish utopian Matti Kurikka (see page 289), Jones saw the family as an enemy to his project and played people off against each other. Essentially, the People's Temple was a structure that attempted to filter its members' personal relationships through the group hierarchy.

Unfortunately, this filter was affected by the increasing power of Jones. Power is usually a game for the cautious and tends to amplify existent paranoia, and Jim Jones was unable to recognise that his urge for total control was a weakness in himself. As a consequence, he lost the capacity to distinguish between real and imaginary threats to himself and the Temple, as well as the ability to deftly

negotiate his way through any negative publicity they received.

To some extent, Jones's paranoia regarding his personal safety was justified. It was a violent era for American politics, and assassinations were not uncommon. John and Robert Kennedy, Malcolm X and Martin Luther King had all been gunned down in the 1960s. Yet for Reverend Jim Jones, rather than the assassin's bullet it was his hypersensitivity to attack by the media that precipitated the wholesale move to South America and his eventual demise.

Jones had used his political influence to quash a number of newspaper and magazine pieces over the years. But in July 1977 he was unable to prevent the publication in *New West* magazine of a series of articles by reporter Marshall Kilduff, which featured interviews with defectors from the Temple, including the infamous Gang of Eight, who'd fled north to Montana in 1973. While the editor of the magazine was reading Jones the articles over the telephone—out of courtesy, because of his political connections—he apparently made the decision to move the People's Temple en masse to Guyana.

Guyana

Jones had first visited Guyana during his sojourn in Brazil in the early 1960s. Since 1964, Guyana had been ruled by tinpot dictator Forbes Burnham, who had been installed by the CIA only to later swing to the hard left of the political spectrum.

By 1970, he had become a Black Power-affiliated communist and declared Guyana a 'co-operative republic'. Burnham had a demographic problem, however, in that most people who could afford to leave the country had done so. For this reason he was particularly amenable to Jim Jones's interest in establishing a co-operative commune for members of the People's Temple, not to mention the man's cash.

In April 1974, against a background of negative publicity and the eight high-profile defections the year before, Jones negotiated a lease on 1500 hectares (3800 acres) of land in the sparsely populated jungles of north-west Guyana, close to the border with Venezuela. The parcel of land was viewed by the increasingly paranoid Temple hierarchy as a bolt-hole in the event of their multiplying enemies (including Nazis, racists and multinational corporations) becoming too powerful in America.

The colony was designated the People's Temple Agricultural Project. Despite this moniker, supplies of drugs and weapons were brought into Jonestown (as the settlement would come to be called) by bribing customs officials. During its early years, the colony was populated by about fifty full-time people, while the Temple also had premises in the capital city of Georgetown, some 150 kilometres (90 miles) to the south-east. Many of these original colonists were former drug addicts who had come to Guyana to dry out. In the jungle, land was cleared for the cultivation of crops such as cassava,

bananas and pineapples. According to Temple publicity films, there were 140 types of tropical plant under cultivation. Families were given huts, while single people slept in dormitories, as was the case in many other nascent colonies.

The initial set-up was a success. Food was grown, the accommodation was presentable, and there was an excellent small hospital to cater for the inevitable problems of tropical living. The major issue facing the colony, in fact, was its leader, back in California. When the order to relocate the Temple ultimately came, the population of Jonestown increased in a series of airlifts to a peak of 1000, a number that included a greater proportion of families than before, as well as senior citizens.

The previously relaxed atmosphere was transformed with the arrival of Jim Jones in July 1977, some members even commenting later that it was as if a dark cloud had suddenly settled over the place. He introduced harsh working conditions: six days a week from 6.30 am to 6 pm, with an hour for lunch, and a half day on Sunday. Although this timetable was subsequently reduced to eight hours a day, five days a week, it was supplemented by a series of lectures and services that could often last until the early hours of the morning. With the population suitably exhausted from their labour, Jones consciously borrowed from Chinese, Stalinist and North Korean mind-control techniques as a means of completing the brainwashing process.

Jonestown contained many vulnerable and impressionable people who had been cut off from the outside world. Driven by Jones' paranoia, mail was read, and there was no telephone. In order to prevent any followers from defecting, Jones posted armed guards, his Red Brigade, around the settlement. Connections in the Guyana government were used to ensure that anyone bearing animosity towards the People's Temple or wanting to persuade family members to leave had trouble obtaining the requisite visas to enter the country. As a result, the man the colonists termed 'Dad', Reverend Jim Jones, was the crazy filter through which they perceived the outside world. And he made no bones about telling them that things were pretty grim out there.

For a good number of his people, however, it's arguable that their life as a devotee was superior to their pre-Temple existence. Given that so many misfits and mentally frail souls were among them, Jonestown and the People's Temple in general provided a sense of community, a structured environment for people who were otherwise incapable of looking after themselves. For a large proportion of those who now found themselves in Guyana, there was simply nowhere else to go.

Jones wasted no time in imposing his increasingly apocalyptic world view on his devotees. He installed a PA system with loudspeakers covering the entire settlement, and only Jones had access to the microphone. The colonists were exposed to his irrational rantings 24 hours a day. Whether eating dinner or working the fields, the voice of Jones was impossible to escape. Even sleeping, the colony was frequently deluged with Jones's nocturnal rants, his voice increasingly slurred by alcohol and the cocktail of medications he was taking for undisclosed ailments.

As time went by, more and more of the colony's energies were absorbed by the black hole of its leader's political agenda. The movies that the original colonists used to borrow from Georgetown were replaced with Soviet propaganda films. With the guards around the perimeter, the constant loudspeaker barrages preaching their lurid conspiracy theories, the backbreaking work, members spying on each other and the ritual humiliation, Jonestown came to resemble a tropical Stalinist work camp, only one that held discotheques at night.

Enemies at the gates

Back in the United States, pressure to investigate the People's Temple had been growing since the latter half of 1976. The publication of Marshall Kilduff's *New West* articles had the roll-on effect of sending most of Jones's influential friends diving for cover in an effort to distance themselves from Reverend Jim and the political time-bomb that his church constituted. Much of this pressure was generated through the lobbying of a group known as the Concerned Relatives, made up of prominent former members of the Temple and families of people who were still among its flock.

The defection of Tim Stoen in June 1977 was a particularly important coup for those looking to shine a light on the dark goings-on at Ukiah and now Jonestown. As Jones's once trusted friend, attorney Stoen had actually designed the plan for the Guyana exodus and had intimate knowledge of the Temple's millions of dollars worth of assets in foreign bank accounts. However, the drama of his defection and that of his wife, Grace, would mainly be played out through the legal battle between the Stoens and Jim Jones for custody of their five-year-old son, John. According to the submissions presented by the Temple's lawyers, Tim Stoen had asked Jones to sleep with his wife and impregnate her, since he himself was infertile. Whether there was any truth in Jones's claim remains unknown. The Stoens would later argue that the statement they had signed to this effect in February 1972 was one of those concocted to be used against members in the event of their attempting to leave the People's Temple. Then again, it was the seventies, and Jones was pretty much able to sleep with any Temple devotee, male or female, he wanted to.

The Stoens had become estranged from each other while still members of the Temple. Grace defected first, in July 1976, but had been unable to get access to her son. She started pursuing the matter through the American courts.

When Tim defected too, he united with his wife in the action. Much to Jones's chagrin, in November 1977 a San Francisco court appointed custody to Grace. By this time, however, young John Stoen had been stashed away in Jonestown. Attempts to have him returned encountered massive local political interference. On the first attempt, the following January, a judge recused himself, saying he had received a death threat over the case. Tim Stoen's visa was then revoked, despite the fact that it was valid for another week at least. With their son inaccessible, the Stoens reverted to exposing the People's Temple in the media.

From his fortified colony in north-western Guyana, Jones railed against the Trotskyite traitors who were trying to bring him undone. He insisted that he was not going to hand over John Stoen, whatever the cost. Perhaps if he had, the events of 18 November might not have occurred, but by this stage Jones was beyond making rational decisions. Although Californian politicians such as Harvey Milk and Willie Brown continued to offer vocal support, the preacher from Indiana was now alone, isolated within his realm of Red Brigade guards, conspiracy theories and savage paranoia.

Jones had already instituted a dummy-run mass suicide, as a loyalty test for his Temple faithful, when he'd made his congregation drink from a vat and then told them it was poison. As 1978 wore on in a flurry of legal exchanges and further media exposés, and the more cornered his deluded mind became, the more attractive the idea of suicide must have seemed. There were other contingency plans open to him, such as moving the People's Temple to the Soviet Union, but as history records, they weren't options he chose to explore.

Cyanide jungle

The catalyst for the sudden and immediate demise of the colony was the visit of US congressman Leo Ryan, along with a few government officials, four members of the Concerned Relatives organisation and a small entourage of journalists. Known for his political showmanship, Ryan had once investigated America's prison system by having himself incarcerated in San Quentin penitentiary for several weeks. He had been approached by the Concerned Relatives early in 1978 and decided to investigate on their behalf. If necessary, the Democrat announced, he was more than prepared to 'free the captives'.

On 14 November, Ryan flew down to Georgetown with his entourage. The lawyers for the People's Temple, Mark Lane and Charles Garry, informed the congressman that he and the others wouldn't be allowed into Jonestown; however, when the two lawyers got word to Jim Jones that Ryan was coming whether he liked it or not, this changed. While Ryan was being given the

The bodies of Congressman Leo Ryan and his companions lie on the Port Kaituma airstrip

runaround in Georgetown, Jones began conducting rehearsals designed to give the visitors the impression that everyone was happy to be in the colony.

Congressman Ryan left the Guyanan capital on 17 November and, sure enough, his party received a warm reception at Jonestown. A function was held that night, where the singing and dancing added to the impression that all was well in this little corner of South America. Having been invited to say a few words, Congressman Ryan declared that he was impressed with Jonestown, that people had been telling him it was by far the best thing that had happened to them. For this speech, he received incredible applause that went on and on.

Not everyone, however, was clapping. During Jim Jones's following speech—a predictably paranoid rant about secret plots and martyrdom at the hands of one's enemies—some of the Temple followers surreptitiously approached members of the congressional party and asked for their help to escape.

Planning to depart late the next day, Ryan and three of his companions stayed overnight in Jonestown, while the other members of the contingent were forced to bunk down in a nearby village. Early in the morning of 18 November, eleven members of the Temple snuck out to the village; during the day, other families sought Ryan's protection to help them defect. Jones had apparently given all of them permission to leave, no doubt because he already had other plans.

A violent tropical thunderstorm served as a harbinger of the chaos that was to follow.

Late that afternoon, Ryan's party and the fourteen would-be defectors headed off towards the airstrip at Kaituma, a short way north, in a dump truck. One of the Temple members, Don Sly, soon showed himself to be a stooge of Jones when he tried to stab Ryan in the truck, but he was pinned down by some of the other defectors. While they waited at Kaituma for a second plane to be readied in addition to their small Cessna, the tension grew. On board the Cessna, defector Larry Layton also proved where his loyalties lay by trying to shoot the passengers. He too was wrestled to the ground after wounding two of the defectors.

The larger plane, a nineteen-seat Twin Otter, was still boarding when a tractor and trailer approached, carrying members of the Temple's Red Brigade security squad, who opened fire. Ryan and four members of the delegation were killed, another nine were injured. The irony was that the attack had been ordered even though Ryan had told Temple attorney Charles Garry that the report he was going to write would be mainly positive.

If Jones hadn't ordered the ambush at Kaituma, it's likely that the People's Temple would have survived. Once it had taken place, however, the situation was irrevocable— which is perhaps exactly what Jim Jones had intended anyway. It is quite likely he was seriously ill, physically as well as mentally, and in his delusional state found it inconceivable that his creation would outlast him. What came next was possibly a disgraceful act of vanity, almost without parallel.

Through the PA system, Jones called a mass meeting in the colony's main pavilion. While the Temple members began to gather, some of Jones's acolytes prepared a vat of poison containing tranquillisers, potassium chloride (used in executions by lethal injection), potassium cyanide (a relatively slow and agonising poison) and Kool-Aid, to conceal the bitter taste. As the subsequently discovered Jonestown Death Tape would reveal, the children were brought up first to drink the potion, at which point some of the members tried to argue with Jones. They were soon shouted down by others loyal to 'Dad'. A few of these doubters were lucky enough to escape, but most of the Jonestown colonists, having been deluged with Jones's charismatic delusions and effectively brainwashed, lacked the ability to refuse.

While some were probably coerced, the vast majority of the 909 people who died from the poison were either children or followers who had voluntarily drunk from the vat. Jones and one of his offsiders were found dead from gunshot wounds. When investigators arrived the following day, they found almost 1000 bodies bloated in the tropical jungle. The body of John Stoen, dead at the age of six and a half, was discovered in Jones's cabin.

Ghost land

It was the strangest, most sickening way for a colony to fail, especially one that could have been a success. A reminder, too, to be sceptical when choosing leaders. If Jim Jones alone had dropped dead, Jonestown might well still be there today, or at least it would gradually have faded into the general fabric of Guyana society. Just as there can be no doubt that Jones was the charismatic glue holding the People's Temple together, there's also no doubt that by the time he got to Guyana he was insane, and with the megalomaniacal will to create a tragic mass delusion. The remnants of the Temple in the United States and the branch in Georgetown understandably disintegrated soon afterwards. Jones left most of the church's liquid assets (around $7.3 million) to the Soviet Union.

Once the bodies had been disposed of, Jonestown was looted by the local Guyana people, who nonetheless refused to inhabit such a haunted place. In the early 1980s, the site became a temporary refuge for the Hmong people, paradoxically refugees from persecution by the communist government of Laos. Today, however, it is deserted, except for the ghosts of the largest mass suicide of modern times.

Jim Jones' throne in front of the stage in the main pavilion at Jonestown, one year after the massacre

✳ EXCERPT FROM THE JONESTOWN DEATH TAPE

JONES: *It's never been done before, you say? It's been done by every tribe in history— every tribe facing annihilation. All the Indians in the Amazon are doing it now. They refuse to bring any babies into the world. They kill every child that comes into the world, because they don't want to live in this kind of a world. So be patient, be patient … I tell you, I don't care how many screams you hear, I don't care how many anguished cries … death is a million times preferable to ten more days of this life. If you knew what was ahead of you … you'd be glad to be stepping over tonight. Death, death, death is common to people … and the Eskimos, they take death in their stride. Let's, let's be dignified. If you'll quit telling them [the children] they're dying, if you adults will stop some of this nonsense … I call on you to quit exciting your children when all they're doing is going to a quiet rest. I call on you to stop this now. If you have any respect at all … Are we black, proud and socialist, or what are we? Now stop this nonsense, don't carry this on anymore, you're exciting your children.*

CROWD: *Right, right.*

JONES: *All over, and it's good. No, no sorrow that it's all over. I'm glad it's over … Hurry, hurry, my children, hurry. All I say, let's not fall in the hands of the enemy. Hurry, my children. Hurry … there are seniors out here that I'm concerned about. Hurry, I don't want to leave my seniors to this mess. Quickly, quickly, quickly, quickly, quickly … Sisters, good knowing you … no more pain now … No more pain I said, Al, no more pain. [Gang of Eight defector] Jim Cobb is laying on the airfield dead at this moment …*

CROWD: *[cheers, shouting and clapping]*

JONES: *… all they're doing is taking a drink, that takes to go to sleep … That's what death is, sleep … I know, but I'm tired of it all.*

UNIDENTIFIED WOMAN: ... *the most loving thing all of us could have done, and it's been a pleasure walking with all of you in this revolutionary struggle. No other way I would rather go than to give my life for socialism, communism, and I thank Dad very, very much.*

UNIDENTIFIED WOMAN: *That, that Dad's love and mercy, goodness and kindness, and bring us to this land of freedom, his love, his mother was the advanced, the advanced guide to socialism and his love, his mercy will go on forever, unto the [unintelligible word] ...*

JONES: *[unintelligible words] ... Where's the vat, the vat, the vat? Where's the vat with the green C thing? CN.*

UNIDENTIFIED WOMAN: *Love is to go on [unintelligible words] ... and thank you, Dad.*

JONES: *The vat, with the green CN, please. Bring it here so the adults can begin ... beg you, don't, don't, fail to follow my advice, you'll be sorry ... you'll be sorry ... [unintelligible word] ... that we'll do it than that they do it.*

VOICES IN THE BACKGROUND: *That's right, that's right.*

JONES: *... you have to step across ... We used to sing: 'This world, this world's not our home'. Well, it sure isn't ... We were saying, it sure wasn't ... Can some people assure these children of the relaxation of stepping over to the next plane? That'd set an example for others. You set 1000 people who say, 'We don't like the way the world is ...'*

CROWD: *That's right, that's right.*

JONES: *[unintelligible words] ... take our life from us, we laid it down, we got tired. We didn't commit suicide. We committed an act of revolutionary suicide, protesting the conditions of an inhumane world ...*

Bibliography

Adams, Charles Francis (ed.). *The New English Canaan of Thomas Morton*. New York: The Prince Society, 1883.

Adams, Charles Francis. *Three Episodes of Massachusetts History: The Settlement of Boston Bay; the Antinomian Controversy; a Study of Church and Town Government*. Boston: Houghton, Mifflin and company, 1892.

Ames, Glenn J. and Love, Ronald S. *Distant Lands and Diverse Cultures: The French Experience in Asia, 1600–1700*. Westport, Connecticut: Praeger, 2003.

Bennett, Ralph (ed.). *Settlements in the Americas*. Newark: University of Delaware Press, 1993.

Bolton, Herbert E. *The Spanish Borderlands: A Chronicle of Old Florida and the Southwest*. New Haven: Yale University Press, 1921.

Bolton, Herbert E. and Maitland Marshall, Thomas. *The Colonization of North America, 1492–1783*. New York: The MacMillan Company, 1920.

Boys, Robert Douglass. *First Years at Port Phillip*. Melbourne: Robertson & Mullens, 1959.

Bushnell Hart, Albert. *Commonwealth History of Massachusetts, Colony Province and State*, vol. 1. New York: States History Company, 1927.

Cave, Alfred. 'Why Was the Sagadahoc Colony Abandoned? An Evaluation of the Evidence', *The New England Quarterly*, vol. 68, no. 4, December 1995, pp 625–640

Cavendish, Richard. 'Founding of the Darien Colony', *History Today*, November 1998.

Chidester, David. *Salvation and Suicide*. Bloomington: Indiana University Press, 1988.

Crook, William Pascoe. *An Account of the Settlement at Sullivan Bay*. Melbourne: The Colony Press, 1983.

Eliot Morison, Samuel. *The European Discovery of America: The Northern Voyages A.D. 500–1600*. New York: Oxford University Press, 1971.

Eliot Morison, Samuel. *The European Discovery of America: The Southern Voyages 1492–1616*. New York: Oxford University Press, 1974.

Foster, W. 'An English Settlement in Madagascar in 1645–6', *The English Historical Review*, vol. 27, no. 106, April 1912.

Grimwade, Russell, et al, *Victoria the First Century*. Melbourne: Ramsay Publishing, 1934.

Knecht, Robert Jean. *The Rise and Fall of Renaissance France, 1483–1610*. Oxford: Blackwell, 2001.

Kuppermann, Karen. *Providence Island 1630–1641: The Other Puritan Colony*. New York: Cambridge University Press, 1993.

Larson, Pier M. 'Colonies Lost: God, Hunger and Conflict in Anosy (Madagascar) to 1674', *Comparative Studies of South Asia, Africa and the Middle East*, vol. 27, no. 2, 2007.

Logan Allen, John (ed.). *North American Exploration: A New World Disclosed*, vol. 1. Lincoln: University of Nebraska Press, 1997.

Logan, F. Donald. *The Vikings in History*. London: Routledge, 1992.

Lowery, Woodbury. *The Spanish Settlements Within the Present Limits of the United States*. New York: G.P. Putnam's Sons, 1905.

McIntyre, Ben. *Forgotten Fatherland: The Search for Elisabeth Nietzsche*. New York: Farrar, Straus & Giroux, 1992.

Miller, Lee. *Roanoke: Solving the Mystery of England's Lost Colony*. London: Jonathan Cape, 2000.

Moree, P. J. *A Concise History of Dutch Mauritius, 1598–1710*. London: Kegan Paul International, 1998.

Moore, Rebecca. *A Sympathetic History of Jonestown: the Moore Family Involvement in Peoples Temple*. Lewiston, New York: Mellen Press, 1985.

Naipaul, Shiva. *Black and White*. London: Hamish Hamilton, 1980.

Oberg, Michael Leroy. *Dominion and Civility: English Imperialism and Native America, 1585–1685*. London: Cornell University Press, 1999.

Parker Pearson, Mike. 'Close Encounters of the Worst Kind: Malagasy Resistance and Colonial Disasters in Southern Madagascar', *World Archaeology*, vol. 28, no.3, February 1997.

Pearson, Michael. *The Indian Ocean*. London: Routledge, 2003.

Prebble, John. *The Darien Disaster*. London: Secker & Warburg, 1968.

Quinn, David B. *England and the Discovery of America, 1481–1620: From the Bristol Voyages of the Fifteenth Century to the Pilgrim Settlement at Plymouth: The Exploration, Exploitation, and Trial-and-error Colonization of North America by the English*. New York: Alfred A. Knopf, 1974.

Quinn, David B. *North America From Earliest Discovery to First Settlements: The Norse Voyages to 1612*. New York: Harper & Row, 1977.

Reiterman, Tim and Jacobs, John. *Raven: The Untold Story of Rev. Jim Jones and His People*. New York: Dutton, 1982.

Rister, Carl Coke. 'Carlota: A Confederate Colony in Mexico', *Journal of Southern History*, vol. 11, no.1, February 1945.

Rolle, Andrew. *The Lost Cause: The Confederate Exodus to Mexico*. London: University of Oklahoma Press, 1992.

Rollins, Patrick J. 'Imperial Russia's African Colony', *Russian Review*, vol. 27, no. 4, October 1968, pp 432–451

Ryder Howe, Ben. 'An Impossible Place to Be', *Outsider Magazine*, September 2004.

Souter, Gavin. *A Peculiar People: the Australians in Paraguay*. Sydney: Angus and Robertson, 1968.

Spillett, Peter G. *Forsaken Settlement: An Illustrated History of the Settlement of Victoria, Port Essington, North Australia, 1838–1849*. Melbourne: Lansdowne, 1972.

Stahle, David W. 'The Lost Colony and Jamestown Droughts', *Science*, vol. 280, no. 5363, April 24 1998, p 564(4).

Stuart Olson, James and Shadle, Robert. *Historical Dictionary of European Imperialism*. Westport, Connecticut: Greenwood Publishing Group, 1991.

Taylor, Alan. *American Colonies: The Settling of North America*. New York: Penguin, 2001.

Thomas Wilson, Edward. *Russia and Black Africa before World War II*. London: Holmes & Meier, 1974.

Tipping, Marjorie. *Convicts Unbound: The Story of the Calcutta Convicts and Their Settlement in Australia*. South Yarra, Victoria: Viking O'Neil, 1988.

Trahair, Richard C. S. *Utopias and Utopians: An Historical Dictionary*. Westport, Connecticut: Greenwood Press, 1999.

Turner, Henry Gyles. *A History of the Colony of Victoria*, vol. 1 *1797–1854*. London: Longmans Green, 1904.

Vaughan, Megan. *Creating the Creole Island: Slavery in Eighteenth-century Mauritius*. Durham, North Carolina: Duke University Press, 2005.

Wafer, Lionel. *A New Voyage and Description of the Isthmus of America*, Elliott Joyce L.E. (ed.). Oxford: Hakluyt Society, 1933.

Weddle, Robert S. *The French Thorn: Rival Explorers in the Spanish Sea, 1682–1762*. College Station, Texas: Texas A&M University Press, 1991.

Williams, John F., Kraus, Daniela and Knowles, Harry. 'Flights from Modernity: German and Australian Utopian Colonies in Paraguay 1886–1896', *Journal of Australian Studies*, no. 69, September 2001.

Wood, Peter H. 'La Salle: Discovery of a Lost Explorer', *The American Historical Review*, vol. 89, no. 2, April 1984, pp 294–323)

Wright Ed. *Lost Explorers*. Sydney: Pier 9, 2008.

Zweig, Stefan. *Brazil: Land of the Future*, trans. Andrew St. James. New York: Viking Press, 1943.

Acknowledgements

Thanks to my commissioning editor Diana Hill, who came up with this clever concept, Emma Hutchinson for her astute editing and superb picture research, as well as Hugh Ford and Susanne Geppert for their excellent design. I'd also like to thank my wife Kumudu for her companionship at the end of the long days chasing ghosts.

Picture credits

Antiquariat Reinhold Berg: page 159
Australpress: pages 7, 17, 37, 53, 63, 74, 82, 89, 96, 104, 142–143, 169, 244–245, 251, 261
Bildagentur für Kunst, Kultur und Geschichte: page 254
Corbis: back cover, pages 25, 71, 164, 195, 241, 247, 257, 303, 308, 311
Getty images: pages 14, 22, 41, 44–45, 135, 300
Maine Historical Society: page 99
Maple Ridge Museum: pages 290, 296
National Library of Australia: pages 2–3, 207, 226–227, 230, 233, 284–285
Photolibrary: front cover, pages 11, 21, 28, 33, 34, 49, 54, 59, 66, 86–87, 91, 127, 139, 147, 148, 152, 172, 177, 182–183, 202, 293
Picture Desk/Art Archive: pages 107, 112–113, 114, 124, 162, 198–199, 264, 268
Son of The South: page 186–187
State Library of Queensland: page 275
State Library of Victoria: pages 213, 214–215

Index

First published in 2009 by Pier 9, an imprint of Murdoch Books Pty Limited

Murdoch Books Australia
Pier 8/9
23 Hickson Road
Millers Point NSW 2000
Phone: +61 (0)2 8220 2000
Fax: +61 (0)2 8220 2558
www.murdochbooks.com.au

Murdoch Books UK Limited
Erico House, 6th Floor
93–99 Upper Richmond Road
Putney, London SW15 2TG
Phone: +44 (0) 20 8785 5995
Fax: +44 (0) 20 8785 5985
www.murdochbooks.co.uk

Chief Executive: Juliet Rogers
Publishing Director: Kay Scarlett

Commissioning Editor: Diana Hill
Project editor: Emma Hutchinson
Cover design: Hugh Ford
Internal design: Susanne Geppert
Text copyright © Ed Wright 2009
Design copyright © Murdoch Books Pty Limited 2009

National Library of Australia Cataloguing-in-Publication Data:
Author: Wright, Ed, 1968–
Title: Ghost colonies : failed utopias, forgotten exiles and
           abandoned outposts of empire / Ed Wright.
ISBN: 9781741964684 (pbk.)
Series: Lost and found in history.
Notes: Includes index.
           Bibliography.
Subjects: Colonies.
           Imperialism.
Dewey Number: 321.08

A catalogue record for this book is available from the British Library.

PRINTED IN 2009.